Research Methods in Anthropology : Qualitative and Quantitative Approaches

ABOUT THE AUTHOR

Prof. Andy.Therborn, is an Ecologist and Social Justice Specialist with more than 20 years of academic and consulting experience. He holds a Ph.D in Human Rights from the Univeristy of Birmingham,UK and wrote the Ph.D and Master Academic Programs of Environmental Sciences for the Universidad de Guayana, Venezuela.

ABOUT THE BOOK

Development anthropology refers to the application of anthropological perspectives to the multidisciplinary branch of development studies. It take international development and international aid as primary object. In this branch of anthropology, the term development refers to the social action made voluntary by different agents (institutions, business, enterprise, state, independent volunteer) who are trying to modify the economic, technical, political or/and social life of a given place in the world, especially in developing nation. Qualitative research seeks out the 'why', not the 'how' of its topic through the analysis of unstructured information - things like interview transcripts, open ended survey responses, e-mails, notes, feedback forms, photos and videos. It doesn't just rely on statistics or numbers, which are the domain of quantitative researchers. Qualitative research is used to gain insight into people's attitudes, behaviours, value systems, concerns, motivations, aspirations, culture or lifestyles. It's used to inform business decisions, policy formation, communication and research. Quantitative research is used widely in social sciences such as psychology, sociology, anthropology, and political science. Research in mathematical sciences such as physics is also 'quantitative' by definition, though this use of the term differs in context. In the social sciences, the term relates to empirical methods, originating in both philosophical positivism and the history of statistics, which contrast qualitative research methods. This book covers a wide arena, and truly reflects the nature of anthropology as an integrated discipline.

Research Methods in Anthropology : Qualitative and Quantitative Approaches

Prof. Andy. Therborn

AMIGA PRESS. INC
Delhi -110051

AMIGA PRESS. INC
H.O :- 28-A, Indra Park, Chander Nagar
Delhi :- 110051 (India)
Tel :- 011-22504028, +91-98736-57000
Email :- info@amigapress.co.in
amigapub@gmail.com
Website :- www.amigapress@co.in

This edition is published by Amiga Press.Inc

ISBN : 978-93-87295-17-9

First Published 2019

Printed and bound by Amiga Press Inc. New Delhi-India

Preface

Social anthropology also explores the role of meanings, ambiguities and contradictions of social life, patterns of sociality, violence and conflict; and the underlying logics of social behaviour. Social anthropologists are trained in the interpretation of narrative, ritual and symbolic behaviour, not merely as text, but with communication examined in relation to action, practice, and the historical context in which it is embedded. Social anthropologists address the diversity of positions and perspectives to be found within any social group.

Qualitative research seeks out the 'why', not the 'how' of its topic through the analysis of unstructured information - things like interview transcripts, open ended survey responses, e-mails, notes, feedback forms, photos and videos. It doesn't just rely on statistics or numbers, which are the domain of quantitative researchers. Qualitative research is used to gain insight into people's attitudes, behaviours, value systems, concerns, motivations, aspirations, culture or lifestyles. It's used to inform business decisions, policy formation, communication and research.

Focus groups, in-depth interviews, content analysis, ethnography, evaluation and semiotics are among the many formal approaches that are used, but qualitative research also involves the analysis of any unstructured material, including customer feedback forms, reports or media clips. Collecting and analyzing this unstructured information can be messy and time consuming using manual methods. When faced with volumes of materials, finding themes and extracting meaning can be a daunting task.

Quantitative research is used widely in social sciences such as psychology, sociology, anthropology, and political science. Research in mathematical sciences such as physics is also 'quantitative' by definition, though this use of the term differs in context. In the social sciences, the term relates to empirical methods, originating in both philosophical positivism and the history of statistics, which contrast qualitative research methods. Qualitative methods produce information only on the particular cases studied, and any more general conclusions are only hypotheses. Quantitative methods can be used to verify, which of such hypotheses are true. A comprehensive analysis of 1274 articles published in the top two American sociology journals between 1935 and 2005 found that roughly two thirds of these objects used quantitative methods.

There are different designs that researchers can chose from to collect data in conducting qualitative, quantitative, and mixed-method research. Exploratory designs are exclusively grounded in qualitative research, and explanatory designs are exclusively grounded in quantitative research. Descriptive designs, evaluative designs, and single-subject designs can draw from either or both types of research.

Research design is different from the method by which data are collected. Many research methods texts confuse research designs with methods. It is not uncommon to see research design treated as a mode of data collection rather than as a logical structure of the inquiry. But there is nothing intrinsic about any research design that requires a particular method of data collection. Although cross-sectional surveys are frequently equated with questionnaires and case studies are often equated with participant observation data for any design can be collected with any data collection method.

Constructive research is perhaps the most common computer science research method. This type of approach demands a form of validation that doesn't need to be quite as empirically based as in other types of research like exploratory research. Nevertheless the conclusions have to be objectively argued and defined. This may involve evaluating the "construct" being developed analytically against some predefined criteria or performing some benchmark tests with the prototype.

This is a reference book. All the matter is just compiled and edited in nature, taken from the various sources which are in public domain.

This book covers a wide arena, and truly reflects the nature of anthropology as an integrated discipline.

—*Editor*

Contents

1

Research in Anthropology

INTRODUCTION

Anthropology is the study of humanity. It has origins in the natural sciences, the humanities, and the social sciences. The term "anthropology", is from the Greek *anthrôpos*, "man", and *-logia*, "discourse" or "study", and was first used in 1501 by German philosopher Magnus Hundt.

Anthropology's basic concerns are "What defines *Homo sapiens*?", "Who are the ancestors of modern *Homo sapiens*?" "What are humans' physical traits?", "How do humans behave?", "Why are there variations and differences among different groups of humans?", "How has the evolutionary past of *Homo sapiens* influenced its social organization and culture?" and so forth.

In the United States, contemporary anthropology is typically divided into four sub-fields: cultural anthropology (also called "social anthropology"), archaeology, linguistic anthropology, and physical (or biological) anthropology. The *four-field* approach to anthropology is reflected in many undergraduate textbooks as well as anthropology programs (e.g. Michigan, Berkeley, Penn, etc.). At universities in the United Kingdom, and much of Europe, these "sub-fields" are frequently housed in separate departments and are seen as distinct disciplines.

The social and cultural sub-field has been heavily influenced by structuralist and post-modern theories, as well as a shift toward the analysis of modern societies (an arena more typically in the remit of sociologists). During the 1970s and 1980s there was an epistemological shift away from the positivist traditions that had largely informed the discipline. During this shift, enduring questions about the nature and production of knowledge came to occupy a central place in cultural and social anthropology. In contrast, archaeology, biological anthropology, and linguistic anthropology remained largely positivist. Due to this difference in epistemology, anthropology as a discipline has lacked cohesion over the last several decades. This has even led to departments diverging, for example in the 1998–9 academic year at Stanford University, where the "scientists" and "non-scientists" divided into two departments: anthropological sciences and cultural & social anthropology; these departments later reunified in the 2008–9 academic year.

Social anthropology is one of the four or five branches of anthropology that studies how contemporary human beings behave in social groups.

Practitioners of social anthropology investigate, often through long-term, intensive field studies (including participant observation methods), the social organization of a particular person: customs, economic and political organization, law and conflict resolution, patterns of consumption and exchange, kinship and family structure, gender relations, childrearing and socialization, religion, and so on.

Social anthropology also explores the role of meanings, ambiguities and contradictions of social life, patterns of sociality, violence and conflict; and the underlying logics of social behaviour. Social anthropologists are trained in the interpretation of narrative, ritual and symbolic behaviour, not merely as *text*, but with communication examined in relation to action, practice, and the historical context in which it is embedded. Social anthropologists address the diversity of positions and perspectives to be found within any social group.

The name social anthropology is used in the United Kingdom but it is a subject closely related to, or even the equivalent of, cultural anthropology, the latter term being more commonly used in other English speaking countries.

BASIC TRENDS

There are several characteristics that tend to unite anthropological work. One of the central characteristics is that anthropology tends to provide a comparatively more holistic account of phenomena and tends to be highly empirical. The quest for holism leads most anthropologists to study a particular place, problem or phenomenon in detail, using a variety of methods, over a more extensive period than normal in many parts of academia. In the 1990s and 2000s, calls for clarification of what constitutes a culture, of how an observer knows where his or her own culture ends and another begins, and other crucial topics in writing anthropology were heard. It is possible to view all human cultures as part of one large, evolving global culture. These dynamic relationships, between what can be observed on the ground, as opposed to what can be observed by compiling many local observations remain fundamental in any kind of anthropology, whether cultural, biological, linguistic or archaeological. Biological anthropologists are interested in both human variation and in the possibility of human universals (behaviours, ideas or concepts shared by virtually all human cultures) They use many different methods of study, but modern population genetics, participant observation and other techniques often take anthropologists "into the field" which means traveling to a community in its own setting, to do something called "fieldwork."

On the biological or physical side, human measurements, genetic samples, nutritional data may be gathered and published as articles or monographs. Due to the interest in variation, anthropologists are drawn to the study of human extremes, aberrations and other unusual circumstances, such as headhunting, whirling dervishes, whether there were real Hobbit people, snake handling, and glossolalia (speaking in tongues), just to list a few. At the same time, anthropologists urge, as part of their quest for scientific objectivity, cultural relativism, which has an influence on all the sub-fields of anthropology. This is the notion that particular cultures should not be judged by one culture's values or viewpoints, but that all cultures should be viewed as relative to each other. There should be no notions, in good anthropology, of one culture being better or worse than another culture. Ethical commitments in anthropology include noticing and documenting genocide, infanticide, racism, mutilation including circumcision and subincision, and torture. Topics like racism, slavery or human sacrifice, therefore, attract anthropological attention and theories ranging from nutritional deficiencies to genes to acculturation have been proposed, not to mention theories of colonialism and many others as root causes of Man's inhumanity to man.

To illustrate the depth of an anthropological approach, one can take just one of these topics, such as "racism" and find thousands of anthropological references, stretching across all the major and minor sub-fields. Along with dividing up their project by theoretical emphasis, anthropologists typically divide the world up into relevant time periods and geographic regions. Human time on Earth is divided up into relevant cultural traditions based on material, such as the Paleolithic and the Neolithic, of particular use in archaeology. Further cultural subdivisions according to tool types, such as Olduwan or Mousterian or Levalloisian help archaeologists and other anthropologists in understanding major trends in the human past.

Anthropologists and geographers share approaches to Culture regions as well, since mapping cultures is central to both sciences. By making comparisons across cultural traditions (time-based) and cultural regions (space-based), anthropologists have developed various kinds of comparative method, a central part of their science. Contemporary anthropology is an established science with academic departments at most universities and colleges. The single largest organization of Anthropologists is the American Anthropological Association, which was founded in 1903.

Membership is made up of Anthropologists from around the globe. Hundreds of other organizations exist in the various sub-fields of anthropology, sometimes divided up by nation or region, and many anthropologists work with collaborators in other disciplines, such as geology, physics, zoology, paleontology, anatomy, music theory, art history, sociology and so on, belonging to professional societies in those disciplines as well.

HISTORY

The first use of the term "anthropology" in English to refer to a natural science of humanity was apparently in 1593, the first of the "logies" to be coined. It took Immanuel Kant 25 years to write one of the first major treatises on anthropology, his Anthropology from a Pragmatic Point of View. Kant is not generally considered to be a modern anthropologist, however, as he never left his region of Germany nor did he study any cultures besides his own, and in fact, describes the need for anthropology as a corollary field to his own primary field of philosophy. He did, however, begin teaching an annual course in anthropology in 1772. Anthropology is thus primarily an Enlightenment and post-Enlightenment endeavor.

Historians of anthropology, like Marvin Harris, indicate two major frameworks within which empirical anthropology has arisen: interest in comparisons of people over space and interest in longterm human processes or humans as viewed through time. Harris dates both to Classical Greece and Classical Rome, specifically Herodotus, often called the "father of history" and the Roman historian Tacitus, who wrote many of our only surviving contemporary accounts of several ancient Celtic and Germanic peoples. Herodotus first formulated some of the persisting problems of anthropology. Medieval scholars may be considered forerunners of modern anthropology as well, insofar as they conducted or wrote detailed studies of the customs of peoples considered "different" from themselves in terms of geography. John of Plano Carpini reported of his stay among the Mongols. His report was unusual in its detailed depiction of a non-European culture

Marco Polo's systematic observations of nature, anthropology, and geography are another example of studying human variation across space. Polo's travels took him across such a diverse human landscape and his accounts of the peoples he met as he journeyed were so detailed that they earned for Polo the name "the father of modern anthropology." Another candidate for one of the first scholars to carry out comparative ethnographic-type studies in person was the medieval Persian scholar Abû Rayhân Bîrûnî in the 11th century, who wrote about the peoples, customs, and religions of the Indian subcontinent. Like modern anthropologists, he engaged in extensive participant observation with a given group of people, learnt their language and studied their primary texts, and presented his findings with objectivity and neutrality using cross-cultural comparisons. However, others argue that he can hardly be considered an anthropologist in the conventional sense. He wrote detailed comparative studies on the religions and cultures in the Middle East, Mediterranean and especially South Asia. Biruni's tradition of comparative cross-cultural study continued in the Muslim world through to Ibn Khaldun's work in the 14th century.

Most scholars consider modern anthropology as an outgrowth of the Age of Enlightenment, a period when Europeans attempted systematically to study human behaviour, the known varieties of which had been increasing since the 15th century as a result of the first European colonization wave. The traditions of jurisprudence, history, philology, and sociology then evolved into something more closely resembling the modern views of these disciplines and informed the development of the social sciences, of which anthropology was a part.

Developments in the systematic study of ancient civilizations through the disciplines of Classics and Egyptology informed both archaeology and eventually social anthropology, as did the study of East and South Asian languages and cultures. At the same time, the Romantic reaction to the Enlightenment produced thinkers, such as Johann Gottfried Herder and later Wilhelm Dilthey, whose work formed the basis for the "culture concept," which is central to the discipline. Institutionally, anthropology emerged from the development of natural history (expounded by authors such as Buffon) that occurred during the European colonization of the 17th, 18th, 19th and 20th centuries. Programmes of ethnographic study originated in this era as the study of the "human primitives" overseen by colonial administrations. There was a tendency in late 18th century Enlightenment thought to understand human society as natural phenomena that behaved according to certain principles and that could be observed empirically. In some ways, studying the language, culture, physiology, and artifacts of European colonies was not unlike studying the flora and fauna of those places.

Early anthropology was divided between proponents of unilinealism, who argued that all societies passed through a single evolutionary process, from the most primitive to the most advanced, and various forms of non-lineal theorists, who tended to subscribe to ideas such as diffusionism. Most 19th-century social theorists, including anthropologists, viewed non-European societies as windows onto the pre-industrial human past.

As academic disciplines began to differentiate over the course of the 19th century, anthropology grew increasingly distinct from the biological approach of natural history, on the one hand, and from purely historical or literary fields such as Classics, on the other. A common criticism has been that many social science scholars (such as economists, sociologists, and psychologists) in Western countries focus disproportionately on Western subjects, while anthropology focuses disproportionately on the "Other"; this has changed over the last part of the 20th century as anthropologists increasingly also study Western subjects, particularly variation across class, region, or ethnicity within Western societies, and other social scientists increasingly take a global view of their fields.

20th Century

In the 20th century, academic disciplines have often been institutionally divided into three broad domains. The natural and biological sciences seek to derive general laws through reproducible and verifiable experiments. The humanities generally study local traditions, through their history, literature, music, and arts, with an emphasis on understanding particular individuals, events, or eras.

The social sciences have generally attempted to develop scientific methods to understand social phenomena in a generalizable way, though usually with methods distinct from those of the natural sciences.

In particular, social sciences often develop statistical descriptions rather than the general laws derived in physics or chemistry, or they may explain individual cases through more general principles, as in many fields of psychology. Anthropology (like some fields of history) does not easily fit into one of these categories, and different branches of anthropology draw on one or more of these domains.

Anthropology as it emerged amongst the Western colonial powers (mentioned above) has generally taken a different path than that in the countries of southern and central Europe (Italy, Greece, and the successors to the Austro-Hungarian and Ottoman empires). In the former, the encounter with multiple, distinct cultures, often very different in organization and language from those of Europe, has led to a continuing emphasis on cross-cultural comparison and a receptiveness to certain kinds of cultural relativism. In the successor states of continental Europe, on the other hand, anthropologists often joined with folklorists and linguists in building nationalist perspectives. Ethnologists in these countries tended to focus on differentiating among local ethnolinguistic groups, documenting local folk culture, and representing the prehistory of what has become a nation through various forms of public education (eg, museums of several kinds).

In this scheme, Russia occupied a middle position. On the one hand, it had a large region (largely east of the Urals) of highly distinct, pre-industrial, often non-literate peoples, similar to the situation in the Americas. On the other hand, Russia also participated to some degree in the nationalist (cultural and political) movements of Central and Eastern Europe. After the Revolution of 1917, anthropology in the USSR, and later the Soviet Bloc countries, were highly shaped by the requirement to conform to Marxist theories of social evolution.

HISTORY OF ANTHROPOLOGY

The anthropologist Eric Wolf once characterized anthropology as the most scientific of the humanities, and the most humanistic of the social sciences. Understanding how anthropology developed contributes to understanding how it fits into other academic disciplines.

Contemporary anthropologists claim a number of earlier thinkers as their forebearers and the discipline itself has many sources. However, anthropology can best be understood as an outgrowth of the Age of Enlightenment. It was during this period that Europeans attempted systematically to study human behavior. Traditions of jurisprudence, history, philology and sociology developed during this time and informed the development of the social sciences of which anthropology was a part. At the same time, the romantic reaction to the Enlightenment produced thinkers such as Herder and later Wilhelm Dilthey whose work formed the basis for the culture concept which is central to the discipline.

These intellectual movements in part grappled with one of the greatest paradoxes of modernity: as the world is becoming smaller and more integrated, people's experience of the world is increasingly atomized and dispersed. As Karl Marx and Friedrich Engels observed in the 1840s:

All old-established national industries have been destroyed or are daily being destroyed. They are dislodged by new industries, whose introduction becomes a life and death question for all civilized nations, by industries that no longer work up indigenous raw material but raw material drawn from the remotest zones; industries whose products are consumed, not only at home, but in every quarter of the globe. In place of the old wants, satisfied by the production of the country, we find new wants, requiring for their satisfaction the products of distant lands and climes. In place of the old local and national seclusion and self-sufficiency, we have intercourse in every direction, universal interdependence of nations.

Ironically, this universal interdependence, rather than leading to greater human solidarity, has coincided with increasing racial, ethnic, religious, and class divisions, and new-and to some confusing or disturbing-cultural expressions. These are the conditions of life with which people today must contend, but they have their origins in processes that began in the 16th century and accelerated in the 19th century.

Institutionally anthropology emerged from natural history (expounded by authors such as Buffon). This was the study of human beings-typically people living in European colonies. Thus studying the language, culture, physiology, and artifacts of European colonies was more or less equivalent to studying the flora and fauna of those places. It was for this reason, for instance, that Lewis Henry Morgan could write monographs on both The League of the Iroquois and The American Beaver and His Works. This is also why the material culture of 'civilized' nations such as China have historically been displayed in fine arts museums alongside European art while artifacts from Africa or Native North American cultures were displayed in Natural History Museums with dinosaur bones and nature dioramas. This being said, curatorial practice has changed dramatically in recent years, and it would be wrong to see anthropology as merely an extension of colonial rule and European chauvinism, since its relationship to imperialism was and is complex.

Museums such as the British Museum weren't the only site of anthropological studies: with the New Imperialism period, starting in the 1870s, zoos became unattended "laboratories", especially the so-called "ethnological exhibitions" or "Negro villages". Thus, "savages" from the colonies were displayed, often nudes, in cages, in what has been called "human zoos". For example, in 1906, Congolese pygmy Ota Benga was put by anthropologist Madison Grant in a cage in the Bronx Zoo, labelled "the missing link" between an orangutan and the "white race"-Grant, a renowned eugenicist, was also the author of The Passing of the Great Race (1916). Such exhibitions were attempts to illustrate and prove in the same movement the validity of scientific racism, which first formulation may be found in Arthur de Gobineau's An Essay on the Inequality of Human Races (1853-55). In 1931, the Colonial Exhibition in Paris still displayed Kanaks from New Caledonia in the "indigenous village"; it received 24 million visitors in six months, thus demonstrating the popularity of such "human zoos".

GROWTH AND DEVELOPMENT

Anthropology grew increasingly distinct from natural history and by the end of the nineteenth century the discipline began to crystallize into its modern form-by 1935, for example, it was possible for T.K. Penniman to write a history of the discipline entitled A Hundred Years of Anthropology. At the time, the field was dominated by 'the comparative method'. It was assumed that all societies passed through a single evolutionary process from the most primitive to most advanced. Non-European societies were thus seen as evolutionary 'living fossils' that could be studied in order to understand the European past. Scholars wrote histories of prehistoric migrations which were sometimes valuable but often also fanciful. It was during this time that Europeans first accurately traced Polynesian migrations across the Pacific Ocean for instance-although some of them believed it originated in Egypt.

Finally, the concept of race was actively discussed as a way to classify-and rank-human beings based on inherent biological difference.

In the twentieth century academic disciplines began to organize around three main domains. The "sciences" seeks to derive natural laws through reproducible and falsifiable experiments. The "humanities" reflected an attempt to study different national traditions, in the form of history and the arts, as an attempt to provide people in emerging nation-states with a sense of coherence. The "social sciences" emerged at this time as an attempt to develop scientific methods to address social phenomena, in an attempt to provide a universal basis for social knowledge. Anthropology does not easily fit into one of these categories, and different branches of anthropology draw on one or more of these domains.

Drawing on the methods of the natural sciences as well as developing new techniques involving not only structured interviews but unstructured "participant-observation"-and drawing on the new theory of evolution through natural selection, they proposed the scientific study of a new object: "humankind," conceived of as a whole.

Crucial to this study is the concept "culture," which anthropologists defined both as a universal capacity and propensity for social learning, thinking, and acting (which they see as a product of human evolution and something that distinguishes Homo sapiens-and perhaps all species of genus Homo-from other species), and as a particular adaptation to local conditions that takes the form of highly variable beliefs and practices. Thus, "culture" not only transcends the opposition between nature and nurture; it transcends and absorbs the peculiarly European distinction between politics, religion, kinship, and the economy as autonomous domains. Anthropology thus transcends the divisions between the natural sciences, social sciences, and humanities to explore the biological, linguistic, material, and symbolic dimensions of humankind in all forms.

In the mid-Twentieth century American anthropology began to methodologically study its own history. In 1967 Marvin Harris published his, The Rise of Anthropological Theory presenting argumentative examinations of anthropology's historical developments, and George W. Stocking Jr., established the historicist school, examining the historical contexts of anthropological movements.

ANTHROPOLOGY AND GLOBAL ENVIRONMENTAL CHANGE

Anthropologists have always been concerned with the relationship between the people they studied and the natural environment. Since the late nineteenth century, the first professional anthropologists focused their research on tribal peoples who were directly dependent on natural resources for their survival. The environment was obviously too important to be ignored. Initially, anthropologists studied how people exploited the environment, then they asked how culture might in turn be shaped by the environment, or by the nature of the human-environment relationship. Nineteenth century anthropologists were often natural historians, and it was common then, and still today, for them to be very broadly interdisciplinary, with interest, and sometimes formal training, in geography, geology, zoology, and botany. During the first half of the twentieth century the anthropological interest in environmental issues led to the identification of cultural ecology as a distinctive sub-discipline. Contemporary prehistoric archaeologists often maintain a focus on environmental issues.

Most early academic anthropologists rejected any simple environmental determinism, but they grouped similar cultures into large culture areas that often reflected underlying common cultural adaptations to generalized natural areas. Before 1950, pioneer cultural ecologist Julian Steward, cautiously observed that over time people tended to organize themselves in similar ways to exploit similar environments, thus producing broadly similar cultural types in widely separate areas of the world. By the late 1960s, cultural ecologists began to apply equilibrium models to small-scale cultures, treating them as human systems in balanced, adaptive relations with natural ecosystems. These functionalist approaches were largely abandoned because they could not explain how systems developed and changed, and they often treated cultures as artificially closed systems. Since the 1980s, cultural ecologists have increasingly situated the peoples they study within the national and international political economy, and interest has shifted to approaches that will help local peoples defend their resources and sub-sistence economies. Many contemporary anthropologists continue an environmental focus, but it has broadened to include contemporary commercially organized, and global scale cultures, as well as existing indigenous peoples with small-scale societies.

CULTURAL EVOLUTION AND HUMAN ADAPTABILITY

One of the longest-running theoretical debates in anthropology concerns the nature of cultural evolution. The orthodox view as originally developed by Morgan (1877), and refined by White (1949, 1959) and others, was that general cultural evolutionary progress was an inevitable and beneficial process of growth and development leading stage by stage to more complex societies, using more energy more efficiently, and with greater adaptability and security. Cultural evolutionists thought that evolutionary progress was such a selfevident human benefit that they did not demonstrate it. White (1949) emphatically declared that culture evolved "as the amount of energy harnessed per capita per year increased." The assumption was that cultural evolution gave people greater control over nature, and this was good for people. However, it is significant that the most enthusiastic anthropological exponents of these measures of cultural progress wrote before the energy shortages of the 1970s, and before the United Nations Brundtland Commission (WCED, 1987) report on sustainable development. Thoughtful reconsideration of all the standard measures of cultural evolutionary progress suggests that it must be a maladaptive process.

Leslie White attributed the most recent step in cultural development to the switch to fossil fuels and nuclear energy, but it is now obvious that the advantages of this may prove illusory. Cultures can be arranged in a progressive general evolutionary sequence of increased energy use running from 5000 to 12 000 kcal per capita per day in small-scale band and village societies, 26000 kcal in pre-capitalist agrarian civilizations, and 230000 kcal consumed by Americans in the 1970s (Cook, 1971). However, critics pointed out that this sequence does not account for the eventual depletion of fossil fuels, the serious deficits in using non-renewable energy to produce food energy, or the costs of the waste by-products of energy production and consumption.

Hubert (1969) predicted that global petroleum production would peak in 1995, and that the supply would be virtually exhausted by 2075. The most telling criticism was the calculation that if energy consumption increased at 5% a year for 200 years, the waste heat produced would equal the heat of incoming solar radiation and the earth would burn up. Fortunately, before such a Sun Day the polar ice caps would melt and rising sea levels would flood out most of the power plants (Luten, 1974). Human reproductive success would also be an unattractive measure of human evolutionary progress. If the production of larger, more complex cultural systems is the measure of evolutionary success, then the process still seems maladaptive for longterm human survival, because fewer, larger, more homogenous, and less durable cultures have replaced more numerous, more diverse, and more durable small cultures.

Greater cultural complexity creates a human survival problem in part because larger, more complex cultural systems incorporate and subordinate smaller systems. Some of the evolutionary theorists recognized that small-scale cultures might actually be better adapted to particular local ecosystems than large-scale cultures. White (1949) observed that foragers, with the simplest cultures, may have had "the most satisfying kind of social environment that man has ever lived in." Sahlins (1968) noted that for-agers were successful because they limited their wants to the consumption levels that their environment and technology could support and they lived satisfying and affluent lives. As the contemporary environmental crisis began to unfold, many anthropologists commented on the connections between self-sufficient small-scale societies and greater social equality, and relative equilibrium with the environment (Bodley, 1975). This suggested the possibility that increased social scale caused inequality, poverty, and global environmental change.

More recent biocultural evolutionary theory shows how cultural evolution could become a maladaptive process that would undermine the resiliency of both natural and human systems. From the biocultural perspective, cultural evolution is produced by changes in culture, which is conceived from the ideas that human behavior is directed in the same way that genes create biological organisms. Cultures change as shared symbolic information changes. The important difference between genes and culture is that individuals intentionally produce and transmit culture, and they can borrow from many sources. However, the scale of culture influences how it is created and transmitted. Cultural transmission is frequently biased, because people emulate the beliefs and behavior that appear to be most successful. Cultural emulation is easy and efficient, but it can lead to maladaptive runaway economic growth and power aggrandizement, which in turn cause global environmental change.

In small, domestically organized societies the members of each household are daily making cultural decisions about technology, production, and consumption. In larger scale, politically organized societies, cultural evolution becomes a political process in which a single ruler can direct the actions of thousands, or even millions of people. Household-level decision making is inherently more responsive to local social and environmental conditions, but it can be over-ridden by political rulers who may be far removed from the environmental consequences of their decisions. Thus, it is not surprising that large scale agrarian civilizations directed by political elites, frequently collapse because they exhaust the resource base, generate social conflict, or become too costly to maintain.

THE CONSTITUTION OF THE LOCAL AND THE POLITICS OF TRANSLATION

What counts as "local" when we speak of "local knowledge"? I want to suggest that when we invoke the "local," we might in fact be speaking about two distinct things. On the one hand are the voices of peasants, farmers, fishers, or indigenous peoples, often living in out-of-the-way places, frequently marginalized politically and economically. These are people we have come to valorize as possessing richly detailed knowledge representing generations of observation and experimentation about medicinal plants, crop varieties, trees, the habits of animals, and much more.

On the other hand are the voices of those who are delegated to speak for local or indigenous communities in national and international fora. They are no less local-it is more the context in which we encounter them. We do not go to them; they come to us. These are actors who have much to say to the scientific community and to decision makers. In an effort to counter long histories of oppression and dispossession, they are forthright in challenging national and international conservation or development agendas, conventions, and assessments and in asserting their rights to lands and livelihoods. These are relatively new actors on the global stage. Though local and indigenous peoples have mobilized in many times and places over the centuries, it has really only been since the 1980s that we have witnessed the emergence of a global indigenous rights movement-what Friedman has referred to as "the rise of the indigenous voice."

These are the people who have increasingly made such a dramatic impression at such international events as the Fifth World Parks Congress, the CBD/COP7, the MA Bridging Scales and Epistemologies conference. Over the last few years at these and similar events, representatives from indigenous and local communities worldwide have appeared in large numbers. At plenary sessions, on panels, and in workshops, indigenous and local community representatives speak of conservation initiatives undertaken without their consent, and of exclusion from ancestral lands. That indigenous issues are increasingly on the agendas of such international events is in no small part the result of extensive preparatory work by indigenous organizations and their allies. They have lobbied to secure prime speaking slots and seats on drafting committees for indigenous representatives, sought funding for indigenous participation, and coordinated regional and preparatory meetings. As a result, indigenous and local representatives have been well prepared to make their voices heard and to ensure they are included in the final outputs of these events.

What this indigenous presence represents is a challenge to many basic assumptions about conservation. Indigenous representatives are suggesting that conservation can be done without externally imposed models, management plans, or monitoring and evaluation. They are also challenging assumptions about the roles of both Western science and major conservation organizations, asserting that conservation goals can be accomplished outside circuits of transnational expertise. Their message is that indigenous and local communities must represent something other than a "transaction cost," that threat assessments that classify their land use practices as disturbances are unacceptable, and that participatory methods that define them as just one more category of stakeholder have no place in their vision of conservation. Though both kinds of actors-"local locals" and local/indigenous advocatesget coded as "local" in international fora, important differences exist between them. When we consider how their words, their insights, and their knowledge move between scales in the process of translation, we must recognize that both are mediated, albeit in very different ways. Making an effective link between local knowledge and policy requires that we recognize these different forms of mediation.

For researchers interested in local or indigenous knowledge, it is those "local locals" that we usually work with the most. After all, these are the people who exist "on the ground" as repositories of the knowledge that interests us. The point, however, is that their knowledge enters circuits of global knowledge production in mediated form through us. Most of us who conduct research on local knowledge are able to do so because powerful institutions are interested in supporting our research, and because these institutions are increasingly interested in what we have to say about particular peoples and places. When they want to learn about local realities and local perspectives, they turn to the social sciences. This is what Gledhill was getting at when he reminded us that "intellectuals are contributing to new regulatory strategies being pursued by states and transnational agencies.

There is a particular danger that anthropologists will reinforce a politics of containment where this offers a new market opportunity for peddling our services as experts on 'culture,' either to the national state as an employer of specialists in the administration of ethnic difference or to the wider world of transnational agencies and NGOs" (1998, 516-17). The key to understanding this process of mediation lies in an understanding of the tools we use. As an anthropologist, I believe in the value of ethnographic research methods. Other social scientists rely on more rapid, formalistic, survey-based methods. Whichever methods we prefer, the social sciences get positioned as speaking for the local. In so doing, the danger is that the representations of those who possess expertise in making the local legible and intelligible to those working at other scales are conflated with local voices themselves. These are not the same thing; we must never conflate data provided by those who work at a local level with local voices themselves. We can offer our translations, our mediated accounts, and these can be very valuable, but we must never presume that we actually ever speak for the local.

The voices of indigenous advocates or representatives are mediated as well, albeit very differently. While they may be unmediated by social science conventions and formalistic methods, they are mediated by transnational discourses of indigeneity. While asserting locality and connection to place, they simultaneously speak with reference to global categories. This does not make their claims any less authentic: there is nothing inauthentic about the solidarity that is emerging from a recognition of shared histories of marginalization. Still, the fact that indigenous representatives are compelled to speak in global categories is a form of mediation.

There is yet another aspect of how the local is constituted that deserves our attention: the pervasive distinction made between local actors and "decision makers." This is achieved in part through what I have elsewhere termed the "topology of simple locality" (Brosius 1999c): a topology that defines the task of the ethnographer as one of inscribing and representing for an audience some actually existing place or set of placesour research sites, the communities in which we work.

It is a kind of focalizing strategy, drawing our attention to particular places as the most significant loci for the production of knowledge, and diverting our attention from the ways in which those places articulate with other places or with actors working at other scales. The topology of simple locality suffers from the same shortcoming that has produced critiques of that other convention of anthropological writing, the "ethnographic present." Anthropologists today are much more alert to the politics and histories that have shaped the communities they study.

However, the "ethnographic present" is a still-extant convention of ethnographic writing wherein an anthropologist describing a particular set of cultural practices writes about them in the present tense, even though their research may have occurred many years in the past and though much of what is described may no longer exist in the same form as it did when it was observed (Fabian 1983).

Just as the ethnographic present acts as a distancing mechanism that relegates our research subjects to a timeless irrelevancy, immune from history and from the effects of our ethnographic presence, so too does the topology of simple locality create a coherent "there" that can be known and represented and kept in its place. As Tawfic Ahmed and Reid (2002, 219) remind us, the Millennium Ecosystem Assessment is "designed to meet the needs of decision-makers." Unspoken here is an assumption about the inherent distance between local actors and decision makers and, therefore, about the relation between scale and hierarchy. Viewed in this way, indigenous knowledge is provided to those in the policy domain, but it speaks only in the passive voice of science rather than in the active voice of advocacy and it speaks from the subordinate position of knowledge solicited and translated up for the purpose of governance.

Whether our goals are purely instrumental (rendering local voices and local knowledge into forms useful in managerial terms) or emancipatory (rendering local voices into compelling narratives designed to secure rights), those local voices are situated in a subject position.

THE CONSTITUTION OF KNOWLEDGE

Now we turn to the question of what counts as "knowledge" when we speak of "local knowledge." As it is used by ethnoecologists and others, reference to indigenous or local "knowledge"-often referred to by the acronyms IK (indigenous knowledge) or TEK (traditional ecological knowledge)-is generally applied to knowledge of the natural world: what such groups know about the resources they exploit, how these societies cognize or interpret natural processes, and so forth. In short, when we speak of indigenous or local knowledge, what we generally mean is environmental knowledge.

That we are at last recognizing the value of local/indigenous knowledge, rather than dismissing it as anecdotal, irrelevant, or merely a lesser form of knowledge, is clearly a positive development. But that we limit our valorization of knowledge largely to that which pertains to the natural world yet again consigns that knowledge to the irrelevancy of the ethnographic present, destined forever to fill what Trouillot has termed the "savage slot" (Trouillot 1991), an epistemological backwater distinct from, and subordinate to, the forms of knowledge possessed by decision makers.

Let us, for a moment, consider the domains of knowledge that concern the Millennium Ecosystem Assessment. One strength of the MA is not only that it is firmly science driven, dedicated to producing and synthesizing reliable scientific data, but that it goes beyond this to identify trends, scenarios, trade-offs, and response options. Central to the MA vision is that it provide information that is not only scientifically credible but salient and legitimate as well.

According to Reid: "Scientific information is salient if it is perceived to be relevant or of value to particular groups who might use it to change management approaches, behavior, or policy decisions.... It is legiti-mate if the process of assembling the information is perceived to be fair and open to input from key political constituencies, such as the private sector, governments, and civil society."

But what might happen, we may ask, if these three criteria were applied not only to objective scientific information but to local and indigenous knowledge as well? What if, when we went out to seek information from local people, we not only asked about their knowledge of the natural world but also sought their analyses of the political world? How might their analyses of drivers and their assessments of threats differ from our own? What if we asked them about trends, scenarios, trade-offs, and response options? In other words, instead of treating our informants as reservoirs of local/indigenous knowledge, what if we treated them as political agents with their own ideas about the salience and legitimacy of various forms of knowledge? And what if we made a more systematic effort to incorporate that into MA outputs? A brief example illustrates what is at stake here. For several years in the 1980s and 1990s, I worked with various groups of Penan hunter-gatherers in the Malaysian state of Sarawak. As traditionally nomadic hunter-gatherers, Penan depend on the forest for virtually every aspect of their existence. They exemplify the depth and richness of environmental knowledge that indigenous peoples hold, with a remarkable knowledge of trees, plants, and animals and of the relations among them. Penan also possess a rich vocabulary for describing landscape and an extensive knowledge of places in the landscape they inhabit. This landscape is more than a reservoir of detailed ecological knowledge or a setting in which they satisfy their nutritional needs. It is also a repository for the memory of past events, a vast mnemonic representation of social relationships and of society. For Penan, landscape, history, and kinship-the bonds linking individuals to households to communities to generations past and future-are part of a larger whole.

In the late 1980s, the Penan became the focus of a high-profile transnational indigenous rights campaign concerned with logging. Since the 1980s, timber companies have expanded their reach throughout virtually every river valley occupied by Penan, and Penan have responded with intermittent blockades. During the first wave of blockades in 1987, images of Penan resisting the approach of logging companies traveled global environmental and indigenous rights circuits, producing an outpouring of support. Penan continue to assert their rights to land using every tool of persuasion available to them, though their efforts have largely been futile. The official government view of Penan is that their way of life is little more than a form of vagrancy in which would-be subjects are able to evade the gaze of the state. The only way Penan can be heard, the only discourse audible to the state, is that of development. The overall effect of the campaign was that the government shifted the debate over logging in Sarawak from a focus on forest destruction and the rights of indigenous communities to an issue of sustainable forest management. The discursive contours of the debate were shifted away from the moral and political domain toward the domain of environmental management. By the mid-1990s, the campaign's momentum had largely dissipated.

The question I want to pose is, in a "policy environment" characterized by dispossession, where the threats to local communities result from the actions of "decision makers," of what relevance is indigenous knowledge of nature by itself, divorced from its significance with respect to the making of claims? What is needed, I would argue, is a more expansive, less fixed notion of knowledge. What matters is not how much Penan know about the landscape they inhabit but how they position that knowledge, and themselves, within the broader contours of power. Whether or not they are actively engaged in explicit acts of resistance, the topic of logging is one that consumes Penan and that they discuss endlessly. Their narratives recount confrontations between themselves and state authorities or company representatives: police, judges, government ministers, camp managers, and others. They recount the arguments put forth by themselves or others: why they decided to blockade, why they should not be blamed for those blockades, and who they believe to be ultimately responsible.

Any effort to understand Penan narratives of dispossession must begin with recognizing the variety of forms they take. Such narratives, and the forms of action they prescribe, exist on a continuum from the concrete to the aesthetic and oblique. Many of the concerns they express are practical in nature-for instance, the simple difficulty of making a living in a logged-over landscape. Penan describe in matter-of-fact terms the destruction of the forest and the hardship this has caused them. They speak of river siltation, the destruction of sago, rattan, and fruit trees, and the depletion of game. At times, Penan make direct claims: they speak of boundaries and of the need to prohibit the entry of outsiders onto their lands. At other times they speak movingly about the qualities of the forest and their life within it.

They speak of the heat, dust, and desolation of logging against the coolness and cleanliness of the forest, the harsh sound of chainsaws versus the squeaking of trees rubbing in the wind. The words and images they employ are contrastive and tinged with nostalgia: what the forest was like before logging and after it. And they speak of loss and pain-at seeing valuable fruit trees destroyed and the graves of loved ones bulldozed. What is further striking about Penan commentaries on landscape and forest destruction is the degree to which the arguments they put forth are about locality and biography. Penan do not talk about the need to preserve rainforests as a generic abstraction; they talk about the need to preserve particular watersheds "from which we eat." It is the transgression of that densely biographical and genealogical locality that Penan find to be such a great injustice.

Often too, Penan speak in metaphors-for example, linking the forest to a supermarket or a bank. Such arguments are meant to appeal to what Penan presume is a shared sense of justice and respect. The arguments that Penan are putting forth should be viewed not exclusively as acts of resistance but simultaneously as efforts at engagement. In making their arguments to loggers, civil servants, environmentalists, and others, Penan are attempting to speak across difference, to familiarize themselves, to frame their arguments in ways that they hope outsiders will recognize. Their purpose is to persuade.

In considering how Penan frame their struggle against logging, it is important to consider not merely the rhetorical elements of these narratives but the forms they take as well: letters addressed to government officials, verbal arguments with timber company managers, maps produced with the aid of local activists, videotaped interviews produced by Euro-American documentary film-makers, and others. What happens when Penan claims are textualized in different ways? How do Penan conceptions of their audience condition the arguments they put forth and the forms of knowledge they deploy? What this points to is the need to foreground notions of agency in narratives of landscape and dispossession. The questions of whom Penan believe to be responsible for their plight and whom they believe is in the best position to help them are as central to this whole domain of discourse as are statements about what is occurring and how it effects their everyday lives. These are as much narratives of culpability as narratives of place.

For instance, in asserting claims to land, arguing for the establishment of reserved areas, attempting to demarcate borders, or contesting the claims of timber companies, Penanoften with the help of nongovernmental organization allies-produce maps or written declarations.

Penan see that loggers bring maps, show them official letters, and try to compel them to sign documents, and that all of these serve to validate company claims to Penan lands. Penan recognize that these methods are the single most effective way to assert their claims in a way that is meaningful to outsiders At the same time they are asserting their own claims to land, Penan deny the validity of maps produced by others. One nomadic headman, referring to map-making practices, described timber companies as "stealing [land] from open places"-that is, from the outside.

He declared government maps a lie because they are made from high above, showing only the shape of the land. The Penan see the fact that these maps are made from a distance as an indication of duplicity. Penan contrast the way companies make maps from a distance with the way they themselves do: by walking through and over every valley and ridge, by filling the place with names, and by sustaining themselves on resources that have been passed down for generations.

As one nomadic Penan man sarcastically told me, he would ask loggers, "If this is your land, why do you always ask us the names of rivers? Do you know the names of places? You and your people are always asking-what is the name of this river?, what is the name of that river? If you don't know these, you don't belong here."

The Penan response to logging is a product not only of the tangible effects of environmental degradation but also of the way Penan perceive themselves to have been treated by those with an interest in its continuation.

They are responding not only to logging as an activity that directly affects their lives but also to the agents of logging. When Penan discuss why they erect blockades, one theme arises more than any other: they say they blockade because "the government does not hear what we say," repeatedly describing the government and companies as being "deaf." Company and government officials do not listen to them, Penan assert, because the officials do not respect them, and they interpret this as a form of insult. Further, because they have made innumerable goodfaith attempts at dialogue, any action they might then take-most often blockades-can no longer be considered their fault. In recent years, we have observed a florescence of scholarship focused on indigenous conceptions of landscape.

This literature has alerted us to the rich variety of narrative forms through which societies inscribe their presence in places. Yet in listening to Penan statements about the forest and its destruction, we should be cautious about assuming that documenting Penan conceptions of landscape as some fixed entity-"indigenous knowledge"-is ever enough. Rather, we also need to try to discern how Penan conceptions of their audience condition the arguments they put forth.

THE UNIQUENESS OF THE CONTEMPORARY ENVIRONMENTAL CRISIS

Bennett (1976) describes a seemingly inevitable ecological transition from environmental equilibrium to disequilibrium. From this viewpoint there is nothing particularly unique about global environmental change. Bennett placed small-scale, tribal societies at the equilibrium end of the continuum, but argued that all people had the same behavioral propensities that would lead to drastic environmental change. However, this mixes human means, ends, and secondary consequences. Biocultural theory maintains that all people are driven by a human nature that seeks domestic security and the future welfare of one's children. People living in small-scale societies achieve these human ends cooperatively by remaining small, consuming resources sustainably, and resisting aggrandizing individuals who would promote security-reducing growth in consumption. Some people in commercially organized cultures competitively elevate their consumption levels in order to obtain these same ends for themselves. Bennett argues that equilibrium cultures are "only pauses in the overall historical tendency toward exponential increases in environmental use and impact." However, historical tendencies are not inevitable; they are the outcome of particular events and individual decision-making.

By the 1980s, as global economic growth and environmental problems intensified, some anthropologists began to argue that people have never been in equilibrium with the environment. For example, Rambo (1985) called Malaysian shifting cultivators "primitive polluters," because they put carbon dioxide into the atmosphere and lived in smoke-filled houses. He declared that primitive and civilized societies interacted with the environment in essentially the same way. In a similar vein, Krech (1999) maintains that Native Americans were not always conservationists, and were in the process of exterminating the bison before Europeans arrived. These revisionist anthropologists, and many others (Headland, 1997) were reacting against the widespread tendency of some environmentalists and deep ecologists to attribute a mystical oneness with nature and an ecological nobility to tribal peoples.

The mistaken implication of such romanticism of the human past, would be that our only salvation is a return to the Stone Age. This is a misleading issue because anthropologists have abundant evidence that tribal peoples were pragmatic materialists who burned on a large scale, sometimes killed more animals than they needed, felled trees to harvest fruit, and were not always guided by the spiritual sanctity of nature. There is also evidence that prehistoric humans hunted some animals to extinction, and may have contributed to the extinction of the Pleistocene megafauna, such as New World elephants, although there is much controversy on the details.

These facts need to be viewed in a larger perspective. The reality is that until 8000 years ago, when the world was still domestically organized and inhabited by only 8 million people living mostly in mobile bands at extremely low densities, there was no need for deliberate conservation practices. Likewise, optimal foraging theory suggests that intentional overhunting would have quickly proven unproductive, because as prey species become scarce, hunting them becomes inefficient.

Archaeological evidence that Australian aborigines successfully lived as hunters and foragers for at least 60 000 years, and aboriginals in Southern Africa successfully survived as a people for 130 000 years leaves little doubt that people living in very small-scale societies produced resilient cultural systems able to successfully maintain very long-term balances with their natural resources. The archaeological record needs to be compared with the estimates at the end of the twentieth century showing a high proportion of plants and animals threatened with extinction, or nearing threatened status. Nothing in human prehistory or history compares with the present rate of global environmental change.

It is remarkable that the scale of global change corresponds directly with increases in the scale of culture. This was dramatically confirmed by the ARCHAEOMEDES project, an interdisciplinary investigation of 30 000 years of environmental change in the Mediterranean region initiated by the European Union in 1992.

Researchers found that the measurable rate at which land degradation could be observed from land clearing, erosion, and dessication increased progressively by orders of magnitude from tens of millennia during the Paleolithic, to millennia during the Neolithic, to centuries during the Roman era, and to decades under industrial capitalism since 1850. In one region of Spain, researchers found that half of all the erosion over the past 10 000 years had occurred in the past 500 years, and it had accelerated over the past 150 years.

THE DRIVING FORCES BEHIND GLOBAL ENVIRONMENTAL CHANGE

The most widely accepted anthropological explanation for the rise of cultural complexity and intensified environmental problems has been population pressure on carrying capacity. Carrying capacity must be defined in relation to particular environments and technologies, and is not a constant. Population pressure is also a variable that can be different under different consumption demands and distribution patterns. Nevertheless, population pressure remains a powerful explanatory model. It is a variation on Malthus' (1895) observation that population has the potential to grow at a faster rate than food production. Population pressure and subsistence intensification have been used to explain the Mesolithic to Upper Paleolithic transition, the domestication of plants and animals leading to the transition from the Upper Paleolithic to the Neolithic, increased energy input and technological innovation in agriculture, and the origin of the state and civilization. All of these changed the environment. Population pressure has also been explicitly linked to contemporary environmental problems.

The problem with all of these population pressure explanations is that often they do not explain population pressure itself, and they do not deal with the social inequality that also produces scarcity. The archaeological record demonstrates that for most of human prehistory population growth was minimal, not because of high mortality, but because fertility was culturally limited. In domesticscale cultures in the absence of political pressures women opted for small families, because extra children were a disadvantage. Only in politically organized and commercial societies are there strong externally imposed incentives for population growth. When anthropologists have looked at extreme examples of supposed population pressure producing environmental stress and human misery, whether in Bangladesh, Brazil or El Salvador, they have found that social inequality, not population, was the problem.

Viewed from a culture scale and biocultural evolutionary perspective, the driving force behind global environmental change is the natural human desire of individuals to improve the material security of their households under cultural conditions of economic scarcity produced by social inequality and competitive striving. The important point is that economic scarcity and environmental problems are produced culturally by social inequality, they are not natural conditions.

ANTHROPOLOGISTS, INDIGENOUS PEOPLES, AND ENVIRONMENTAL CHANGE

Cultural ecological researchers have often helped indigenous people defend their ecosystems and natural resources against deterioration caused by the uninvited intrusion of outside commercial interests. The most important anthropological support, from both archaeologists and cultural anthropologists, has been in helping indigenous communities document their long-term use of particular places and resources, in order that extensive, traditionally owned and used territories can be legally titled to communities and protected. In some cases it has been useful to document that traditional uses were sustainable. Anthropologists have also helped demonstrate that indigenous communities have highly developed knowledge of their ecosystems, including the names and natural histories of plants and animals. Some indigenous communities have asked researchers to help them with the difficult problem of managing natural resources for both subsistence and commercial uses. Other communities have sought to protect portions of their territories for eco-tourism.

LOCAL KNOWLEDGE IN GLOBAL ENVIRONMENTAL ASSESSMENTS AND CONVENTIONS

Second, I consider the constitution of "knowledge," showing how scientists interested in local/indigenous knowledge have focused overwhelmingly on environmental knowledge and ignored other domains of knowledge that are salient in the effort to link scales of analysis The 1980s and 1990s showed remarkable growth and proliferation in indigenous movements worldwide. Much of the momentum for this movement was built around opposing the presence of extractive industries on indigenous lands, and the indigenous movement forged alliances with, among others, the global rainforest movement. Somewhat later, as the term indigenous knowledge began to appear on international agendas, the issues of bioprospecting and intellectual property rights became central concerns around which indigenous activists organized (Brush 1993).

Shifts in the conservation field have been equally significant. As global environmental change proceeds at an unprecedented pace, conservation has emerged as a central element in civic and political debates in the nations of both the North and the South. Responding to these debates, new forms of conservation practice are continually emerging. In the early 1990s, we witnessed the proliferation of bottom-up models under the rubric of community-based conservation. Since then, the "requiem for nature" argument has questioned the effectiveness of community-based approaches and called for stricter enforcement of protected area boundaries (Terborgh 1999). Simultaneously, we are seeing a host of new strategic priority-setting approaches that fall under the rubric of ecoregional conservation. Taking developments such as these into consideration, I conclude by offering an alternative approach to integrating local/indigenous knowledge into global scientific assessments that is premised on distinguishing several forms of mediation of local perspectives, and that incorporates a more expansive definition of knowledge.

LOCAL KNOWLEDGE, INDIGENOUS PEOPLES, AND ENVIRONMENTAL GOVERNANCE

In the past decade or so, it has become axiomatic to state that indigenous peoples "possess, in their ecological knowledge, an asset of incalculable value: a map to the biological diversity of the earth on which all life depends.

Encoded in indigenous languages, customs, and practices may be as much understanding of nature as is stored in the libraries of modern science". As selfevident as this may now seem, it does not provide much guidance with respect to how one moves between local knowledge and global science. That is the question that animates this volume and the Millennium Ecosystem Assessment as a whole.

In our efforts to bridge scales and epistemologies, we stand at a critical crossroad. For today we are confronted with two apparently contradictory trends in the domain of environmental governance. On the one hand, we have witnessed a trend toward valorizing indigenous/local forms of knowledge and mobilizing indigenous peoples. The Bridging Scales and Epistemologies conference, the outputs of the World Parks Congress, the World Conservation Congress, and the CBD/COP7-all of which express some form of support for indigenous priorities-are four manifestations of this trend.

On the other hand, in the last few years we have witnessed a decisive move by major conservation organizations toward cartographically enabled regional land use planning approaches under the rubric of ecoregional conservation. Along with this, we have witnessed the emergence of the field of "conservation finance" and the proliferation of social science-based metrics and models designed to monitor and manage social and political processes in conservation.

These three are linked discursively, strategically, and institutionally in a broader process of consolidation, and together they are reshaping the way conservation is conceptualized, planned, and administered. The comprehensive visions being promoted and the proprietary data-bases being produced in the emerging complementarities of spatial planning, investment, and social metrics have the potential to reshape the contours of the relationship between humanity and nature for generations to come.

Events such as the World Parks Congress and the World Conservation Congress can be seen, in essence, as exercises devoted to normalizing and reinforcing these complementary manifestations of consolidation. Attending these events, one is left with the impression that an enormous weight of managerialism has descended over conservation, much as it once did on development, and that this state of affairs is in large part due to the efforts of major conservation organizations to consolidate their authority over global conservation practices. They are achieving this consolidation by establishing administrative technologies in which they are taken for granted as methodological gatekeepers. Increasingly, conservation has become a gated community that one can enter only by accepting the methodological terms promulgated by major conservation organizations. This has occurred as tools or approaches that originated as emancipatory moves-stakeholder analysis, participatory mapping, community-based natural resource management-have been incorporated into the managerial apparatus of conservation. Once incorporated, they become tied to the imperatives of funding cycles, scaling up, accountability to donors, and more.

This situation is ironic, and it has major implications for integrating local and indigenous perspectives into conservation. Just when local voices and local forms of knowledge are being invoked as relevant to the setting of global conservation strategies and local conservation management, the institutional structures of global conservation that are now emerging are preventing them from being meaningfully included. What then becomes of alternative forms of conservation that are informed by local ways of knowing?

This consolidation of conservation practices by major conservation organizations is being achieved by the shift in scale that I have described. As Smith (1992) and Harvey (1996) remind us, scale is always political. Left unspoken in contemporary conservation is the relation between scale and hierarchy. Higher-level scales of visualization require higher-level structures of governance.

Ecoregional conservation is fundamentally about scale-both enlarging the scale of environmental interventions and linking information created at different scales into a single strategic blueprint for the future at an extended temporal scale. All the talk about scaling up in conservation is accompanied by a concern for improving "efficiencies" and reducing "transaction costs." Indigenous knowledge, when it moves up the scale, becomes both simplified and embedded in a range of other agendas. The former reifies the distinction between local/indigenous peoples living their lives in particular places and policy makers who are making sometimes momentous decisions about those peoples' lives.

Local/indigenous advocates, on the other hand, are refusing that distinction. Making meaningful progress in the future will entail a willingness on the part of conservation scientists and practitioners to work with indigenous/local communities in new ways, ways in which the tools of Western science are offered in support of local conservation priorities. What that means for how conservation initiatives are planned, implemented, and governed is not yet clear, but it is an effort that we must take seriously. The challenge is to seek productive terms of engagement. We cannot afford to perpetuate the polemic that the goals of conservation and indigenous rights are at odds with each other, or that indigenous knowledge is something to be packaged and passed up to "decision makers." The fate of biodiversity rests in part on how the conservation community responds to the challenge posed by indigenous and local communities and whether it is able to embrace this as an opportunity to create new alliances for conservation.

STUDY OF ANTHROPOLOGY

Anthropology consists of the study of humanity. It is holistic in two senses: it is concerned with all human beings at all times and with all dimensions of humanity.

In principle, it is concerned with all institutions of all societies. Since the work of Franz Boas and Bronislaw Malinowski in the late 19th-and early 20th-centuries, anthropology has been distinguished from other social science disciplines by its emphasis on cultural relativity, in-depth examination of context, cross-cultural comparisons, and the importance it places on long-term, experiential immersion in the area of research, often known as participant-observation.

In the United States, and to a lesser extent in Britain and other English-speaking countries, anthropology has often been traditionally conceived as comprising four related fields of study:

- Biological or physical anthropology seeks to understand the physical human being through the study of genetics, inherited traits and variations thereof, evolution, adaptation, etc. Subfields or related fields include primatology, nutritional anthropology, and human and population genetics.
- Socio-cultural anthropology is the investigation, often through long term, intensive field studies, of the culture and social organization of

a particular people: language, economic and political organization, kinship, gender relations, religion, mythology, symbolism, etc. (U.S. universities more often use the term cultural anthropology; British universities have tended to call the corresponding field social anthropology, and for much of the 20th century emphasized the analysis of social organization more than cultural symbolism.) In some European countries, socio-cultural anthropology is known as ethnology (a term also used in English-speaking countries to denote the comparative aspect of socio-cultural anthropology.) Subfields and related fields include psychological anthropology, folklore, anthropology of religion, ethnic studies, and cultural studies.

- Linguistic anthropology seeks to understand the processes of human communications, verbal and non-verbal; it identifies the many subtle elements of the world's languages and documents their structure, function and history. Linguistic anthropologists often draw on related fields including semeiotics, cognitive linguistics, discourse analysis, and narrative analysis.
- Archaeology is the study of the human past through the exploration, discovery, excavation, dating, and methodological analysis of material remains left by past humans; it includes prehistoric cultures and their development as well as historically documented cultures.

In countries of the British Commonwealth, social anthropology has often been institutionally separate from physical anthropology and primatology, which may be connected with departments of biology or zoology; and from archaeology, which may be connected with departments of Classics, Egyptology, and the like. In various times and places, anthropologists have also found themselves institutionally linked with scholars of folklore, museum studies, geography, sociology, social relations, ethnic studies, and cultural studies.

Some anthropologists have used anthropological studies to frame cultural critiques. This has been particularly prominent in America, from the popular critiques of Victorianism by Margaret Mead and Ruth Benedict through contemporary attacks on post-colonialism under the heading of postmodernism.

Anthropology is a methodologically diverse discipline, incorporating both qualitative methods and quantitative methods. Ethnographies-intensive case studies based on field research-have historically had a central place in the literature of the discipline. Currently, advancements across the scientific disciplines such as in physics and chemistry have aided anthropologists in their efforts to better understand all of humanity. Radiocarbon dating is just one of many technologies used regularly in the field of anthropology.

HISTORICAL AND INSTITUTIONAL CONTEXT

The anthropologist Eric Wolf once described anthropology as "the most scientific of the humanities, and the most humanistic of the sciences." Contemporary anthropologists claim a number of earlier thinkers as their forebears, and the discipline has several sources; Claude Lévi-Strauss, for example, claimed Montaigne and Rousseau as important influences. Anthropology can best be understood as an outgrowth of the Age of Enlightenment, a period when Europeans attempted systematically to study human behavior. The traditions of jurisprudence, history, philology, and sociology then evolved into something more closely resembling the modern views of these disciplines and informed the development of the social sciences, of which anthropology was a part. At the same time, the romantic reaction to the Enlightenment produced thinkers, such as Johann Gottfried Herder and later Wilhelm Dilthey, whose work formed the basis for the "culture concept," which is central to the discipline.

Institutionally, anthropology emerged from the development of natural history (expounded by authors such as Buffon) that occurred during the European colonization of the 17th, 18th, 19th and 20th centuries. Programs of ethnographic study originated in this era as the study of the "human primitives" overseen by colonial administrations. There was a tendency in late 18th century Enlightenment thought to understand human society as natural phenomena that behaved in accordance with certain principles and that could be observed empirically. In some ways, studying the language, culture, physiology, and artifacts of European colonies was not unlike studying the flora and fauna of those places. Saartje Baartman, a Namaqua woman, was examined by anatomist Georges Cuvier. This being said, curatorial practice has changed dramatically in recent years, and it would be inaccurate to see anthropology as merely an extension of colonial rule and European chauvinism, since its relationship to imperialism was and is complex.

Anthropology grew increasingly distinct from natural history, and by the end of the nineteenth century, it had begun to crystallize into its modern form; by 1935, for example, it was possible for T. K. Penniman to write a history of the discipline entitled "A Hundred Years of Anthropology." Early anthropology was dominated by proponents of unilinealism, who argued that all societies passed through a single evolutionary process, from the most primitive to the most advanced. Non-European societies were thus seen as evolutionary "living fossils," which could be studied in order to understand the European past. Scholars wrote histories of prehistoric migrations that were sometimes valuable but often also fanciful. It was during this time that Europeans, such as Paul Rivet, first accurately traced Polynesian migrations across the Pacific Ocean-though some of them believed those emigrations had originated in Egypt. Finally, concepts of race were developed with a view to better understanding the nature of the biological variation within the Human species, and tools such as Anthropometry were devised as a means of measuring and categorizing this variation, not just within the genus Homo, but in fossil Hominids and primates as well. Racialistic concepts were advocated by a few and gave rise to theories of Scientific racism.

Anténor Firmin wrote De l'égalité des races humaines (1885) as a direct rebuttal to Count Arthur de Gobineau's polemical four-volume work Essai sur l'inegalite des Races Humaines (1853-1855), which asserted the superiority of the Aryan race and the inferiority of blacks and other people of color. Firmin's work argued the opposite, that "all men are endowed with the same qualities and the same faults, without distinction of color or anatomical form. The races are equal" (pp. 450). Firmin grew up in Haiti, and was admitted to the Societé d' Anthropologie de Paris in 1884 while serving as a diplomat. His persuasive critique and rigorous analysis of many of that society's leading scholars made him an early pioneer in the so-called vindicationist struggle in anthropology. Many scholars also associate his work with the very first ideas of Pan-Africanism. Many modern anthropologists no longer refer to races as biological realities and may instead refer to the idea of clines.

In the twentieth century, academic disciplines began to organize around three main domains. The domain of the sciences seeks to derive natural laws through reproducible and falsifiable experiments; that of the humanities reflects an attempt to study different national traditions, in the form of history and the arts, as an attempt to provide people in emerging nation-states with a sense of coherence; the social sciences emerged at this time as an attempt to develop scientific methods to address social phenomena and provide a universal basis for social knowledge. Anthropology does not easily fit into one of these categories, and different branches of anthropology draw on one or more of these domains.

Drawing on the methods of the natural sciences and developing new techniques involving not only structured interviews, but unstructured participant observation, and drawing on the new theory of evolution through natural selection, the branches of anthropology proposed the scientific study of a new object: humankind, conceived of as a whole. Crucial to this study is the concept of culture, which anthropologists defined both as a universal capacity and a propensity for social learning, thinking, and acting (which they saw as a product of human evolution and something that distinguishes Homo sapiens-and perhaps all species of genus Homo-from other species), and as a particular adaptation to local conditions, which takes the form of highly variable beliefs and practices. Thus, culture not only transcends the opposition between nature and nurture, but absorbs the peculiarly European distinction among politics, religion, kinship, and the economy as autonomous domains. Anthropology thus transcends the divisions between the natural sciences, social sciences, and humanities to explore the biological, linguistic, material, and symbolic dimensions of humankind in all forms.

Anthropology in the United States

Anthropology in the United States was influenced by the availability of Native American societies as ethnographic subjects and the political debates around the definition of humanity and citizenship.

Jacksonian America and Polygenism

Late eighteenth century ethnology established the scientific foundation for the field, which began to mature when Andrew Jackson was President of the United States (1829-1837). Jackson was responsible for implementing the Indian Removal Act, the coerced and forced removal of an estimated 100,000 American Indians during the 1830s to Indian Territory in present-day Oklahoma; for insuring that the franchise was extended to all white men, irrespective of financial means while denying virtually all black men the right to vote; and, for suppressing abolitionists' efforts to end slavery while vigorously defending that institution. Finally, he was responsible for appointing Chief Justice Roger B. Taney who would decide, in Scott v. Sandford (1857), that Negroes were "beings of an inferior order, and altogether unfit to associate with the white race... and so far inferior that they had no rights which the white man was bound to respect." As a result of this decision, black people, whether free or enslaved, could never become citizens of the United States.

It was in this context that the so-called American School of Anthropology thrived as the champion of polygenism or the doctrine of multiple origins-sparking a debate between those influenced by the Bible who believed in the unity of humanity and those who argued from a scientific standpoint for the plurality of origins and the antiquity of distinct types. Like the monogenists, these theories were not monolithic and often used words like races, species, hybrid, and mongrel interchangeably. A scientific consensus began to emerge during this period "that there exists a Genus Homo, embracing many primordial types of 'species.'" Charles Caldwell, Samuel George Morton, Samuel A. Cartwright, George Gliddon, Josiah C. Nott, and Louis Agassiz, and even South Carolina Governor James Henry Hammond were all influential proponents of this school. While some were disinterested scientists, others were passionate advocates who used science to promote slavery in a period of increasing sectional strife. All were complicity in establishing the putative science that justified slavery, informed the Dred Scott decision, underpinned miscegenation laws, and eventually fueled Jim Crow. Samuel G. Morton, for example, claimed to be just a scientist but he did not hesitate to provide evidence of Negro inferiority to John C. Calhoun, the prominent pro-slavery Secretary of State to help him negotiate the annexation of Texas as a slave state.

TYPES OF MANKIND, 1854

The high-water mark of polygenitic theories was Josiah Nott and Gliddon's voluminous eight-hundred page tome titled Types of Mankind, published in 1854. Reproducing the work of Louis Agassiz and Samuel Morton, the authors spread the virulent and explicitly racist views to a wider, more popular audience. The first printing sold out quickly and by the end of the century it had undergone nine editions. Although many Southerners felt that all the justification for slavery they needed was found in the Bible, others used the new science to defend slavery and the repression of American Indians. Abolitionists, however, felt they had to take this science on its own terms. And for the first time, African American intellectuals waded into the contentious debate.

In the immediate wake of Types of Mankind and during the pitched political battles that led to Civil War, Frederick Douglass (1818-1895), the statesman and persuasive abolitionist, directly attacked the leading theorists of the American School of Anthropology. In an 1854 address, entitled "The Claims of the Negro Ethnologically Considered," Douglass argued that "by making the enslaved a character fit only for slavery, [slaveowners] excuse themselves for refusing to make the slave a freeman.... For let it be once granted that the human race are of multitudinous origin, naturally different in their moral, physical, and intellectual capacities... a chance is left for slavery, as a necessary institution.... There is no doubt that Messrs. Nott, Glidden, Morton, Smith and Agassiz were duly consulted by our slavery propagating statesmen" (p. 287).

Boasian Anthropology

Cultural anthropology in the United States was influenced greatly by the ready availability of Native American societies as ethnographic subjects. The field was pioneered by staff of the Bureau of Indian Affairs and the Smithsonian Institution's Bureau of American Ethnology, men such as John Wesley Powell and Frank Hamilton Cushing. Lewis Henry Morgan (1818-1881), a lawyer from Rochester, New York, became an advocate for and ethnological scholar of the Iroquois. His comparative analyses of religion, government, material culture, and especially kinship patterns proved to be influential contributions to the field of anthropology. Like other scholars of his day (such as Edward Tylor), Morgan argued that human societies could be classified into categories of cultural evolution on a scale of progression that ranged from savagery, to barbarism, to civilization. Generally, Morgan used technology (such as bowmaking or pottery) as an indicator of position on this scale.

Franz Boas established academic anthropology in the United States in opposition to this sort of evolutionary perspective. Boasian anthropology was politically active and suspicious of research dictated by the U.S. government and wealthy patrons. It was rigorously empirical and skeptical of overgeneralizations and attempts to establish universal laws. Boas studied immigrant children to demonstrate that biological race was not immutable, and that human conduct and behavior resulted from nurture, rather than nature.

Influenced by the German tradition, Boas argued that the world was full of distinct cultures, rather than societies whose evolution could be measured by how much or how little "civilization" they had. He believed that each culture has to be studied in its particularity, and argued that cross-cultural generalizations, like those made in the natural sciences, were not possible.

In doing so, he fought discrimination against immigrants, African Americans, and Native North Americans. Many American anthropologists adopted his agenda for social reform, and theories of race continue to be popular targets for anthropologists today. The so-called "Four Field Approach" has its origins in Boasian Anthropology, dividing the discipline in the four crucial and interrelated fields of sociocultural, biological, linguistic, and prehistoric anthropology.

Boas used his positions at Columbia University and the American Museum of Natural History to train and develop multiple generations of students. His first generation of students included Alfred Kroeber, Robert Lowie, Edward Sapir and Ruth Benedict, all of whom produced richly detailed studies of indigenous North American cultures.

They provided a wealth of details used to attack the theory of a single evolutionary process. Kroeber and Sapir's focus on Native American languages helped establish linguistics as a truly general science and free it from its historical focus on Indo-European languages.

The publication of Alfred Kroeber's textbook, Anthropology, marked a turning point in American anthropology. After three decades of amassing material, Boasians felt a growing urge to generalize. This was most obvious in the 'Culture and Personality' studies carried out by younger Boasians such as Margaret Mead and Ruth Benedict. Influenced by psychoanalytic psychologists such as Sigmund Freud and Carl Jung, these authors sought to understand the way that individual personalities were shaped by the wider cultural and social forces in which they grew up. Though such works as

Coming of Age in Samoa and The Chrysanthemum and the Sword remain popular with the American public, Mead and Benedict never had the impact on the discipline of anthropology that some expected. Boas had planned for Ruth Benedict to succeed him as chair of Columbia's anthropology department, but she was sidelined by Ralph Linton, and Mead was limited to her offices at the AMNH.

Anthropology in Britain

Whereas Boas picked his opponents to pieces through attention to detail, modern anthropology in Britain was formed by rejecting historical reconstruction in the name of a science of society that focused on analyzing how societies held together in the present.

The two most important scholars in this tradition were Alfred Reginald Radcliffe-Brown and Bronislaw Malinowski, both of whom released seminal works in 1922. Radcliffe-Brown's initial fieldwork, in the Andaman Islands, was carried out in the old style of historical reconstruction. After reading the work of French sociologists Émile Durkheim and Marcel Mauss, Radcliffe-Brown published an account of his research (entitled simply The Andaman Islanders) that paid close attention to the meaning and purpose of rituals and myths.

Over time, he developed an approach known as structural-functionalism, which focused on how institutions in societies worked to balance out or create an equilibrium in the social system to keep it functioning harmoniously. Malinowski, in contrast, advocated an unhyphenated functionalism, which examined how society functioned to meet individual needs. He is better known, however, for his detailed ethnography and advances in methodology. His classic ethnography, Argonauts of the Western Pacific, advocated getting "the native's point of view" and an approach to fieldwork that became standard in the field.

Malinowski and Radcliffe-Brown's influence stemmed from the fact that they, like Boas, actively trained students and aggressively built up institutions that furthered their programmatic ambitions. This was particularly the case with Radcliffe-Brown, who spread his agenda for "Social Anthropology" by teaching at universities across the Commonwealth. From the late 1930s until the postwar period appeared a string of monographs and edited volumes that cemented the paradigm of British Social Anthropology. Famous ethnographies include The Nuer, by Edward Evan Evans-Pritchard, and The Dynamics of Clanship Among the Tallensi, by Meyer Fortes; well-known edited volumes include African Systems of Kinship and Marriage and African Political Systems. Contemporary social anthropology is international and has branched in many directions.

Anthropology in France

Anthropology in France has a less clear genealogy than the British and American traditions. Most commentators consider Marcel Mauss to be the founder of the French anthropological tradition. Mauss was a member of Durkheim's Année Sociologique group, and while Durkheim and others examined the state of modern societies, Mauss and his collaborators (such as Henri Hubert and Robert Hertz) drew on ethnography and philology to analyze societies which were not as 'differentiated' as European nation states. In particular, Mauss's Essay on the Gift was to prove of enduring relevance in anthropological studies of exchange and reciprocity.

Throughout the interwar years, French interest in anthropology often dovetailed with wider cultural movements such as surrealism and primitivism which drew on ethnography for inspiration. Marcel Griaule and Michel Leiris are examples of people who combined anthropology with the French avant-garde. During this time most of what is known as ethnologie was restricted to museums, such as the Musée de l'Homme founded by Paul Rivet, and anthropology had a close relationship with studies of folklore.

Above all, however, it was Claude Lévi-Strauss who helped institutionalize anthropology in France. In addition to the enormous influence his structuralism exerted across multiple disciplines, Lévi-Strauss established ties with American and British anthropologists. At the same time he established centers and laboratories within France to provide an institutional context within anthropology while training influential students such as Maurice Godelier and Françoise Héritier who would prove influential in the world of French anthropology. Much of the distinct character of France's anthropology today is a result of the fact that most anthropology is carried out in nationally funded research laboratories (CNRS) rather than academic departments in universities.

Other influential writers in the 1970s include Pierre Clastres, who explains in his books on the Guayaki tribe in Paraguay that "primitive societies" actively oppose the institution of the state. Therefore, these stateless societies are not less evolved than societies with states, but took the active choice of conjuring the institution of authority as a separate function from society. The leader is only a spokeperson for the group when it has to deal with other groups ("international relations") but has no inside authority, and may be violently removed if he attempts to abuse this position.

Canadian Anthropology

Canadian anthropology began, as in other parts of the Colonial world, as ethnological data in the records of travellers and missionaries. In Canada,

Jesuit Missionaries such as Fathers LeClercq, Le Jeune and Sagard, in the 1600s, provide the oldest ethnographic records of First Nations in what was then the Domain of Canada.

True anthropology began with a Government department: the Geological Survey of Canada, and George Mercer Dawson (director in 1895). Dawson's support for anthropology created impetus for the profession in Canada. This was expanded upon by Prime Minister Wilfrid Laurier, who established a Division of Anthropology within the Geological Survey in 1810. Anthropologists were recruited from England and the USA, setting the foundation for the unique Canadian style of anthropology.

Early scholars include the brilliant linguist and Boasian, Edward Sapir, also Oxford graduates Marius Barbeau and Diamond Jenness. Born in rural Québec, Barbeau became a Rhodes scholar and eventually a classmate of Jenness. The two studied under Tylor and Marett at Oxford. In Canada, Barbeau and Jenness worked at the National Museum (as it became known later). In 1944, Canada's first home-grown anthropologist established the archive which has become an key source of ethnographic and folklore material.

Following George Mercer Dawson (of McGill, Montreal) and Franz Boas, Sapir and Barbeau conducted ethnographic research and collected material culture from the peoples of the Northwest Coast, especially Haida. Jenness is best known for his research in the Arctic among the Copper Inuit. However, in actuality, they all worked in a variety of areas in Canada, recording traditions and songs, studying languages, and collecting artifacts for the museum. They essentially had sole responsibility for the development of the profession in Canada from 1910 until 1925 when Sapir left. The development was slow relative to expansion (due to the colonizing needs) of Britain and the USA. The first academic position in anthropology at a Canadian university was awarded to Thomas McIlwraith. The next universities to hire anthropologists, UBC and McGill, did so only in 1947. The first PhD in anthropology was granted in 1956, with only a few more being granted until the late 1960s. The 1970s brought a boom in university development and in professional anthropology, and by 1980 about 400 people with doctorates in anthropology were employed in Canada, and many more with a master's degree. Harry Hawthorne built the department at UBC and set a standard for the use of anthropological research as a guide to public policy in his classic report to the federal government, coauthored by M.-A. Tremblay, "A Survey of the Contemporary Indians of Canada" (1966, 1967).

Canadian Anthropology is characterized by a combination of Americanist Boasian-influenced interest in First Nations, British Anthropological concerns with social function and process, and Francophone concerns with small, rural and ethnically isolated community studies. Issues of disparity, continuity and change, political-economy, environment and cultural ecology, and personality, culture and symbolism predominated the discourse from World War I to the Vietnam War era.

Post World War Anthropology

Before second World War British 'social anthropology' and American 'cultural anthropology' were still distinct traditions. It was after the war that the two would blend to create a 'sociocultural' anthropology.

In the 1950s and mid-1960s anthropology tended increasingly to model itself after the natural sciences. Some anthropologists, such as Lloyd Fallers and Clifford Geertz, focused on processes of modernization by which newly independent states could develop.

Others, such as Julian Steward and Leslie White, focused on how societies evolve and fit their ecological niche-an approach popularized by Marvin Harris. Economic anthropology as influenced by Karl Polanyi and practiced by Marshall Sahlins and George Dalton focused on how traditional economics ignored cultural and social factors. In England, British Social Anthropology's paradigm began to fragment as Max Gluckman and Peter Worsley experimented with Marxism and authors such as Rodney Needham and Edmund Leach incorporated Lévi-Strauss's structuralism into their work.

Structuralism also influenced a number of developments in 1960s and 1970s, including cognitive anthropology and componential analysis. Authors such as David Schneider, Clifford Geertz, and Marshall Sahlins developed a more fleshed-out concept of culture as a web of meaning or signification, which proved very popular within and beyond the discipline.

In keeping with the times, much of anthropology became politicized through the Algerian War of Independence and opposition to the Vietnam War; Marxism became a more and more popular theoretical approach in the discipline. By the 1970s the authors of volumes such as Reinventing Anthropology worried about anthropology's relevance.

In the 1980s issues of power, such as those examined in Eric Wolf's Europe and the People Without History, were central to the discipline. Books like Anthropology and the Colonial Encounter pondered anthropology's ties to colonial inequality, while the immense popularity of theorists such as Antonio Gramsci and Michel Foucault moved issues of power and hegemony into the spotlight. Gender and sexuality became popular topics, as did the relationship between history and anthropology, influenced by Marshall Sahlins (again), who drew on Lévi-Strauss and Fernand Braudel to examine the relationship between social structure and individual agency.

In the late 1980s and 1990s authors such as George Marcus and James Clifford pondered ethnographic authority, particularly how and why anthropological knowledge was possible and authoritative. They were reflecting trends in research and discourse initiated by Feminists in the academy, although they excused themselves from commenting specifically on those pioneering critics. Nevertheless, key aspects of feminist theorsing and methods became de rigeur as part of the 'post-modern moment' in anthropology: Ethnographies became more reflexive, explicitly addressing the author's methodology, cultural, gender and racial positioning, and their influence on his or her ethnographic analysis.

This was part of a more general trend of postmodernism that was popular contemporaneously. Currently anthropologists have begun to pay attention to globalization, medicine and biotechnology, indigenous rights, and the anthropology of industrialized societies.

2

Sociological Research in Development Anthropology

In their study on "The modern anthropology of Southeast Asia", Victor King and William Wilder raise the question in how far the region can be taken as a field of anthropological enquiry. After their initial discussion of cultural and social trends as well as anthropological studies, they conclude that the common issue of the region is its diversity.

They come to the rather pragmatic solution that "South-East Asia constitutes a convenient unit of study,... but... we should not think of it in terms of a bounded, unified and homogenous socio-cultural area". We doubt that there are homogenous socio-cultural areas anywhere else. These are usually constructed through the invention of traditions and ideological simulations. The interesting case with regards to Southeast Asia is, why no such homogeneity has been constructed, not even by anthropologists or sociologists.

Africa f.e. is as heterogeneous, but on the ideological-political level as well as in social science discourses the region has been constructed as comparatively homogenous. In contrast to Southeast Asia we do have some basic paradigms like segmentary society, rentier- (or even failed) state, etc. These emerged from comparative studies and discussions. Concerning Southeast Asia, we have f.e. a prominent production of theory regarding kinship issues and ritual speech2 but this is mainly focused on Indonesia.

Looking at Southeast Asia common ignorance is rather wide spread. Those working on Indonesia tend to ignore concepts based on research on the mainland

1. Prior to the Asian crisis Sharon Siddique argued that with the economic boom in East- and Southeast Asia, such a homogenization process in terms of an "Asian" identity might emerge. The discussion of Asian values and the community culture approaches of several NGO or the

post-colonial anti-westernization discourses of W. Bello, C. Mustafa Theerayuth Boonmee aim into such a direction.

2. The centre of this approach was formerly related to the "Leiden school of Anthropology" (van Wouden, de Josselin de Jong etc.) and had shifted to Canberra (Fox) at the end of the 20th century. A telling exception is the old discussion on the "plural society" and the "dual economy" or of the "Indianized states" during the first half of the last century. In contrast, later research is far more localized. Geertz "involution" has, as far as we know, never been applied for the analysis of development in Thailand, Vietnam, or anywhere outside of Indonesia. On the other hand the "loosely structured social system" or "patron-client" perspective has not received any attention outside of the discussion of Thailand. In these cases it can be discussed whether this really is a loss or not. However, it is surprising that the studies of Leach or Condominas of the minorities in the Mekong uplands, have received far more attention within anthropology than as stimulations for further research in Southeast Asia. Even in the later ethnographies of the "hill-tribes" one hardly finds any reference to Leach or Condominas.

As King and Wilder (2003) indicate, this has a lot to do with the colonial past when the initial paradigms for the study of Indonesia, Burma and Malaysia or Indochina were formed. This tradition of colonial fragmentation perpetuated by the languages used in publications, and teaching courses at the Universities, is one reason why no paradigm of Southeast Asian Studies has emerged, from which it might be possible to define the region as such as a field for anthropological enquiry. An additional more pragmatic reason certainly is the need to be fluent in quite a few rather difficult languages to do comparative field research.

Even globalization has not really lead to socio-cultural homogenization or stimulated comparative studies on a larger scale. A structural discrepancy among those working on Southeast Asia might have its root in this: Firstly, this discrepancy concerns the status of the researchers with regards to their discipline. In the European social science discussion Southeast Asian studies are marginal. In sociological research in Europe, the so-called "own society" still reigns supreme. Less so in anthropology and ethnology where field research in a far away location has always been part of the initiation rites. Most social science research in Southeast Asian universities or research institutes has in common with European institutions the focus on the own society and culture, which is in this case the own country. As mentioned, studies comparing processes in Thailand with Indonesia or Malaysia and vice versa are hardly found outside of the NUS (National University of Singapore). Thereby mainstream research in Southeast

Asia is marginal for Europe and vice versa mainstraem research in Southeast Asia is ignored in Europe. This is probably one reason why except theoretical discourses hardly any aspects of "European studies" feed into Southeast Asian studies and vice versa nothing much from Southeast Asian studies is cited by the great social scientists like Luhmann, Giddens, Bourdieu not to speak of Foucault, Baudrillard or others. Here Castells has to be cited as an important exception!

SOCIAL ANTHROPOLOGY

Social anthropology was founded in Britain following World War I through a methodological revolution pioneered by Bronislaw Malinowski's meticulous process-oriented fieldwork in the Trobriand Islands of Melanesia between 1915 and 1918 and through Alfred Radcliffe-Brown's theoretical program for systematic comparison that was based on a conception of rigorous fieldwork and the structure-functionalist conception of Durkheim's sociology. Other intellectual founders include W. H. R. Rivers and A. C. Haddon, whose orientation reflected the contemporary Volkerpsychologie of Wilhelm Wundt and Adolph Bastian, and Sir E. B. Tylor, who defined anthropology as a positivistic science following Auguste Comte. Edmund Leach (1962) defined social anthropology as a kind of comparative micro-sociology based on intensive fieldwork studies. There was never a settled theoretical orthodoxy on the nature of science and society but always a tension between several views that were seriously opposed.

Following World War II, sociocultural anthropology as comprised by the fields of ethnography and ethnology diverged into an American school of cultural anthropology while social anthropology diversified in Europe by challenging the principles of structure-functionalism, absorbing ideas from Claude Levi-Strauss's structuralism and from Max Gluckman's Manchester school, and embracing the study of conflict, change, urban anthropology, and networks. A European Association of Social Anthropologists (EASA) was founded in 1989 as a society of scholarship at a meeting of founder members from fourteen European countries, supported by the Wenner-Gren Foundation for Anthropological Research. The Association seeks to advance anthropology in Europe by organizing biennual conferences and by editing its academic journal, Social Anthropology/Anthropologie Sociale.

Other universities outside Britain do have departments of Social Anthropology, including in the United States (e.g., Stanford University, Harvard University, University of Chicago) and many non-European anthropologists identify themselves as social anthropologists, and often in ways not anticipated by the founders of the field, as for example in the subfield of structure and dynamics.

DEFINITION OF SOCIAL ANTHROPOLOGY

A single-sentence definition of social anthropology is of doubtful utility. Nevertheless, anthropology, in general, as we have defined it earlier, as the empirical and scientific study of man in his totality. Social anthropology, as we find it in India, South Africa and elsewhere outside the US, originates from England. Evans-Pritchard has elaborated the origin and development of social anthropology in England. He says that the subject was taught at Oxford since 1885 under the name of anthropology (not social anthropology) or ethnology. It was started at Cambridge and in London in 1900 and 1908, respectively. But the first university chair which bore the title of social anthropology was started in 1908. Sir James Frazer was made the honorary professor at Liverpool in 1908. Since then, the subject has received wider recognition and it is now taught under the name of social anthropology in Great Britain.

According to Evans-Pritchard, social anthropology includes the study of all human cultures and societies. The basic idea is that it tries to find out the structure of human societies all over the world. What social anthropology seeks to establish is that all societies notwithstanding any country are an organized whole. It is not just the separate customs or beliefs that are different, but the whole pattern of working, living, marrying, worshipping, organizing politically, keeping order and so on. Everything is different from the way we do things because the structure, the plan and the idea behind them are different.

Let us take the case of different tribal groups of India. The POI survey has identified 461 tribal groups in the country. In terms of customs, folkways, food habits and rituals no one tribe is similar to another. Despite this diversity all the tribal groups constitute a society whcih may be called as tribal society. In This tribal society, there are some traits of institutions which bear a close similarity or uniformity. There is a legitimate way of acquiring a mate, some system of succession and some kind of polity. It is here that social anthropology, on one hand, accounts for the social and cultural variation among, the different tribal groups, but on the other hand, it also conceptualizes the similarities found between tribal social systems and human relationship. As a matter of fact, when we try to understand the tribal economy as a particular group, say Santhal, we try to find out how this economy is connected with other aspects of the Santhal society. If we are required to define social anthropology in a comprehensive way, we would say that this discipline seeks to find out institutional relations within the society and relations between societies. In other words, we try to find out the social institutions of the Santhals as connected with the tribe and also the relations of these institutions with the institutions of other tribes and wider non-tribal society or the national society.

The British social anthropology, as Evans-Pritchard observed, is a branch of sociology. He writes :

> *When people speak of sociology they generally have in mind studies of particular problems in civilized societies. If we give this sense to the word, then the difference between social anthropology and sociology is a difference of field, but there are also important differences of method between them. The social anthropologist studies primitive societies directly, living among them for month or years, whereas sociological research is usually from documents and is largely statistical.*

Evans-Pritchard, by comparing social anthropology with sociology, brings out a clear definition of social anthropology. According to him, "social anthropology has primitive societies as its subject matter. In other words, it is concerned with the affairs of the primitive, indigenous people, hills and forest people, scheduled tribes and other such groups of people". Another part of the definition of social anthropology is the fieldwork. Data in social anthropology are generated in the field and not on the desk of a study room in a library. It is because of this that M. N. Srinivas lived for months together in Rampura village. Similar fieldwork was done by Mackim Marriot in Kishnagarhi of Alighar district.

The definition of social anthropology, as given by Evans-Pritchard is as under :

> *It is the relation to this general body of theory to primitive social life which constitutes the subject of social anthropology. In other words, social anthropology studies: (1) primitive societies, and (2) generates data by doing fieldwork.*

John Lewis, another British social anthropologist, has also defined social anthropology on the pattern of the definition given by the British social anthropology school. In a very straightforward manner, he says that anthropology is the study of the way of life of primitive people as they can still be found today, or not too much altered by contact with civilization.

Lewis has defined social anthropology is a very conservative style. He argues that social anthropology studies primitives but these primitives are qualified by a statement that they should remain unaffected by social change.

In other words, only those primitives according to Lewis need to be studied who remain outside the impact of social and cultural change. Such a study would bring out only those characteristics of the tribal society whcih are queer and rigid. For Lewis, anthropology is nothing but the study of other cultures, as advocated by John Beattie. This makes social anthropology a comparative discipline of the study of social institutions. However, despite limiting the field of social anthropology to the study of primitive communities,

Lewis suggests for establishing a pattern of indigenous society. Eriksen puts all emphasis on the study of small places in social anthropology. He argues that social anthropology intensively is concerned with the small places. But these small places relate to large issues. Defining social anthropology in a new perspective, Eriksen writes :

> *One may, therefore, say that anthropology asks large questions, while at the same time it draws many of its insights from small places... it has been common to regard social anthropology's traditional focus on small scale non-industrial societies, compared with other subjects dealing with culture and society. However, because of changes in the world and in the discipline itself, this is no longer an accurate description. Practically, and social system can be studied anthropologically contemporary anthropological research displays an enormous range, empirically as well as thematically.*

Eriksen's definition of social anthropology contests Lewis' definition. Lewis says that social anthropology studies primitive people as they can still be found, uninfluenced by social change. Eriksen rejects it objects to it and says that social anthropology does not remain restricted to primitive people. It studies any social system, the qualification of such a social system is that it is of a small-scale non-industrial kind of society. Thus, according to Eriksen, social anthropology studies.

(1) small-scale society,
(2) non-industrial society, and
(3) small and larger issues of the society.

Early Social Anthropology

The students of sociology generally talk about the founding fathers of the discipline. It is unanimously agreed all over the world that Emile Durkheim, Max Weber and Karl Marx are the architects of sociology. They have constituted the tradition and culture of sociology. It is argued that historically, early anthropology started sometime during the 18th century. If we are able to identify the thinkers who founded anthropology, we would be able to define the discipline.

According to some historians, the origin of social anthropology is traced to David Hume and Immanuel Kant who were the first philosophers to define social anthropology. Hume was a British empiricist who argued that "experience was the only trustworthy source of valid knowledge". It was through the initiation of Hume that empiricism entered the social sciences including social anthropology. Empiricism literally means "based on experience". Thus, according to Hume, social anthropology studies the society out of empiricism, that is, experience.

Kant contested the empirical approach to social anthropology as given by Hume. He argued that people had certain shared innate faculties, which were assumed to be embedded in their mode of thought. In other words, he held that human beings were born with certain 'formulas' for thinking; from idea, it follows that people all over the world would think in roughly the same way.

The definitions of anthropology given by Hume and Kant, though quite vague, boil down to the fact that anthropology records the experiences of people. It is not a desk social science. It builds on data coming out of experience. However, the approach taken by Kant is highly philosophical and psychological. He propounds that anthropology should study the universal mental traits of human beings. If a serpent spreads it hood, it frightens a man; and if a locality is gutted, the inhabitants run in panic. Such a behaviour is universal; it is found all over the world and in all societies. According to Kant, anthropology, therefore, identifies the human universal mental traits.

It is also amazing to know that the history of anthropology neither begins with Herodotus nor with any other thinker. It is said that the systematic history of anthropology rightly begins from Henry Maine and henry Morgan. These two thinkers could be said to be the founding fathers of social anthropology. How did they define social anthropology? For them,, social anthropology was the study of social evolution. These thinkers tried to find the origin and development. Let us now turn to the definition of social anthropology in terms of evolution which remained pervasive and dominant all through the 19th century.

The 19th Century Evolutionary Approach

The 19th century social anthropologists were greatly influenced by the findings of Darwin and his associates. The biological evolutionists established that the origin of man has passed through several stages—from *homo sapiens* to apes. Darwinism promoted Social Darwinism. The anthropologist following the logic fo Dawinsim tried to establish the origin of social institutions. It would not be wrong to say that Social Darwinism prevailed throughout the 19th century and first quarter of the 20th century.

The definition of social anthropology given by Social Darwinists is a landmark in the development of this discipline. The foundations of present anthropology go back to Henry Maine's *Ancient Law* (1861) and Lewis Henry Morgan's books, including *Ancient Society* (1877). "Both of these authors developed theories of primitive society which were to wield influence far into the 20th century. Maine, who had worked in India, proposed a distinction between status and contract societies, a conceptual pair which is reminiscent of many later distinctions between 'modern' and 'traditional' societies. In status-based or traditional societies, Maine argued, kinship was usually crucial in determining one's position in society; in contract-based societies, on the contrary, it would rather be the individual achievements of persons that provided them with their positions.'

The contributions of Morgan to early anthropology was, however, a beginning of the theory of social evolution. The theory says that anthropology studies the human society which has passed through the stages of savagery, barbarism and civilization. At the savagery stage human beings had an economy characterized by subsistence. Man earned his livelihood through hunting and food gathering. At the stage of barbarism agriculture and animal husbandry were the sources of living while those societies which reached the stage of civilization, developed literacy, technology, industry and the state.

The theory expounded by Morgan was one, there wee other theories too; for instance, Westermark set out the theory of human marriage; Brifault propounded the theory of family. What we intend to conclude here is that there was a team of evolutionists which established theories of culture, including religion and other fields of social anthropology. These evolutionists included. W.H.R. Rivers, Tylor, Frazer, William James, A.C. Haddon and Charles Seligman. All these early social anthropologists defined social anthropology as a science of social evolution. In other words, social anthropology studies the origin and evolution of social institutions such as society, religion, marriage, kinship and so on.

EMERGENCE OF MODERN SOCIAL ANTHROPOLOGY

Before discussing the emergence of modern social anthropology we would like to observe that the social anthropology as we teach and research today has to be relevant to the reality of society, if it has to survive. With this current perspective in kind we propose to discuss historically the meaning and definition of sociology as it has come after the arrival of modern anthropology. Franz Boas and Bronishlaw Malinowski are often regarded as the first modern anthropologists. Boas belonged to Germany but he came to the US in 1880 to study the American Indians. He conducted field research by himself and founded modern American cultural anthropology. Alfred Kroeber, Ruth Benedict and Margarete Mead students of Boas. Boas contributed substantially to the field of anthropology. His most important contribution seems to be the doctrine of 'cultural relativism'. It is a concept which argues that each group should be studied according to its own culture. In other words, culture is specific to a group. Even today, Boas' contribution of cultural relativism is considered to be an indispensable methodological tool of social and cultural anthropology. Thus, Boas defined anthropology as a social science of culture study. This is one aspect of modern anthropology.

Malinowski hailed from Poland who later on emigrated to Britain in 1910. He is known for his work on the Trobrianders living in the islands of New Guinea. He conducted fieldwork among these tribals between 1915 and 1918. This kind of work, where he had close and enduring contact with the local community, contributed a lot to the knowledge kit of social anthropology and sociology. As a matter of fact, the method of functionalism which Robert Merton developed in sociology draws heavily from Malinowski. He emphasized the importance of studying the interrelationships of various aspects of society, and therefore, held that long field studies were absolutely necessary.

According to Malinowski, social anthropology is concerned with the interrelationships of various parts of tribal society. In other words, tribal economy, politics, kin are all interrelated. Social anthropology is interested to study functional relations among the members of tribal society.

Yet another thinker who substantially contributed to British social anthropology and helped to define it was A.R. Radcliffe-Brown. He was profoundly inspired by Durkheim's writings on social integration. Durkheim made important studies about the division of labour in primitive societies and about religion and totemism.

Radcliffe-Brown was a functionalist and considered society as an organic whole. He is said to be the founder of structural-functionalism in anthropology. This is a doctrine about the ways in which the various institutions of society contribute to its stability. Malinowski was no structural-functionalist although he described himself as a functionalist. Radcliffe-Brown and his followers regarded individuals and their actions as 'side-effects' of society, whose deepest meaning constituted in contributing to social integration, Malinowski was instead inclined to argue that society exists to satisfy the needs of the individuals. The contrast between these leading in early modern anthropology can be traced up to this very day: some tend to regard society as an unintended consequence of the actions of individuals, whereas, others regard persons largely as products of their society.

Besides Boas, Malinowski and Radcliffe-Brown, there are also others who have shaped the subject matter and definition of modern social anthropology. These include Marcel Mauss, Levy-Bruhl and Sigmund Freud.

As pointed out earlier, social anthropology, as we find it in India and other Asian countries, is the offspring of British social anthropology. In order to define social anthropology in a scientific and precise way, Evans-Pritchard makes a list of the titles of these which were awarded degrees. All these titles indicate the kind of work social anthropologists were doing. On the strength of the research work done, it could be said that the students of social anthropology are concerned with the study of political institutions, religious, institutions, class distinctions based on colour, sex, or rank, economic institutions, legal or quasi-legal institutions and marriage, and also of social adaptation, and of the entire social organization or structure, of one or other people. On the basis of the sample of these titles Evans-Pritchard observes:

> *Social anthropology, thus not only covers societies round the globe but also a number of different studies... Social anthropologists study a primitive society in the same way whether it is in Polynesia, Africa or Lapland; and whatever they are writing about—a kinship system, a religions cult or a political institution it is examined in its relation to the total social structure in which it is contained.*

Evans-Pritchard's approach to the understanding of the subject draws only from the earlier modern anthropologists, mainly, Malinowski and Radcliffe-Brown. His definition does not go further: it is the study of the interrelations in a primitive society.

Evans-Pritchard was the product of the forties. During this decade and earlier also, the British colonial empire had wider horizons extending to India and Africa. The prevailing social reality, therefore, inspired Evans-Pritchard and his generation to define social anthropology in terms of the social status of primitive societies. It also brought home the fact that fieldwork in colonial societies was easier to carry out. For instance, in India, the British administrators-turned-anthropologists never had to bear the brunt of the rough and tough life of India's villages. The fieldwork was done by the petty Indian bureaucrats. Evans-Pritchard's approach to social anthropology was quite suitably not only to him but also other British social anthropologists. His definition was, thus, historically conditioned.

Development of Social Anthropology

Every age of geographical discovery has seen a burst of interest in the new kinds of society that the explores have found; we are reminded today by the descendants of these peoples that were there all along, and were only 'new' to foreigners who had lived for centuries in ignorance of their existence. The explorers and colonizers, however, being accustomed to take it for granted that they were themselves the standard of what people ought to be like, were always prompted to ask why other peoples were so unlike themselves.,

THE EARLY TRAVELLERS

The sixteenth century was one period, the eighteenth another. The French essayist Montaigne (1533-92) was much interested in the apparently paradoxical contrasts between the customs of his own country and others. His essay on cannibals was one of the sources of Shakespeare's *Tempest.* The attitude of Prospero to Caliban, the hardly-more-than-monster who repaid his master's attempt to educate him by trying to rape his daughter, is a paradigm of the cruder form of colonialist attitude, so close to contemporary experience as to be horrifying. A slightly subtler approach to the question of the meaning of physical differences between population was the theological arguments whether people with browns skins who wore no clothes could really be descendants of Adam.

Eighteenth-century Europeans were less certain than sixteenth-century ones that all the advantage was on their side. Interest was now directed to North America and Polynesia. The Indians were taken to represent the pristine condition of man—though Rousseau's 'noble savages' of the golden age of natural man were those same Caribs who the Spanish missionaries had thought could not have souls. Hobbes in the seventeenth-century had already thought the American Indians approached pretty closely to his imagined state of nature where every man's hand was against his neighbour and men's lives were 'solitary, poor, nasty, brutish and short'.

Reports of the manners and customs of distant lands now began to be treated not just as bits of interesting information but as data for constructing historical schemes of the development of society. Some writers start the history of comparative ethnography with the Jesuit missionary Lafitau, who in 1724 published a book comparing American Indian customs with those of the ancient world as described by Latin and Greek writers. A little later (1760) Charles de Brosses wrote on parallels between ancient Egyptian religion and that of West Africa—a subject that occupies that the attention of a new school of historians today. In 1748 Montesquieu published his *Espit des Lois,* based on reading and not on travel, and thus became for some the first theorist of our subject. He considered that differences in legal systems could be explained by relating them to differences in other characteristics of the nations which possessed them, population, temperament, religious beliefs, economic organization, and customs generally, as well as to their environment. This could entitle him to be described as the first functionalist.

In Scotland a number of men were seeking to trace the evolution of society from—as one of them put it—'a state little better than mere brutality to that most perfect state... in ancient Greece'. The most famous of them, Adam Ferguson and Adam Smith, based their generalizations, as did Montesquieu, on the widest reading about the institutions of different societies that was available in their day. The idea of such an evolution did not have to wait, as is popularly supposed, for Darwin's discovery of the principle of natural selection in the evolution of biological species, and indeed the influence of Darwin's work was on the whole unfortunate when it led to attempts to fit societies and races—the latter not always clearly distinguished from societies—into evolutionary schemes.

Diffusionism

The nineteenth century saw the beginning of travel for the sake of the observation of different examples of human society. The most famous of the nineteenth-century travellers was Bastian (1826-1995), who engaged as a ship's doctor in order to see the world, and succeeded in visiting a remarkable number of places. He was interested in ideas as such, and particularly religious beliefs, and was struck and the similarities which he found in places far apart. He attributed this to psychological qualities common to all human beings — the 'psychic unity of mankind', which leads people independently to think of similar myths and rituals.

His younger contemporary Ratzel (1844-1904), also a great traveller, opposed his theories root and branch. Ratzel was more interested in implements than in ideas, and he argued that since most people are not inventive, these must have been invented by individuals in a few places and spread over the world by migration. He looked therefore for similarities between objects found in places far apart, but did not seek for further evidence of the migration by whcih they wee supposed to have spread over the world. His theory is called *diffusionism.* It was developed further by his more sophisticated pupil Frobenius (1873-1938), who held that 'culture-complexes'—combinations of objects and items of behaviour—must have been diffused as whole, since there was no other reason why the items should be found in association. He made it his business to trace the path of their diffusion. This approach to the history of civilization reached its *reductio ad absurdum* with the theory that all the basic inventions were made in one place, namely Egypt.

As we in this century see symbolism more and more as the reflection of universal human experience, at any rate when considering mythology and religious beliefs, we are likely to range ourselves with Bastian against the diffusionists. Not much need really be said about the war of the diffusionists and evolutionists, but it must be mentioned because the writers to whom contemporary social anthropology owes most were still caught up in it. No one today would argue either that *all* social institutions, techniques, and myths were spread through the world by diffusion, or that *every* society has independently evolved every aspect of its own culture. The whole discussion now seems rather unreal, ignoring as it does the obvious fact that the imitation of tools and techniques is something very different from the 'taking over' of institutions or myths. In fact most of the writers whose work has lived have recognized that the history of society must have been a mixture of independent development and the effects of external influences. Most of them, also, have been evolutionists in the sense that they have been more interested in the development of institutions than in the question of their geographical spread.

Theories of Evolution

The most famous of the early evolutionists was the American Lewis H. Morgan (1818-81). He was a member of a student whcih purported to imitate the rituals of the Iroquois, and this inspired him to spend some time living among the Iroquois so as to find out what their society was really like. In 1851 he published *The League of the Iroquois,* the first description of a political system based on the relations between autonomous lineages, like those later analysed by Evans-Pritchard and others.

In the process of learning the languages of the Iroquois Morgan discovered that the names they used to describe kin relationships—father, brother, etc.—were applied to a much wider range of people than they are in English. His method of recording the names by looking at them all from the point of view of one individual, whom he called *Ego,* has become the standard anthropological technique. He was surprised to find that several other Indian tribes had a system of terminology identical with that of the Iroquois, though their languages were quite different. He was so much impressed by this that he started collecting lists of minship terms from all over the world, and in 1871 he published, in *Systems of Consanguinity and Affinity,* an account of these with a theory explaining them. The extension outside the individual family of the words for parents seemed to him to indicate a confusion about who people's parents were; and as there was clearly no such confusion among the Iroquois, he supposed the terminology must have been carried over from an earlier state of things when there was. This led him to postulate as series of stages in the development of the family from complete promiscuity to monogamous marriage.

Meanwhile other writers were seeking evidence for earlier stages of society in the Greek and Latin, and, in one important case, the Indian classics. Bachofen (1815-87), a Swiss jurist, first developed a theory about societies which trace descent through women. He supposed that they consisted of people who did not recognize male parenthood. On a combination of mythology and the examples in Herodotus he built a picture of a 'matriarchal' society which was a sort of mirror-image of what we are used to; women exercised authority, the left hand was superior to the right, the moon to the sun, female deities were worshipped, and so, on. He argued that patriarchal Roman society must have been established as the result of a male revolt against this.

J. F. McLennan (1827-81) believed that apparently anomalous usages could be explained as symbolic representations of actions that had really been performed at earlier stages of social development. In his *Studies in Ancient History* he observed that marriage customs often involved a mock capture of the bride, although she and her family had agreed to the marriage. He concluded that at one time men must in fact have seized their wives by force. Why, he asked? Because they were not allowed to marry within their own tribe (to him a tribe was a roaming band of about a thousand people, like the American Indian tribes) and were at war with all outsiders. McLennan gave us the words *exogamy* and *endogamy* for marrying *outside,* and *inside,* a defined group.

Henry Sumner Maine (1822-88), a jurist who was a member of the Viceroy's council in India, was struck by the similarities between the recorded laws of ancient Rome and ancient India(and later on ancient Ireland). All these were patrilineal societies. This inclined him to think that patriliny was the original rule of descent, but he was primarily interested in the development of legal rules from a starting point within recorded history. His central theme is the change from societies based on status, where an individual's rights and obligations are given in virtue of his status, and particularly his status in the descent group, and one based on contract, in which he deliberately enters into new relationships for specific purposes. Modern anthropologists recognize that there is room for contractual, or freely chosen, relationship in the simplest societies. Marriage is one, clientship, or voluntary dependence, another. But we still find the idea of the contrast useful, and observe that the weight of *ascribed status,* as it was defined in this study is much heavier in societies of simple technology. Maine's most famous book is *Ancient Law.* We owe to him the terms taken from Roman law: *agnation* for the recognition of relationship by descent through males, and *cognation* for the recognition of relationship between all descendants of one father and mother.

Edward Burnet Tylor (1832-1917) is often described as the father of British anthropology, though some of us might prefer to trace our paternity to Maine or even Morgan. Tylor's influence at the present day is stronger among American than among British anthropologists. He was greatly interested in religion, which he sought to define as broadly as possible, in opposition to those who supposed that religion must be concerned with gods conceived as separate from and superior to humanity, or must involve a particular emotional attitude towards its object, or required that a system of beliefs should have some other feature in common with the world religions before it was entitled to be put in the same category with them. Tylor offered as a 'minimum definition' of religion 'the belief in Spiritual Beings.' This he expected would be found everywhere, and his expectation was justified. The experience of dreaming, he argued, led people to suppose that they themselves had some non-corporeal part which could be separated from their bodies; while the belief that spirits inhabited inanimate objects was, he though, an expression of the child's tendency to personify all the objects around him. Like all his contemporaries Tylor thought of humanity in the mass as growing through the ages from childhood to maturity, and of primitive peoples as being all still in the stage of childhood.

Tylor also sought to make anthropology scientific by the use of what the called 'social arithmetic', or the tabulation of customs in order to see how they were correlated. Thus he might be regarded as the founder of the 'comparative method', thought he did not use this term. In discussing the question whether patriliny or matriliny came earlier, he remarked that in matrilineal societies authority was not exercised by women, and therefore he rejected the terms 'matriarchal' and 'patriarchal'.

He noted that in the simple societies it was very common for the children of a brother and a sister to marry and gave us the term *cross-cousin marriage* to describe such unions. In the context of exogamy he made observations which anticipate by some sixty years recent discussions on the feud and the circumstances which keep it within bounds, as well as one of the basic generalizations of Fortes' and Evans-Pritchard's introduction to *African Political Systems* (1940). Exogamy, he said, 'cements....uncultured population... into nations capable of living together in peace....till they reach the period of higher military and political organization'; and 'By binding together a whole community with ties of kinship and affinity, and especially by the peacemaking of the women how hold to one clan as sisters and to another as wives, it tends to keep down feuds and heal them when they arise, so as at critical moments to hold together a tribe which under endogamous conditions would have split up'.

Tylor introduced into anthropology the term 'survival', though the notion that social usages could be adequately explained as survival from earlier stages of society was implicit in the theories of Morgan and McLennan. He defined survivals as 'processes, customs, opinions, and to forth, state of society different from that in which they had their original home, and they thus remain as proofs and examples of an older condition of culture out of which a newer has been evolved'. By defining the subject-matter of anthropological study as 'culture' Tylor became the founder of a whole school.

Robertson-Smith (1846-94) was one of the scholars who in the nineteenth-century began to interpret the Old Testament in its historical context. He also travelled widely in Arabia an so was able to reinforce his theories from observation of contemporary Arab society. His best-known work, *The Religion of the Semite* (1889), makes the point that in 'traditional' religions—those not purporting to have been founded as the result of a revelation—ritual is much more important than dogma. There is an obligation to participate in rites, but people are not called upon to express adherence to specific beliefs. Robertson-Smith saw religion as an extension of the social field of include divine beings, relations with whom were patterned on those between living men. Accordingly he saw the essence of sacrifice in the feast shared by the worshippers with the their god.

J.G. Frazer (1854-1941) first made the general public aware of anthropology. His *Golden Bough* is still the most widely read book on the subject. Frazer's interests were largely confined to the field of religion. Within that field he assembled a vast mass of data illustrating different themes of myth or ritual, which he found first in the Greek and Latin authors, and then come to see as characteristic of the religions of simple societies all over the world. He showed how universal was the concern of religion with the fertility of men, their herbs, and their land; and his theory of 'sympathetic magic' drew attention to the symbolism whereby magical rites imitate the effect they are intended to produce. He interpreted this as the result of a mistaken process of reasoning to which he gave the name of 'bastard science'; such an explanation is no longer found convincing, but in recent years Levi-Strauss (1908 -) in Franc has revived our interest in the kind of classification by analogy that Frazer was describing.

Around the turn of the century the line of descent of anthropology in Britain began to diverge from that in America. The great figure in the immediate past of America is that of Franz Boas (1858-1942), who was trained in the natural sciences, and turned to the study of human society after an expedition to the Eskimo country which was primarily geographical in intention. Boas' scientific training caused him to look very sceptically at current theories of the evolution of society or the diffusion of culture. He would have none of their conjectures, but he was still interested in discovering how particular cultures grew up rather than how living men organized life in society. He was one of the last scholars to do valuable work in all the different branches of anthropology.

FRENCH SOCIOLOGISTS AND THEIR INFLUENCE

In France, meantime, there was growing up a school of sociology which profoundly influenced the leading British anthropologists of the early twentieth-century, and caused them to direct their interest wholly to the study of contemporary societies, neglecting archaeology and physical anthropology, which up to that time had been thought of as integral parts of our subject. The French scholars were led by Emile Durkheim (1858-1917) and published much of their important work in a periodical, *L'Annee Sociologique,* which they found in 1898 as a vehicle for their point of view.

Durkheim followed the British sociologist Herbert Spencer in asserting that there was a specifically social aspect of reality which could not be reduced to the behaviour of individual organisms. Social facts, he said, were to be studied as 'things', with an existence independent of the consciousness of the individual people who make upon society (*Regles de la Methode Sociologique.* 1895). The social facts are rules of behaviour, *norms,* standard fo value, expectations that society has of its members, behaviour that corresponds to them, and reactions to deviant behaviour. As far as any particular person is concerned, they are given. He finds himself in a world where thee are certain rules, and where he will suffer if he breaks them. Of course people do sometimes break rules, either on calculation or no impulse. This can be called, if you like, expressing their individuality. But the rules themselves do not express anyone's individuality, and social behaviour— the behaviour that is thought appropriate to particular people in particular circumstances—is a response to complex pressures and not the expression of a kind of personality. This is the principle of social analysis that laymen find hardest to grasp, but it is fundamental.

Much of Durkheim's work was concerned with industrialized Europe, but be applied himself also to some of the problems of the simpler societies. In *De la Division duTravail Social* (1893) he contrasted the type of solidarity to be found in societies in with a simple and a complex division of labour. In the former, he said, *solidarity* (a word which is difficult to define, but which indicates the way a society is held together) is *mechanical.* That is to say, society is held together by the association of *like* units. He gave as an example the rings of the earthworm. An earthworm lives as one organism, but if you cut it in half it does not die; the head and tail are not organically interdependent. Where the division of labour is complex, solidarity is organic, you cannot cut up the society into independent parts; you cannot even picture how this could be done. The solidarity of such a society is the product of the links between *complementary* units. The solidarity of brothers mechanical, that of husband and wife organic. Brothers have *like* interests in their common patrimony and should join in defending their rights; but brothers who have grown up together can separate and form independent households; indeed they usually do. But one cannot conceive a household apart from the Co-operation of the husband and wife.

In his *Formes Elementaires de la Vie Religieuse* (1912) Durkheim used the results of field studies of the Australian aborigines, Following Robertson-Smith's emphasis on the importance of ritual, he argued that ritual reflects the order of society, and indeed that the god who is worshipped is in fact society—a personification of the rules of conduct and values that the society most cherishes. Periodic rituals bring its members together in a highly charged emotional atmosphere, and thus impress upon them their interdependence and the importance of keeping the rules which maintain it. Although most anthropologists today would say that this approaches does not exhaust the study of religion it drew attention of an aspect of it that had been neglected until then; and every fieldworker now must look out for those aspects of religious ritual— and they are many—that do symbolize social relationships.

Those of Durkheim's contemporaries who are read by students of social anthropology are Marcel Mauss (on the exchange of gifts and the principle of social relationships that we now call reciprocity) and Van Gennep (on various types of ritual). Their successor in the present generation, Levi-Strauss, has developed the idea of reciprocity as the fundamental principle of social structure, which Malinowski had demonstrated from his work in the Trobriand Islands.

The work of the French sociologists influenced the two leading British anthropologist of the twentieth-century, Malinowski and Radcliffe-Brown, whose theories are so much a part of the body of thought of contemporary anthropology that they are better dealt with in the contest of current problems. Malinowski's theories relied more on psychology than Durkheim's, but Radcliffe-Brown, for whom the concept of social structure was central, followed very closely in Durkheim's footsteps.

As social anthropologists have cast their nets wider, have studied societies of larger scale and have sought to draw comparisons between the non-industrialized societies of today and those of which there is historical record, they have sought inspiration in the work of writers who treat historical data from a sociological point of view. Chief among these is Max Weber (1864-1920), whose work on different types of political system has suggested many interesting problems to people studying societies with well-developed institutions of government.

Field Studies

The idea that anthropologists should go out and find their own data instead of relying on what travellers could tell them became current at the end of the last century. Boas' work among the Eskimo was done in 1883-4; from 1897 to 1902 he was in charge of the Jesup North Pacific expedition which aimed establishing the relationship between the aboriginal peoples of North-eastern Asia and North America. One product of this study was his interest in the Kwakiutl Indians of Vancouver Island, whom he revisited at intervals for nearly fifty years. His collection of 'texts'—statements made by informants—is said to be the largest ever made for a single society, but he do not have the experience of living continuously among them, and recording actual events. Contemporary with this was the Torres Straits and New Guinea expedition of 1898, in which six British scientists, trained in anthropology) took part. The anthropological work was done by A.C. Haddon, C.G. Seligman, and W.H.R. Rivers, and all three went on to do independent fieldwork, Haddon and Seligman in Papua, Seligman later in Ceylon and in the Southern

Sudan, Rivers among the Todas in Madaras. In all these expeditions the anthropologists worked mainly by questioning informants, sometimes through the medium of interpreters. But when they knew the local language they did write down verbatim what their informants said. Boas in particular insisted on the importance of these 'vernacular texts'.

Rivers was the last British field anthropologist to interpret usages that the actually observed as survivals of an earlier stage of society; he built up out of such interpretations of indigenous and invading cultures. The Royal Society awarded him a gold medal for his *History of Melanesian Society* published in 1914. This is worth bearing in mind by anyone who thinks that Malinowski, when he published his *Argonauts of the Western Pacific* in 1922, overemphasized the importance of looking at customs in their contemporary context.

Nevertheless we owe to Rivers a number of concepts that are still fundamental in the analysis of kinship. He first gave a technical meaning to *descent* as membership of the social group of either the mother or the father, and distinguished *secession* as the transmission of rank or office from *inheritance* as the transmission of property. Rivers held that rules of marriage were the determinants of differences between kinship systems. It was Mrs. Seligman who in 1922 pointed out that the most important distinguishing factor was the rule of descent itself.

The next big advance in fieldwork was Malinowski's expedition to the Trobriand Islands. There was an element of chance in this. Malinowski, as an Austrian subject, was allowed as an alternative to stay in the Trobriands. This long stay in one little island enabled him to see the actual processes of Trobriand social life, the differences between professed norms and usual behaviour, the kind of social pressures brought to bear on offenders, as well as making an exhaustive analysis of the language. Every anthropologist now is expected to spend at least a year in the society he is studying, preferably two with an interval between to collect himself and find what questions he has forgotten to ask. Few have been able to rival the standard of thoroughness set by Malinowski, whose data can be used by students today to answer questions that he himself had not thought of.

The development of knowledge in any field proceeds by the questioning of what is taken for granted at any one time. That is why laymen often find it easier to disregard the knowledge of specialists because 'they don't agree' than to ask what they are disagreeing about or how much common ground they have. But students seeking knowledge sometimes fall into the opposite error of thinking that there must somewhere be one right answer to all the disputed questions. A few of the controversies described in this study have been settled by showing that some assumption was contrary to observed fact. But in the main rival theories express different ways of looking at facts.

Experience may show that the one way is more fruitful than others, but none claims to have attained finality.

SCOPE OF SOCIAL ANTHROPOLOGY

While defining social anthropology, Beals and Hoizer write, "It is concerned with culture *per se*, whether it belongs to the primitive men of the stone age or the European City-dwellers of today," Although it is more properly a definition of cultural anthropology yet is surely and clearly shows that the field of social anthropology is very wide. It includes a study of different parts of culture, social institutions, economic institutions and political administration. The main branches of social anthropology are given below :

Ethnography : Ethnography is the main field fo social anthropology. As is clear from its name, it studies the human races. Its scope also includes the study of cultures of different races.

Familial Anthropology : Family is the basic institution of society. Social anthropology, therefore, studies the family also. This branch of social anthropology is known as familial anthropology. It takes up a comparative study fo the families of different cultures and societies. It studies the different forms of family along with its progress.

A family is based on marriage. Familial anthropology, therefore, includes a study of different forms or marriage. It also includes other blood relations along with marriage.

Economic Anthropology : Economic rules play an important part in social organization. Some radical changes take place in social structure along with a change in economic administration Social anthropology, therefore, minutely studies economic administration of primitive and civilized human societies and of different levels of evolution in them.

Political Anthropology : Political administration also has an important place in social structure along with economic administration. Social anthropology, therefore, studies all types of political administration, laws, governments and rules of punishment, etc. This branch of social anthropology is known as political anthropology.

Symbiology and Linguistics : The study of different symbols of human behaviour, which are current in languages of different societies, supplies many important facts for the study of society. Social anthropology, therefore, studies; all these also. The whole linguistics field falls within this branch of social anthropology. The main branches of linguistics are given below :

(i) *Descriptive linguistics* : It studies the individual and regional languages.

(ii) *Historical linguistics* : It is a historical study of languages;

(iii) *Comparative linguistics* : It studies the contemporary facts about language;

(iv) *Common linguistics* : It studies the between the minimum and maximum roots of some languages.

Thought and Art : The study of thoughts in theoretical study is very important. Thought includes religion, magic, science, even legends. Social anthropology is a comparative study of all these things in ancient human societies. Art is an important par of culture and culture depicts the interior of a society. Social anthropology studies, sculpture, metallurgy, and even dancing and instrumental and vocal music.

Social Anthropology and Religion

Religion is a universal and pervasive institution in human society. Of all the manifestations of man's intellectual and social life, religion stands most elusive. The belief, thought, and action with which religion is concerned could be found at all levels of culture, primitive or civilized.

Religion may be defined as a 'system of beliefs, emotional attitudes, and practices by means of which a group of people attempt to cope with ultimate problems of human life.' Religion is the institutionalized set of belief men hold about supernatural forces.

Theories of Religion

Social anthropologists have endeavoured to construct theories of religion which provide an explanation to human behaviour. The religious life of any people is manifested in outward form, in beliefs and in rites. The beliefs are about sacred things and rites addressed to them. Mere beliefs do not constitute religion, it is rites which make religion a living force. The shape of the supernatural power varies from society to society. Some religions believe that the supernatural power is abstract (*nirakar*) and can only be experienced and imagined. On the other hand, there hand, there are religions which argue that the supernatural power has a definite shape, a dimension, it is an idol. It is a form, a shape (*sakar*). On the basis of some such notions anthropologists have formed the following explanations about religion :

(1) Animism
(2) Polytheism
(3) Monotheism
(4) Naturalism

Animism

About a century has passed Edward B. Tylor pointed out that all peoples in primitive societies believed in animism. It means there is existence of intangible, non-material or spiritual beings which may be souls, ghosts, ancestral spirits, fauna, flora, ogres or monsters, or simply objects. The origins of beliefs in such spiritual beings are probably multiple, as Tylor believes. The presence of vitality in a living person, which is unquestionably absent from a corpse, results in an animistic interpretation. The persons and things heard, seen or felt in dreams or in temporary hallucinatory experiences as in hot weather or when a person is exhausted, or when he is under the influence of drugs, yield the same result. Additional experiences which bring about or reinforce animistic beliefs are echoes, reflections in quiet pools, or other natural phenomena. Tylor contended that "once the basic premise of an animistic ideology—belief in the existence of spiritual beings and souls—had been developed, the path was laid for eventual development to later stages of religious ideology. But before the second stage was reached, the original belief in souls and spirits had come to include beliefs in malevolent spirits or demons, and in the spirits of ancestors."

Tylor presumed that the souls, ancestral spirits and other supernatural beings of the first developmental stage tended to change as a second stage into other higher or more grandisose forms of supernatural beings such as nature gods. Neither proof nor disproof is available economic level are not well enough known to indicate that they are largely or exclusively animistic. In fact, other forms of supernatural concepts, such as that of a single deity, also appear along with animistic concepts among such peoples. Animism thus has passed through several stages of development. And, these stages very from tribe to tribe and country to country. In our country, the form of animism that we find is based on ancestor worship.

Polytheism

Literally, polytheism means belief in more than one great spiritual power. This type of religious belief is found at all socio-economic levels. Defining polytheism John Lewis says that it is "believing in and worshipping in several gods". Polytheism is widely prevalent in advanced agricultural-pastoral socio-economic systems and in cultures like those of ancient Egypt, Mesopotamia, Greece and Rome. Tylor has tried to establish an evolutionary formulation of religion. In this context, he says that among the tribals, the beginning of religion started with animism. At the second stage of development it took the form of animitism. The concept of animitism holds that a non-material, impersonal, non-individualized spiritual essence pervades all things, manifests itself in inanimate and animate things. This spirit is considered to be a source of great power. It has miraculous efficacy.

The third stage of the evolution of religion is polytheism. This form of religious belief—belief in plural gods—is rarely found. However, when the simple agricultural economy develops, polytheism emerges. In the simple, small-sized societies, there is prevalence of animism and animitism, but polytheism is associated with higher level of development attained by a particular tribal group.

Monotheism

Monotheism means belief in a single deity. Its propitiators believe that the cosmos is a unity, with one god who created and ordered all. Monotheism is the widely held idea that the belief in only one god is of recent development. It has not definitely been proved to be correct. "However, no absolutely pure monotheism has ever developed among peoples in primitive economies and has never characterized any such society.

This is known for societies of primitive economy because of available evidence regarding the universality of animistic ideologies among them. Yet, the synchronous occurrence of such animistic ideologies along with a monotherisitic-like belief in a high god is certain."

Naturalism

Yet another form of animism is found in naturalism. It is believed that the supernatural power has its manifestation in things of nature. The roaring of clouds, lightening in the clouds and earthquakes are nothing but the expressions of the supernatural power. When there are floods in the rivers, the supernatural power expresses its wrath. The wrath of the power, therefore, has to be propitiated by animal sacrifice. It is believed, especially by the tribals, that nature has supernatural power which has to be respected. Because of this power there is awe for nature and people worship nature in the form of earth, fire, water, stars, floods, etc.

CONSTITUTION OR NATURE OF THE PERSON

Historically, Christian theologians have differed on how many components make up the human being.

Two Parts (Dichotomism)

The traditional Christian view, still held by a large number of lay Christians and theologians, is that the human being is made up of 2 components: material (body/flesh) and spiritual (soul/spirit). The soul or spirit departs from the body at death, and will be reunited with the body at the resurrection.

Three Parts (Trichotomism)

A minority of theologians have argued that human beings are made up of three distinct components: body/flesh, soul, and spirit. This is technically known as trichotomism. The biblical texts typically used to support this position are 1 Thessalonians 5:23 and Hebrews 4:12.

One Part (Monism)

Modern theologians increasingly hold to the view that the human being is an indissoluble unity. This is known as holism or monism. The body and soul are not considered separate components of a person, but rather as two facets of a united whole. It is argued that this more accurately represents Hebrew thought, whereas body-soul dualism is more characteristic of Greek philosophy and Platonic thought. Monism also appears to be more consistent with modern neuroscience, which has revealed that the so-called "higher functions" of the mind are emergent from the brain, rather than being based in an immaterial soul as was previously thought. An influential exponent of this view was liberal theologian Rudolf Bultmann. Oscar Cullmann was influential in popularizing it.

Origin of Humanity

The Bible teaches in the book of Genesis the humans were created by God. Some Christians believe that this must have involved a miraculous creative act, while others are comfortable with the idea that God worked through the evolutionary process.

God's Image in the Human

The book of Genesis also teaches that human beings, male and female, were created in the image of God. The exact meaning of this has been debated throughout church history.

Origin/Transmission of the Soul

There are two opposing views about how the soul originates in each human being. *Creationism* teaches that God creates a "fresh" soul within each human embryo at or some time shortly after conception. The Roman Catholic Church officially teaches the creationist position. Notably, this is not to be confused with creationism as a view of the origins of life and the universe.

Traducianism, by contrast, teaches that the soul is inherited from the individual's parents, along with his or her biological material.

Sinful Nature

Christian theology traditionally teaches the corruption of human nature. However, there have been a range of views held throughout church history. Pelagius taught that human nature is not so corrupt that we cannot overcome sin. Arminians believe that our nature is corrupt, but that free will can still operate. Saint Augustine believed that all humans are born into the sin and guilt of Adam, and are powerless to do good without grace. John Calvin developed the doctrine of total depravity.

Death and Afterlife

Christian anthropology has implications for beliefs about death and the afterlife. The Christian church has traditionally taught that the soul of each individual separates from the body at death, to be reunited at the resurrection. This is closely related to the doctrine of the immortality of the soul. For example, the Westminster Confession (chapter XXXII) states:

"The bodies of men, after death, return to dust, and see corruption: but their souls, which neither die nor sleep, having an immortal subsistence, immediately return to God who gave them"

Intermediate State

The question then arises: where exactly does the disembodied soul "go" at death? Theologians refer to this subject as the intermediate state. The Old Testament speaks of a place called *sheol* where the spirits of the dead reside. In the New Testament, *hades*, the classical Greek realm of the dead, takes the place of *sheol*. In particular, Jesus teaches in Luke 16:19-31 (Lazarus and Dives) that *hades* consists of two separate "sections", one for the righteous and one for the unrighteous. His teaching is consistent with intertestamental Jewish thought on the subject.

Fully developed Christian theology goes a step further; on the basis of such texts as Luke 23:43 and Philippians 1:23, it has traditionally been taught that the souls of the dead are received immediately either into heaven or hell, where they will experience a foretaste of their eternal destiny prior to the resurrection. (Roman Catholicism teaches a third possible location, Purgatory, though this is denied by Protestants.) "The souls of the righteous, being then made perfect in holiness, are received into the highest heavens, where they behold the face of God, in light and glory, waiting for the full redemption of their bodies. And the souls of the wicked are cast into hell, where they remain in torments and utter darkness, reserved to the judgment of the great day." (*Westminster Confession*)

Some Christian groups which stress a monistic anthropology deny that the soul can exist consciously apart from the body. For example, the Seventh-day Adventist church teaches that the intermediate state is an unconscious sleep; this teaching is informally known as "soul sleep".

DISCOURSE

Discourse is a term used in semantics and discourse analysis, but it also refers to a social conception of discourse, often linked with the work of French philosopher Michel Foucault (1926-1984) and Jürgen Habermas' The Theory of Communicative Action (1985). Each thinker had personal conceptions of discourse which are thought to be incompatible with the other. They remain two important figures in this field; Habermas trying to find the transcendent rules upon which speakers could agree on a groundworks consensus, while Foucault was developing a battle-type of discourse which opposed the classic marxist definition of ideology as part of the superstructure.

Discourse Analysis

The Social Conception of Discourse

In the social sciences, a discourse is considered to be an institutionalized way of thinking, a social boundary defining what can be said about a specific topic, or, as Judith Butler puts it, "the limits of acceptable speech"-or possible truth. Discourses are seen to affect our views on all things; it is not possible to escape discourse. For example, two notably distinct discourses can be used about various guerrilla movements describing them either as "freedom fighters" or "terrorists". In other words, the chosen discourse delivers the vocabulary, expressions and perhaps also the style needed to communicate. Discourse is closely linked to different theories of power and state, at least as long as defining discourses is seen to mean defining reality itself. According to Foucault's definition, discourse must be heard rather as synonym of his concept of episteme, notwithstanding important theoretical displacements (episteme was first thought as the condition of possibility of discourses).

In other words, Foucault's discourse must both be understood as a singular discourse, as defined above, and as a more general discourse, meaning the boundaries given to any particular discourse. In this more general sense, discourse is not composed only of words, which would be to limit oneself to a dualist conception: as he demonstrated in Discipline and Punish, discourse is also composed of architectural dispositifs, such as Jeremy Bentham's panopticon or the map of a classroom, etc. A dispositif is "a resolutely heterogeneous assemblage, containing discourses, institutions, architectural buildings, reglementary decisions, scientific statements, philosophical, moral, philanthropic propositions, in one word: said as well as non-said, those are the dispositif's elements. The dispositif in itself is the network that we can establish between those elements."

According to Foucault, discourse can't be reduced to an ideological reflexion, it is to be thought as itself a Kampfplatz or battlefield. Against Kant's conception, Foucault argues that truth is not the objective bounty that the winners can take; truth is not an absolute, it is on the contrary produced in this battle with strategic aims. This conception of truth may be related to Althusser's theory on the "epistemological break" between science and ideology (the "epistemological break" is not an event, but a process; "science" always has to fight for its truth against ideology, which keeps coming back). Since knowledge and power are intrinsically related, according to Foucault, he can thus say that power relations are immanent to discourses, whereas in the classic marxist conception, the discourse is conceived as the ideological superstructure-which, of course, interacts with the base, as Marx wrote, but this does not impede the power relations being essentially located in the economic base, afterward reflected in the superstructure.

Furthermore, as he showed in Society Must Be Defended (1976-77), discourse is not anyone's property and thus has no essentialist meaning. The same discourse may change political sides quite often, being reappropriated and endlessly modified, as did Foucault show in his analysis of the historical and political discourse; there is a "polymorphic tactics" of discourses. In other words, specific discourses are not tied to the subject; rather, the subject is a social construction of the discourse, or, as Nietzsche said, a "grammatical fiction". Judith Butler would maintain this ambivalency of discourse, which can be performed in various contexts by different subjectivities. In psychology critical perspectives on discourse have been developed in relation to developmental psychology by Erica Burman and in relation to social theory and psychoanalysis by Ian Parker (psychologist), and a critical research group, the Discourse Unit, was founded by these two. This perspective has also then had an influential bearing on critical psychology.

Philosophy and religion are often closely interwoven in Eastern thought. Many Asian religious and philosophical traditions originated in India and China and spread across Asia through cultural diffusion and the migration of peoples. Hinduism is the wellspring of Buddhism, the Mahayana branch of which spread north and eastwards from India into Tibet, China, Mongolia, Japan and Korea and south from China into Vietnam. Theravada Buddhism spread throughout Southeast Asia, including Sri Lanka, parts of southwest China, Cambodia, Laos, Myanmar, and Thailand.

Indian philosophy includes Hindu philosophy. They contain elements of nonmaterial pursuits, whereas another school of thought from India, Carvaka, preached the enjoyment of material world. Confucianism and Taoism, both of which originated in China have had pervasive influence on both religious and philosophical traditions, as well as statecraft and the arts throughout Asia.

During the 20th century, in the two most populous countries of Asia, two dramatically different political philosophies took shape. Gandhi gave a new meaning to Ahimsa, a core belief of both Hinduism and Jainism, and redefined the concepts of nonviolence and nonresistance. During the same period, Mao Zedong's communist philosophy became a powerful secular belief system in China.

Folk Religions

Folk religions practiced by tribal groups are common in Asia, Africa and the Americas. Their influence can be considerable; may pervade the culture and even become the state religion, as with Shintoism. Like the other major religions, folk religion answers human needs for reassurance in times of trouble, healing, averting misfortune and providing rituals that address the major passages and transitions in human life.

The "American Dream"

The American Dream is a belief, held by many in the United States, that through hard work, courage, and self-determination, regardless of social class, a person can gain a better life. This notion is rooted in the belief that the United States is a "city upon a hill, a light unto the nations," which were values held by many early European settlers and maintained by subsequent generations.

Marriage

Most Christian churches give some form of blessing to a marriage; the wedding ceremony typically includes some sort of pledge by the community to support the relationship. In marriage, Christians draw a parallel with the relationship between Jesus Christ and His Church. The Roman Catholic Church believes it is morally wrong to divorce, and divorcées cannot remarry in a church marriage (without a formal annulment of the previous marriage).

Cultural Studies

Cultural studies developed in the late 20th century, in part through the re-introduction of Marxist thought into sociology, and in part through the articulation of sociology and other academic disciplines such as literary criticism. This movement aimed to focus on the analysis of subcultures in capitalist societies. Following the non-anthropological tradition, cultural studies generally focus on the study of consumption goods (such as fashion, art, and literature). Because the 18th-and 19th-century distinction between "high" and "low" culture seems inappropriate to apply to the mass-produced and mass-marketed consumption goods which cultural studies analyses, these scholars refer instead to "popular culture".

Today, some anthropologists have joined the project of cultural studies. Most, however, reject the identification of culture with consumption goods. Furthermore, many now reject the notion of culture as bounded, and consequently reject the notion of subculture. Instead, they see culture as a complex web of shifting patterns that link people in different locales and that link social formations of different scales. According to this view, any group can construct its own cultural identity. Currently, a debate is underway regarding whether or not culture can actually change fundamental human cognition. Researchers are divided on the question.

Cultural Change

Cultures, by predisposition, both embrace and resist change, depending on culture traits. For example, men and women have complementary roles in many cultures. One gender might desire changes that affect the other, as happened in the second half of the 20th century in western cultures. Thus there are both dynamic influences that encourage acceptance of new things, and conservative forces that resist change. Three kinds of influence cause both change and resistance to it:

1. forces at work within a society
2. contact between societies
3. changes in the natural environment.

Cultural change can come about due to the environment, to inventions (and other internal influences), and to contact with other cultures. For example, the end of the last ice age helped lead to the invention of agriculture, which in its turn brought about many cultural innovations.

In diffusion, the form of something (though not necessarily its meaning) moves from one culture to another. For example, hamburgers, mundane in the United States, seemed exotic when introduced into China. "Stimulus diffusion" refers to an element of one culture leading to an invention in another. Diffusion of innovations theory presents a research-based model of why and when individuals and cultures adopt new ideas, practices, and products.

"Acculturation" has different meanings, but in this context refers to replacement of the traits of one culture with those of another, such as happened to certain Native American tribes and to many indigenous peoples across the globe during the process of colonization. Related processes on an individual level include assimilation (adoption of a different culture by an individual) and transculturation.

Cultural invention has come to mean any innovation that is new and found to be useful to a group of people and expressed in their behavior but which does not exist as a physical object. Humanity is in a global "accelerating culture change period", driven by the expansion of international commerce, the mass media, and above all, the human population explosion, among other factors. The world's population now doubles in less than years.

Culture change is complex and has far-ranging effects. Sociologists and anthropologists believe that a holistic approach to the study of cultures and their environments is needed to understand all of the various aspects of change. Human existence may best be looked at as a "multifaceted whole." Only from this vantage can one grasp the realities of culture change.

DEVELOPMENT ANTHROPOLOGY

Development anthropology refers to the application of anthropological perspectives to the multidisciplinary branch of development studies. It take international development and international aid as primary object. In this branch of anthropology, the term development refers to the social action made voluntary by different agents (institutions, business, enterprise, state, independent volunteer) who are trying to modify the economic, technical, political or/and social life of a given place in the world, especially in developing nation.

For development anthropology, development is neither a goal, an ideal nor a failure. It is an object of study. With researches on the field, the anthropologist can describe, analyze and understand the different actions of development that took and take place in a given place. The various impacts on the local population, environment, social and economic life are to be examined.

Development Criticism

Most of the development anthropologists severely criticize what had been done before in development effort since 1960. They blame the different agents to have only considered a small aspect of the local people's lives without analyzing the consequences on a larger scale. Again, international development is often seen in anthropology as an extension of the colonialism era or as post-colonialism. Some author, like Arturo Escobar even see international development as a means for the occident to keep control over the resources of the former colonies. In fact, between 1945 and 1960, the former colonies were going through the decolonization era, and the development plan helped to maintain dependency from the formers colonies to the old metropole. This point of view is largely supported by the dependency theory. Mainly, the development project is seen as an effort of modernization and an eradication of the indigenous culture.

Applied Anthropology in Development

On the other side, some anthropologist while contribute directly on the field to some projects development. They'll put in use their perspective of development. This method differ from economists in some areas in which this is evaluated. Economists look at aggregate measures like gross national product and per capita income, as well as measures of income distribution and inequality in a society. Anthropology can provide a more fine-grained analysis of the qualitative information behind these numbers, such as the nature of the social groups involved and the social significance of the composition of income. Thus, development anthropologists often deal with assessing the important qualitative aspects of development sometimes ignored by an economic approach.

DIFFUSION (ANTHROPOLOGY)

The diffusion of innovations within a single culture applies, for example, to the acceptance of new technological products like the wristwatch and the personal computer, foods like tomato sauce and California sushi, music styles like opera and bossa nova, dressing styles like the top hat and blue jeans, ideals like democracy or feminism, and so on. Diffusion across cultures, too, is a well-attested and uncontroversial phenomenon. For example, the practice of agriculture is widely believed to have diffused from somewhere in the Middle East to all of Eurasia, less than 10,000 years ago, having been adopted by many pre-existing cultures. Other established examples of diffusion include the spread of the war chariot and iron smelting in ancient times, and the use of cars and Western business suits in the 20th century.

Mechanisms for Inter-cultural Diffusion

Inter-cultural diffusion can happen in many ways. Migrating populations will carry their culture with them. Ideas can be carried by trans-cultural visitors, such as merchants, explorers, soldiers, diplomats, slaves, and hired artisans.

Technology diffusion has often occurred by one society luring skilled scientists or workers by payments or other inducement. Trans-cultural marriages between two neighboring or interspersed cultures have also contributed. Among literate societies, diffusion can happen through letters or books (and, in modern times, through other media as well).

Diffusion Theories

The many models that have been proposed for inter-cultural diffusion are:

- Heliocentric diffusionism--the theory that all cultures originated from one culture.
- Culture circles diffusionism (Kulturkreise)--the theory that cultures originated from a small number of cultures.
- Evolutionary diffusionism--the theory that societies are influenced by others and that all humans share psychological traits that make them equally likely to innovate, resulting in development of similar innovations in isolation.

- Biblical diffusionism--all culture started with Adam; during the Renaissance, this theory was formalized as the great chain of being.

A concept that has often been mentioned in this regard, which may be framed in the evolutionary diffusionism model, is that of "an idea whose time has come"-whereby a new cultural item appears almost simultaneously and independently in several widely separated places, after certain prerequisite items have diffused across the respective communities.

This concept has been invoked, for example, with regard to the development of calculus by Newton and Leibnitz, or the inventions of the airplane and of the electronic computer.

The Theory Applied to Middle Ages Europe

One of the most remarkable examples of diffusion theory is the massive technology addition into Europe in the period 1000 to 1700 AD. In the prior Dark Ages period, Byzantine and Asian cultures were far more advanced than Europe: however, this era beginning in the High Middle Ages reversed that balance and resulted in a Europe which greatly surpassed Asian, Byzantine and Muslim cultures in pre-industrial technology.

In the Dark Ages, many important basic inventions had their roots elsewhere, notably: gunpowder, clock mechanisms, shipbuilding, paper and the windmill; however, in each of these cases Europeans not only adopted the technologies, but improved the manufacturing scale, inherent technology and applications to a point clearly surpassing the evolution of the original invention in its country of origin.

For example, by the late fourteenth century, European fleets. Armed with advanced cannons, decimated Arab and Chinese fleets, paving the way for unfettered domination of the seas that led to the colonial era.

Diffusion Disputes

While the concept of diffusion is well accepted in general, conjectures about the existence or the extent of diffusion in some specific contexts have been hotly disputed.

An example of such disputes is the proposal by Thor Heyerdahl that similarities between the culture of Polynesia and the pre-Columbian civilizations of the Andes are due to diffusion from the latter to the former-a theory that currently has few supporters among professional anthropologists.

Attempts to explain similarities between two cultures by diffusion are often criticized for being ethnocentric, since they imply that the supposedly "receptors" would not be capable of innovation. In fact, some authors made such claims explicitly-for example, to argue for pre-Columbian trans-oceanic contact as the "only possible explanation" for the origin of the great civilizations in the Andes and of Central America. Those disputed are fueled in part by the overuse of cultural diffusion, starting in the late 19th century, as a blanket explanation for all similarities between widely dispersed cultures. The most famous proponent of this theory was William Graham Sumner, who argued that civilization first formed in Ancient Egypt and then diffused to other places.

Diffusion theories also suffer from being inherently speculative and hard to prove or disprove; especially for relatively simple cultural items like "pyramid-shaped buildings", "solar deity", "row of standing stones", or "animal paintings in caves". After all, the act of diffusion proper is a purely mental (or at most verbal) phenomenon, that leaves no archaeological trace.

Therefore, diffusion can be deduced with some certainty only when the similarities involve a relatively complex and partly arbitrary collection of items-such as a writing system, a complex myth, or a pantheon of several gods.

Another criticism that has been leveled at many diffusion proposals is the failure to explain why certain items were not diffused. For example, attempts to "explain" the New World civilizations by diffusion from Europe or Egypt should explain why basic concepts like wheeled vehicles or the potter's wheel did not cross the ocean, while writing and stone pyramids did.

KINSHIP

Kinship is the most basic principle of organizing individuals into social groups, roles, and categories. It was originally thought to be determined by biological descent, a view that was challenged by David M. Schneider in his work on Symbolic Kinship (1984, A Critique of The Study of Kinship).

The crux of his argument was that anthropologists had founded the domain of "kinship" on the notions of human reproduction and the biologically defined relatedness of their own Euro-American culture. Human reproduction and notions of biological relatedness cannot be presumed to structure people's social relationships in other cultural contexts.

The word kinship can refer more broadly to any emotional relationship. This can also refer to ideas which are mathematically related.

In its most general sense, kinship can be used in reference to similarity; for instance, a car is akin to a truck. In some cultures, the formal establishment of kinship involves various customs and obligations. Anthropologists have studied different systems of kinship in a wide variety of cultures.

Many codes of ethics consider the bond of kinship as creating obligations between the related persons stronger than those between strangers, as in Confucian filial piety and the Christian injunction that charity begins at home.

ANTHROPOLOGY IN PUBLIC HEALTH

Public health is often described as having the population or community as its patient, in contrast to the individual-level focus of clinical medicine. This focus on community creates a natural foundation for partnership between public health and anthropology, which takes as its primary focus the study of people in groups, and especially in local communities. Anthropology has four major subfields: cultural anthropology, physical or biological anthropology, archeology, and linguistics. Crosscutting the subfields are several subdisciplinary foci that have much to contribute to the achievement of public health objectives. The most important for public health is medical anthropology, a field that first emerged as a coherent subdiscipline in the 1950s and has rapidly grown to become one of the largest areas of research and practice within anthropology. The richness of this subdiscipline is apparent in the range of theoretical perspectives encompassed by it.

Anthropology has also made important methodological contributions to public health, especially with regard to the use of ethnography for the systematic collection of field data; qualitative methods for the collection and analysis of descriptive, interpretative, and formative data; and the integration of qualitative and quantitative approaches. The ability to translate scientific knowledge into effective practice at the community level is a third area where anthropological approaches have much to offer public health.

THEORETICAL CONTRIBUTIONS

As with anthropology and public health, the basic unit of study in ecology is the population. The medical-ecological approach links biomedicine with biological and cultural anthropology, resulting in important contributions to understanding health and disease as dynamic, adaptive, population-based processes. The ecological model builds on three key assumptions:

1. There are no single causes of disease; rather, disease is ultimately due to a chain of factors related to ecosystem imbalances.
2. Health and disease are part of a set of physical, biological, and cultural subsystems that continually affect one another.
3. The ecological model provides a framework for the study of health in an environmental context, but it does not specify what factors maintain health within any given local system.

Critical medical anthropology raises important questions about the impact of global political and economic structures and processes on health and disease. It expands the context within which medical anthropology operates and brings it closer to the perspective of public health practice by explicitly seeking to contribute to the creation of global health systems that "serve the people." Critical medical anthropology focuses on health care systems and how they function at multiple levels, including the individual level of patient experience, the microlevel of physician-patient relationships, the intermediate level of local health care systems, particularly hospitals and clinics, and the macrosocial level of global political-economic systems. At each of these levels, the goal is to understand how existing social relations structure the relationships among the participants in the systems. In particular, critical medical anthropologists study the way health care is embedded within dominant relations such as those of class, race, and gender.

The individual level of patient experience has been the focus of interpretative anthropology approaches. A. Kleinman (1997) introduced the cultural interpretative model to provide a means of balancing the externalized, objective view of disease with the subjective experience of illness. M. Lock and N. Scheper-Hughes (1990), in turn, developed the concept of "sufferer experience" as an important dimension to the study of health. They developed a metaphorical framework of "the three bodies" to facilitate understanding of the multiple layers of health and illness. The individual body constitutes the layer of lived experience, with an explicit rejection of Cartesian mind-body dualism. The social body encompasses the way in which the individual body becomes a kind of canvas upon which nature, society, and culture is represented. The body politic refers to "the regulation, surveillance, and control of bodies (individual and collective) in reproduction and sexuality, work, leisure, and sickness" (Lock and Scheper-Hughes 1990, p.51). Sickness, in this framework, is understood as a "form of communication" among all three levels, a kind of individual-level expression of social truths and social contradictions. It then follows that, in order to effectively treat the individual expression of sickness, the role of social and political factors in generating sickness must also be considered.

The microlevel of physician-patient relationships and the intermediate level of local health care systems have been the focus of clinical anthropology. M. Konner (1993) provides a global overview of the many political and economic factors that impact the way doctors are trained and socialized, as well as how they shape the way medical care is enacted in clinics and hospitals. P. Farmer (1999) examines inequalities in the distribution and outcome of infectious diseases such as tuberculosis, AIDS (acquired immunodeficiency syndrome), Ebola, and malaria, as well as social responses such as quarantine and accusations of sorcery that often are associated with infectious diseases. His particular concern is with the emergence of disease from socially produced phenomena such as poverty and political upheaval, which he describes as the "biological reflections of social fault lines" (p. 5). Farmer also critiqued simplistic models of disease causality that fail to incorporate dynamic, systematic global factors and, therefore, slight the need for preventive models that target the social determinants of health.

In a similar mode, M. Singer (1994) proposed a synthesis of two key concepts from the ecological model-that health and disease are ultimately due to a chain of factors, and that they are part of a set of interacting subsystems-with the broader global perspective of critical medical anthropology to describe and explain the dynamics of the AIDS pandemic. Singer coined the term "syndemic" to describe the synergistic interaction of social factors, especially local and global inequities, with the epidemiological risk factors for HIV (human immunodeficiency virus), TB, hepatitis, and substance abuse. The syndemic model provides an important intermediate model that frames the investigation of community-level outcomes in terms of individual behavior, local processes, and higher level processes. This model raises difficult questions, and it challenges public health to address the root causes of health disparities. By introducing a multilevel, dynamic epidemiological perspective, it points toward the need to develop and evaluate systems-and community-level interventions that target linked processes.

METHODOLOGICAL CONTRIBUTIONS

The application of anthropological methods to public health problems has been another important area of contribution. The use of systematic, descriptive, and qualitative methods has proven effective in identifying context-specific factors that contribute to health and disease outcomes. Another important methodological contribution is the use of triangulation, or the systematic application of multiple methods in order to reduce bias in situations where controlled comparison is not feasible. For example, anthropologists typically use natural observation of behavior along with self-report data and descriptions of normative expectations to obtain highly accurate descriptions of events and social relationships.

The development of rapid assessment techniques, variously called rapid appraisal, rapid assessment, and rapid rural appraisal, is a prime example of anthropological contributions to the public health methodological toolkit. As described by J. Beebe (1995) this is a multidisciplinary team-based approach designed to generate reasonably valid, reliable, and qualitative results within a short time frame. Rapid assessments can provide the contextual information needed to design in-depth community-level and community-based public health research and to guide decisions about implementing programs in local settings.

J. A. Trostle and J. Sommerfeld (1996) describe a number of mutual methodological benefits to be gained from combining anthropological and epidemiological approaches, including:

- Anthropological knowledge of cross-cultural variability can be used to improve the development and measurement of epidemiologic variables.
- Research results can be communicated more effectively to policymakers and to a public audience when both anthropological and epidemiological descriptions are employed.
- Conceptual and experimental work can be undertaken to determine the best measures of complex cultural and behavioral variables.
- Ethnographic and epidemiological information can be used to design health surveillance systems that return data to communities in more comprehensible forms, creating new meanings for the "popular epidemiology."

The authors also provide a useful overview of the way anthropologists and epidemiologists have approached key social and cultural concepts relevant to the study of health and disease, including culture change and stress; social stratification; risk vulnerability; behavior; and illness constructs. They also review a number of areas of mutual methodological interest. They propose the label of "cultural epidemiology" to describe "cross-cultural analyses of the distribution and determinants of disease and illness and with unpacking variables (e.g., race, class, religion, time) to illustrate and specify their theoretical context and meaning" (p. 266).

OTHER DISCIPLINES OF ANTHROPOLOGY

Ecological Anthropology

Ecological anthropology deals with human-environmental (nature-culture) relationships over time and space. It investigates the ways that a population shapes its environment and the subsequent manners in which these relations form the population's social, economic, and political life (Salzman and Attwood 1996:169). Ecological anthropology applies a systems approach (Ellen 1982; Hardesty 1997; McGee 1996) to the study of the interrelationship between culture and the environment. At the heart of contemporary ecological anthropology is "an understanding that proceeds from a notion of the mutualism of person and environment" (Ingold 1992:40) and the reciprocity between nature and culture (Harvey 1996).

In the 1960s, ecological anthropology first appeared as a response to cultural ecology a sub-field of anthropology headed by Julian Steward. Steward focused on studying different modes of subsistence as methods of energy transfer and then analysed how they determine other aspects of culture. Culture became the unit of analysis. The first ecological anthropologists explored the idea of that humans as ecological populations should be the unit of analysis and culture became the means by which that population alters and adapts to the environment. It was characterised by systems theory, functionalism and negative feedback analysis.

From the beginning various scholars criticised the discipline saying it inherently was too focused on static equilibriums which ignored change, that it used circular reasoning, and that it oversimplified systems. One of the current criticisms is that, in its original form, ecological anthropology relies upon cultural relativism as the norm (Kottak 1999). However, in today's world, there are few cultures who are isolated enough to live in a true culturally relative state. Instead, cultures are being influenced and changed by governments, NGOs, businesses, etc. In response the discipline has seen a shift towards applied ecological anthropology, political ecology and environmental anthropology.

One of the leading practitioners within this sub-field of anthropology was Roy Rappaport. He delivered many outstanding works on the relationship between culture and the natural environment in which it grows, especially concerning the role of ritual in the processual relationship between the two. He conducted the majority, if not all of his fieldwork amongst a group known as the Maring, who inhabit an area in the highlands of Papua New Guinea. His magnum opus, Ritual and Religion in the making of humanity (1999), was not published until two years after his death. Rich in content and rigorous in analysis, many feel that this work cannot be fully comprehended upon first blush but needs to be absorbed slowly over time.

Economic Anthropology

Economic anthropology is an approach to the central questions of anthropology through the lens of economics. Thus, it is similar to evolutionary psychology in that it attempts to use one scientific discipline to explain another. There are three major paradigms within the field of economic anthropology: formalism, substantivism and culturalism.

Formalism

The formalist model is the one most closely linked to neoclassical economics, defining economics as the study of utility maximisation under conditions of scarcity. As an attempt to use neoclassical theory to analyze subjects outside of its traditional purview, formalist economic anthropology can be linked with new institutional economics. This approach usually makes the following central assumptions:

- Individuals pursue utility (or preference) maximisation by choosing between alternative means. They will always choose alternatives that maximise their utility (or that yields a given amount of utility for the least possible amount of inputs or effort required), often within specific informational or transaction cost constraints.

- Individuals will do so based on rationality, using all available information to measure the cost and utility of each means and considering the opportunity costs involved compared to spending their time and effort on other utility maximising pursuits. Lack of information can be modelled as information asymmetry or as a transaction cost. Whether by conscious forethought, instincts, or traditions, individuals are able to undertake the relevant calculations. In order to make rational choices individuals will seek to obtain all relevant information up to a point where the opportunity cost of information-gathering equals the additional utility gained from having been able to make better informed choices.
- All individuals live under conditions of scarcity of means while at the same time having unlimited wants.
- Underlying individuals' pursuit of utility maximisation is the principle of diminishing marginal utility, meaning that additional resources allocated towards a particular end will tend to achieve that end less and less efficiently. Rational actors will allocate their resources first towards those opportunities that provide the greatest payoff for them, and as opportunities get used up, allocate them towards progressively less efficient ends.

Some formalists use game theory as a model of rational behavior under specific cultural or interpersonal constraints. Formalists such as Firth and Schneider assert that the neoclassical model of economics can be applied to any society if appropriate modifications are made, arguing that the principles outlined above have universal validity. All human cultures are therefore a collection of "choice making individuals whose every action involves conscious or unconscious selections among alternatives means to alternative ends" (Burling, 1962, quoted from Prattis, 1982:207), whereby the ends are culturally defined goals. Goals refer not only to economic value or financial gain but to anything that is valued by the individual, be it leisure, solidarity or prestige.

In the context of hunter-gatherer and Neolithic cultures, formalist models usually must deal with high transaction costs and are thus sometimes simplified to a model of bilateral monopoly.

Since a formalist model usually states what is to be maximized in terms of preferences, which often but not necessarily include culturally expressed value goals, it is deemed to be sufficiently abstract to be capable of explaining human behavior in any context. A traditional assumption many formalists borrow from neoclassical economics is that the individual will make rational choices based on full information, or information that is incomplete in a specific way, in order to maximize whatever that individual considers being of value. While preferences may vary or change, and information about choices may or may not be complete, the principles of economising and maximising still apply.

The role of the anthropologist may then to analyse each culture in regards to its culturally appropriate means of attaining culturally recognized and valued goals. Individual preferences may differ from culturally recognized goals, and under economic rationality assumptions individual decisions are guided by individual preferences in an environment constrained by culture, including the preferences of others. Such an analysis should uncover the culturally-specific principles that underlie the rational decision-making process. In this way, economic theory has been applied by anthropologists to societies without price-regulating markets (e.g. Firth, 1961; Laughlin, 1973). Besides cultural values, formalists may also use evolutionary psychology to help model preferences.

Substantivism

The substantivist position, first proposed by Karl Polanyi in his work The Great Transformation, argues that the term 'economics' has two meanings: the formal meaning refers to economics as the logic of rational action and decision-making, as rational choice between the alternative uses of limited (scarce) means. The second, substantive meaning, however, presupposes neither rational decision-making nor conditions of scarcity. It simply refers to study of how humans make a living from their social and natural environment. A society's livelihood strategy is seen as an adaptation to its environment and material conditions, a process which may or may not involve utility maximisation. The substantive meaning of 'economics' is seen in the broader sense of 'economising' or 'provisioning'. Economics is simply the way society meets their material needs.

Polanyi's term "great transformation" refers to the divide between modern, market-dominated societies and non-Western, non-capitalist preindustrial societies. Polanyi argues that only the substantive meaning of economics is appropriate for analysing the latter. Without a system of price-making markets formal economic analysis does not apply, for example in centrally planned economies or preindustrial societies. Individual choice in such places is not so much based on the maximisation of economic profit but rather on social relationships, cultural values, moral concerns, politics or religion. Production in most peasant and tribal societies is for the producers, also called 'production for use' or subsistence production, as opposed to 'production for exchange' which has profit maximisation as its chief aim. These types differ so radically that no single theory can describe them all.

According to Polanyi, in modern capitalist economies the concepts of formalism and substantivism coincide since people organise their livelihoods based on the principle of rational choice. However, in non-Capitalist, pre-industrial economies this assumption does not hold. Unlike their Western capitalist counterparts, they are not based on market exchange but on redistribution and reciprocity.

Reciprocity is defined as the mutual exchange of goods or services as part of long-term relationships. Redistribution implies the existence of a strong political centre such as kinship-based leadership, which receives and then redistributes subsistence goods according to culturally-specific principles. In societies that are not market-based reciprocity and redistribution usually occur together. Conversely, market exchange is seen as the dominant mode of integration in modern industrial societies, while reciprocity may continue in family and inter-household relations, and some redistribution is undertaken by the state or by charitable institutions. Each of these three systems of distribution requires a separate set of analytical concepts. Another key concept in substantivism is that of 'embeddedness'. Rather than being a separate and distinct sphere, the economy is embedded in both economic and non-economic institutions. Exchange takes place within and is regulated by society rather than being located in a social vacuum.

For example, religion and government can be just as important to economics as economic institutions themselves. Socio-cultural obligations, norms and values play a significant role in people's livelihood strategies. Consequently, any analysis of economics as an analytically distinct entity isolated from its socio-cultural and political context is flawed from the outset. A substantivist analysis of economics will therefore focus on the study of the various social institutions on which people's livelihoods are based.

The market is only one amongst many institutions that determine the nature of economic transactions. Polanyi's central argument is that institutions are the primary organisers of economic processes. The substantive economy is an "instituted process of interaction between man and his environment, which results in a continuous supply of want satisfying material means" (1968:126).

The concept of embeddedness has been very influential in the field of economic anthropology. In his study of Chinese ethnic business networks in Indonesia, Granovetter found individual's economic agency embedded in networks of strong personal relations. In processes of clientelization the cultivation of personal relationships between traders and customers assumes an equal or higher importance than the economic transactions involved.

Economic exchanges are not carried out between strangers but rather by individuals involved in long-term continuing relationships. Granovetter describes the neo-liberal view of economic action as separating economics from society and culture, thereby promoting an 'undersocialized account' that atomises human behavior: "Actors do not behave or decide as atoms outside a social context, nor do they adhere slavishly to a script written for them by the particular intersection of social categories that they happen to occupy. Their attempts at purposive action are instead embedded in concrete, ongoing systems of social relations." (1985:487).

Culturalism

For some anthropologists the substantivist position does not go far enough in its criticism of the universal application of Western economic models on societies all around the globe. Gudeman, for example, argues that the central processes of making a livelihood are culturally constructed. Therefore, models of livelihoods and related economic concepts such as exchange, money or profit must be analyzed through the locals' ways of understanding them.

Rather than devising universal models rooting in Western understandings and using Western economic terminologies and then applying them indiscriminately to all societies, one should come to understand the 'local model'. In his work on livelihoods Gudeman seeks to present the "people's own economic construction" (1986:1); that is, not just examining the cultural construction of values as in which products people like to buy and how much they value leisure, but people's own conceptualizations or mental maps of economics and its various aspects, i.e. their understanding of concepts such as exchange, property or profit. His description of a peasant community in Panama reveals that the locals did not engage in exchange with each other in order to make a profit but rather viewed it as an "exchange of equivalents", with the exchange value of a good being defined by the expenses spent on producing it. Only outside merchants made profits in their dealings with the community, and it was a complete mystery to the locals how they managed to do so...Gudeman not only rejects the formalist notion of the universal 'economic man'; he also criticizes the substantivist position for imposing their universal model of economics on all preindustrial societies and so making the same mistake as the formalists.

While conceding that substantivism rightly emphasises the significance of social institutions in economic processes, Gudeman considers any derivational model that claims to be of universal nature, be it formalist, substantivist or Marxist, to be ethnocentric and essentially tautological. In his view they all model human relationships as mechanistic processes by taking the logic of natural science based on the material world and applying it to the human world.

Rather than to "arrogate to themselves a privileged right to model the economies of their subjects", anthropologists should seek to understand and interpret local models (1986:38). Such local models may differ radically from their Western counterparts. To quote Gudeman: "Gaining a livelihood might be modelled as a causal and instrumental act, as a natural and inevitable sequence, as a result of supernatural dispositions or as a combination of all these." (1986:47). For example, the Iban only use hand knives to harvest rice. Even though the use of sickles would speed up the harvesting process, their concern that the spirit of the rice may flee is greater than their desire to economize the harvesting process.

Gudeman brings post-modern cultural relativism to its logical conclusion. Generally speaking, however, culturalism can also be seen as an extension of the substantivist view, with a stronger emphasis on cultural constructivism, a more detailed account of local understandings and metaphors of economic concepts, and a greater focus on socio-cultural dynamics than the latter (cf. Hann, 2000).

Culturalists also tend to be both less taxonomic and more culturally relativistic in their descriptions while critically reflecting on the power relationship between the ethnographer (or 'modeller') and the subjects of his or her research. While substantivists generally focus on institutions as their unit of analysis, culturalists lean towards detailed and comprehensive analyses of particular local communities. Both views agree in rejecting the formalist assumption that all human behaviour can be explained in terms of rational decision-making and utility maximisation.

Critics of the Approaches

There have been many critics of the formalist position. Its central assumptions about human behavior have been questioned. In particular, it has been argued that the universality of rational choice and utility maximization cannot be assumed across all cultures. But also with regards to modern Western societies the economic reductionism in explaining human behaviour has been critiqued. Prattis notes that the premise of utility maximisation is tautological; whatever a person does, may it be work or leisure, is declared to be utility maximization. If he or she doesn't maximize money then it must be pleasure or some other value.

To quote: "This post hoc reasoning back to a priori assumptions has minimal scientific value as it is not readily subject to falsification." (1989:212). For example, a person may sacrifice his or her own time, finances or even health to help others. Formalists would then pronounce that s/he does so due to placing a high value on helping others, and so sacrificing other goals in order to maximize this value and thereby to gain utility (e.g. meaning, satisfaction of having helped, approval from others etc.). But this simply an assumption, the motivation of this person may or may not coincide with this inferred explanation pattern. Similarly, Gudeman argues that Western economic anthropologists will invariably "find" the people they study to behave "rationally" since that is what their model leads them to do. Conversely, formalism will consider any behavior that does not maximize utility based on available means as irrational. However, such "non-maximising acts" may seem perfectly rational and logical for the acting individual whose actions may have been motivated by a completely different set of meanings and understandings.

Finally, there is the substantivist point that both economic institutions and individual economic activities are embedded in the socio-cultural sphere and can therefore not be analysed in isolation. Social relationships play an essential role in people's livelihood strategies; consequently, a narrow focus on atomised individual behavior to the exclusion of his or her socio-cultural context is bound to be flawed.

Substantivism has not been without its critics, either. Prattis (1982) argues that the strict distinction between primitive and modern economies in substantivism is problematic. Constraints on transactional modes are situational rather than systemic (he therefore implies that substantivism focuses on social structures at the expensive of analyzing individual agency). Non-maximizing adaptation strategies occur in all societies, not just in "primitive" ones. Similarly, Plattner (1989) argues that some generalization across different societies are still possible, meaning that Western and non-Western economics are not entirely different. In an age of globalization there are probably hardly any "pure" preindustrial societies left. Conditions of resource scarcity can be said to exist anywhere in the world. It is significant to note anthropological fieldwork that demonstrates rational behavior and complex economic choices amongst peasants (cf. Plattner, 1989:15). Also, individuals in e.g. communist societies can still engage in rational utility maximizing behavior, e.g. by building relationships to bureaucrats who control distribution, or by using small plots of land in their garden to supplement official food rations. Cook thinks that there are significant conceptual problems with the substantivists' theorizing: "They define economics as an aspect of everything that provisions society but nothing that provisions society is defined as economic." (1973:809).

While market exchange is dominant in the West, redistribution can also play a very significant role particularly in the more socialist or welfare-state Western societies such as France, Germany or Sweden. State and charity or religious organizations collect donations and then distribute them to needy groups (or use the funds to offer free or inexpensive social services).

Culturalism can also be criticized from various perspectives. Marxists would argue that culturalists are too idealistic in their notion of the social construction of reality and too weak in their analysis of external (i.e. material) constraints on individuals that affect their livelihood choices. If, as Gudeman argues, local models cannot be objectively appraised or held against a universal standard, then there is also no way of deconstructing them in terms of ideologies propagated by the powerful that serve to neutralise resistance through hegemony. This is further complicated by the fact that in an age of globalization most cultures are being integrated into the global capitalist system and are influenced to conform to Western ways of thinking and acting. Local and global discourses are mixing and the distinctions between the two are beginning to blur. Even though people will retain aspects of their existing worldviews, universal models can be used to study the dynamics of their integration into the rest of the world.

Ethnobiology

Ethnobiology is the study of the past and present interrelationships between human cultures and the plants, animals, and other organisms in their environment, including relationships with ecosystems as a whole. It is an interdisciplinary subject which draws on knowledge from many different fields of knowledge such as linguistics, anthropology, biology, chemistry.

The field itself focuses on the study of how human societies relate to the biosphere. It is therefore conventionally centered in the use of diverse flora and fauna by indigenous societies. Humans relate to plants and animals both in space and time. Therefore, this relationship encompasses human cultures worldwide and it includes the past and the present human interactions with the living environment.

The term ethnobiology did not come into use until the twentieth century (Sillitoe, 2006). It was originally and is still being referred to as biological anthropology by many scholars in related disciplines.

However, unlike the traditional biological anthropology which primarily studies humans and the nonhuman primates as biological organism, ethnobiology is wider in scope, both in academic and practical aspects. Most importantly, ethnobiology makes apparent academic connection between human cultural practices and subdisciplines of biology.

The principal disciplines of enthnobiology include ethnobotany, ethnomycology, ethnolichenology, ethnozoology (e.g. ethnoentomology, ethnoichthyology, ethnoornithology), ethnoecology, paleoethnobotany, and zooarchaeology.

The academic and practical aspects of the sub-field ethnobotany are remarkably apparent in its historical review of human cultural evolution right from gathering, gardening and various levels of ethnomedical practices. It also evaluates plant as a medicine and how it got blended into spiritual uses of various cultures. Many ethnobotanists are therefore interested in researching on the use of traditional "plant medicines" and why they are culturally linked to the spirit world.

The subfield ethnozoology generally focuses on the relationship between animals and humans throughout human history. It therefore studies human practices such as hunting, fishing and animal husbandry in space and time. In all its disciplines, ethnobiology satisfies its anthropological aspect by considering classified cultural and cognitive issues. The biological component is manifested by its eminent focus on historical evolution and utilization of the living resource.

Ethnobiology-is an interdisciplinary subject that focuses on the study of how human societies relate to the biosphere. It is therefore conventionally centred in the use of diverse flora and fauna by indigenous societies. Humans' interrelationship with plant and animals can be delineated both in space and time. This relationship therefore encompasses human cultures worldwide and it includes the past and the present human interactions with living environment.

Theological Anthropology

Theological anthropology is the branch of theology which is concerned with the study of humankind, or anthropology, in relation to the divine. In a theological context, it is usually referred to simply as anthropology.

CHRISTIAN ANTHROPOLOGY

In the context of Christian theology, theological anthropology refers to the study of the human ("anthropology") as it relates to God. It differs from the social science of anthropology, which primarily deals with the comparative study of the physical and social characteristics of humanity across times and places. One aspect studies the innate nature or constitution of the human, known as the nature of humankind (known as the nature of man before the popularity of gender-neutral language). It is concerned with the relationship between notions such as body, soul and spirit which together form a person, based on their descriptions in the Bible. There are three traditional views of the human constitution – trichotomism, dichotomism and monism (in the sense of anthropology).

Body

The body is the corporeal or physical aspect of a human being. Christians have traditionally believed that the body will be resurrected at the end of the age.

Rudolf Bultmann states the following:

"That soma *belongs inseparably, constitutively, to human existence is most clearly evident from the fact that Paul cannot conceive even of a future human existence after death, `when that which is perfect is come' as an existence without* soma *– in contrast to the view of those in Corinth who deny the resurrection (1 Cor. 15, especially vv. 35ff.)."*

"Man does not have a soma*; he is a* soma*"*

Soul

The semantic domain of Biblical soul is based on the Hebrew word *nepes* which presumably means "breath" or "breathing being". This word never means an immortal soul or an incorporeal part of the human being that can survive death of the body as the spirit of dead.

This word usually designates the person as a whole or its physical life. In the Septuagint *nepes* is mostly translated as *psyche* (øõ÷Þ) and, exceptionally, in the Book of Joshua as *empneon* that is "breathing being". The New Testament follows the terminology of the Septuagint, and thus uses the word *psyche* with the Hebrew semantic domain and not the Greek, that is an invisible power (or ever more, for Platonists, immortal and immaterial) that gives life and motion to the body and is responsible for its attributes.

In Patristic thought, towards the end of the 2nd century *psyche* was understood in more a Greek than a Hebrew way, and it was contrasted with the body.

In the 3rd century, with the influence of Origen, there was the establishing of the doctrine of the inherent immortality of the soul and its divine nature. Origen also taught the transmigration of the souls and their preexistence, but these views were officially rejected in 553 in the Fifth Ecumenical Council. Inherent immortality of the soul was accepted among western and eastern theologians throughout the middle ages, and after the Reformation, as evidenced by the Westminster Confession.

On the other hand, a number of modern Protestant scholars have adopted views similar to conditional immortality, including Edward Fudge and Clark Pinnock; however the majority of adherents hold the traditional doctrine. In the last six decades, conditional immortality, or better "immortality by grace" of the soul has also been widely accepted among Eastern Orthodox theologians, by returning to the views of the late 2nd century, where immortality was still considered as a gift granted with the value of Jesus' death and resurrection.

Spirit

The spirit (Hebrew *ruach*, Greek *pneuma*, which can also mean "breath") is likewise an immaterial component. It is often used interchangeably with "soul", although trichotomists believe that the spirit is distinct from the soul. "When Paul speaks of the *pneuma* of man he does not mean some higher principle within him or some special intellectual or spiritual faculty of his, but simply his self, and the only questions is whether the self is regarded in some particular aspect when it is called *pneuma*. In the first place, it apparently is regarded in the same way as when it is called *psyche* – viz. as the self that lives in man's attitude, in the orientation of his will."

Flesh

"Flesh" is usually considered synonymous with "body", referring to the corporeal aspect of a human being. The apostle Paul contrasts flesh and spirit in Romans 7-8.

GIDDENS OR FRENCH POST-MODERNISTS

So far the impact of the Asian – European Centres established at Southeast Asian universities, namely at Universiti Malaya and Chulalongkorn University can not be evaluated. Very interesting is the establishment of the "Centre for Occidental Studies" at Universiti Kebangsaan Malaysia (UKM). In difference to the other centres, this is entirely funded by UKM. Perhaps these regional studies centres might stimulate the exchange of knowledge and cooperation. Perhaps, the social science discussion in Europe might receive some new ideas. Secondly, there is an important implication to this different status of Southeast Asian Studies within the region and outside. Research by those working in Southeast Asia has to address issues defined politically as relevant.4 The findings have to be fed into the local discussion of future development and of how to solve problems. In contrast, not the least due to the marginalization of foreigners doing research on Southeast Asia, they can, and quite often do, focus on quite specific and sometimes "exotic" topics that are not that closely connected to local social science discourses in the region.

Exotic topics are a general problem of anthropologists, or at least for those anthropologists who follow the traditional path of our mighty ancestors. As a novice the anthropologist comes to his or her field site, ideally in a village located in a remote area. He or she is isolated from other foreigners, has a hard time to learn the local language which can take years, suffers from culture shock and recovers, tries to grasp every detail of the local culture which definitely takes years or the whole life, becomes more and more part of the local society and With scientists working in Southeast Asia we mean those working in universities or research institutes within the region regardless of whether they are nationals of Southeast Asian countries or aliens. In contrast, with those working outside the region we refer to those employed at universities or research institutes outside of the region proper. In most cases these are foreigner. A special case are Southeast Asian Ph.D students enrolled in European, American or Australian Universities.

An example is the Tsunami. We were quite surprised when we started to do some research in Aceh, Khao Lak and Sri Lanka that we did not meet other foreign researchers in some cases even goes native. Finally, the anthropologist becomes an expert for his or her particular people. Ideally, he or she is the only expert for this culture in the whole world. He or she imposes a copy right and struggles over gate keeping. Somebody who is trained in such a manner is not very keen to engage in a wider debate with colleagues and to contribute to area studies. It seems that in times where post-modern anthropologists develop ideas of fragmented identities and multi-sited ethnographies on one hand an intensified particularism can be observed on the other hand.

A remarkable exception of this is gender studies. Influential theories on gender and power relationships have been drawn from comparison of SE-Asian societies. We indicate "Power and difference. Gender in island southeast Asia", edited by Jane Monning Atkinson and Shelly Errington, a pioneer work which came out in1990.

Since then Southeast Asian anthropological findings have constantly fuelled anthropological and interdisciplinary gender discourse. We will mention only a few of them: Aihwa Ong's and Michael Peletz's book (1995) on body politics in SE-Asia, Lenore Manderson's and Pranee Liamputtong's volume on adolescence in SE-Asia (Manderson/Liamputtong 2002), and a study published by Lenore Manderson with Linda Rae Bennett on Violence against women in Asian societies, with examples drawn mainly from Southeast Asia (Manderson/Bennett 2003).

Thirdly, the research work of the scholars is embedded in different structures. Europeans scholars are in Southeast Asia for their field research, for conferences etc. in other words outside of their usual work and everyday life. In contrast, those working in Southeast Asian universities etc. hardly find time for field research due to the manifold demands in terms of administrative work, teaching load, consultancies and political engagement. For them the region is the space of everyday life. Still the number of European "Southeast Asianists" who work for extended periods in universities of the region is surprisingly small, as well as the number of Southeast Asians working in European universities outside of the language departments. This seems to be changing though, as more and more young researchers start to work with NGO etc. in Southeast Asia. At least a few Europeans who worked in universities of the region for longer periods are doing comparative studies or focus on Southeast Asia wide processes. Evers analysis of strategic group formation can be cited as well as Mulders work on "everyday life in Southeast Asia" or the studies of Evers, Nas and others on southeast Asian urbanism, to refer to just a few.

NEW RESEARCH TRENDS

The different life styles and research conditions of local and foreign scholars can lead to meconnaissance as Wazir (1996) notes, "how representative are the images of the developing world which are created through the globalization of knowledge and how distinctly different are these from the images that the developing world conceives of knowledge produced from Europe and the United States" (2003:135). A way out of such misreckoning is mutual working together. This faces problems resulting from the mentioned discrepancies, and the valorisation of knowledge on a global scale especially in publications.

In a recent study on social science research in Southeast Asia, Evers and Gerke show that during the last decades publications dealing with the region have nearly tripled (Evers/Gerke (2003). Still most publications on Southeast Asia are produced by scholars associated to universities or institutes outside of the region, especially the US and Western Europe. But, the proportion produced within the region is rising relatively faster then publications outside. This shows that possibilities for cooperation are improving, which has and will have the effect that the issues addressed by research might become more comparable. However, the social science capacities are highly unequally distributed among the countries. Most publications on Singapore are produced in Singapore. In Malaysia and the Philippines about a quarter of publications are "home grown" and in Thailand a bit less than one fifth. This rank order of local studies on the own country contrasts with global research on the respective country. Here more than 30% of the publications refer to the Philippines. Second comes Vietnam (26%), thereafter Indonesia (24%), Thailand (23%) and Malaysia (20%). Concerning Vietnam and Indonesia we thus find a strong contrast between local social science capacities and international attention. Whether this indicates that international – local cooperation is less in these countries is a question of further enquiry. With regards to Myanmar, Cambodia,6 Laos and Brunei7 less than 5% of publications deal with these countries.

Unfortunately, Evers and Gerke do not differentiate whether the publications referring to Southeast Asia were published in journals of Southeast – or Asian studies, i.e. regional studies journals, or in disciplinary oriented journals. Using Ingenta during the last ten years 29 articles referring to Southeast Asia were Certainly, these very rough data have to be taken with caution, but nevertheless they do indicate the marginal status of Southeast Asian studies regardless of their origin within disciplinary discourses. To overcome this marginalization requires improved funding of research especially of cooperative research. However, money does not solve the problem. As important is that Southeast Asian studies (regardless of whether it is local or global) moves out of the niches of regional studies and faces the challenges to get published in disciplinary journals. Leach, Firth and a few others might be taken as example. Thereby the social processes in Southeast Asia might receive more attention by others, as the case of Castells indicates. In other words, the mutual boundaries of ignorance should be overcome.

Would the establishment of Southeast Asian Centres facilitate such a development? Looking through the internet it seems that most universities in the US have Southeast Asian Centres. In Germany the situation is quite different. With a few exceptions (Passau, Bonn, Münster, Freiburg)9 the centres for Southeast Asian Studies have their focus on language, literature and history, neither on political science, anthropology or sociology. In the lists of larger scale interdisciplinary research programmes funded by the DFG,10 only two deal explicitly with South-east Asia namely the "uplands programme" of the University of Hohenheim and STORMA of the University of Göttingen. No Southeast Asia Centre has been involved in these. To put Southeast Asia on the agenda, more engagement of the regional institutes and individual scholars to involve in such large scale projects is necessary and, what is as or even more important, to get together and establish such a programme as international cooperation focusing on Southeast Asia. For us as relative newcomers to the regional studies scene, this rather limited involvement of the regional institutes is slightly surprising.

Taking all these arguments together, the question emerges whether the marginalization of regional studies within the global social science discourses is accompanied by a wider marginalization within the process of knowledge production in general. Keeping in mind the argument raised before that research of foreigners on Southeast Asia is embedded in structures different from those working in Southeast Asia, who tend to be far more oriented towards local problems, it might be that regional studies in Europe are as well marginal to the Southeast Asian discussion of Southeast Asia. Here a closer examination of publications (including translations) might provide more information.

We will not go into a discussion of anthropological and sociological research in this presentation. On one hand the study of King and Wilder provides a detailed overview at least on anthropological research, and as the data by Evers and Gerke indicate, the fields has far expanded during the last decades. The focus will be on what has not become a field of anthropological or sociological enquiry. The regions left out (Cambodia, Laos, Myanmar) have been mentioned already, as well as the lack of comparative studies and the need for closer working together.

With a comparative perspective we do not mean the comparison of one country with another one. A comparative perspective requires a theoretical perspective by which similarities and differences can be identified, or by which socio-cultural units can be defined. In other words, there is still, even after the postmodern deconstruction the need for a "sociology" or "anthropology" of Southeast Asia. Sociology and anthropology are reflective sciences, what means that the research topics evolve from current processes and have effects on them, especially when social science findings are applied in development projects and scientists are involved in these development processes, what is commonly the case in Southeast Asia. In these processes theories of culture and society are created. Currently, the national mindedness implies that Malaysian scholars construct their national theory of Malaysian society as base for research and development strategies, Indonesian create an Indonesian theory of Indonesian society and Thai's of Thai society etc. Thereby the wider regional perspective is lost on the way. This attempt to create "national" theories for "national" development is a highly relevant topic for research namely in the framework of a sociology or anthropology of knowledge. How are concepts and theories adapted to the social circumstances within the countries, and under what circumstances do which concepts emerge? In how far reflect these theories syncretism so commonly seen in Southeast Asian religious practises?

The creation of "national" theories has one focus on "identity," which forms one background for the popularity of "Asian values" among anthropologists and sociologists. Here a comparative perspective centred on notions of identity, power and the construction of the person in hierarchical and egalitarian systems in Southeast Asia can provide a wider, regional perspective. Especially with regards to identity this has turned into an important background for local conflicts within Southeast Asia.

Sociology and anthropology, in difference to economics and political science do not take political boundaries for natural or as constituting socio-cultural units. As always, political boundaries usually disconnect integrated societies, and only with the rise of nationalism a social correspondence had been created. An example is the straits of Malacca, the northern states of what is today Malaysia and southern Thailand, or the mountainous Mekong region, where only since the end of the last century a process of integration into the surrounding states has taken place. In how far do these cross-boundary regions constitute fields for anthropological enquiry? How do the interactions between the different groups, the minorities and majorities as well as the majorities that are minorities change? How does 15 Perhaps only at the NUS an attempt is made towards a theory of Southeast Asian society. New Research Trends national integration lead to new differentiations or fragmentations and conflicts? Here the Mountainous Mekong Southeast Asia (MMSEA) conferences are an example for approaches to overcome existing political boundaries and to focus on socio-cultural and political processes within the region. This approach is as well different from the traditional studies of a specific ethnic group, in which the interactions are often less analysed. While in this perspective comparison means the analysis of more or less integrated socio-cultural units, it is as important to do comparative research in not related regions that share common characteristics like minorities living in mountainous areas in the Mekong uplands as well as in Borneo or the Philippines.

Similarly, no comparative research that we know of has been conducted on the "sea-nomads" in the Indonesian archipelago and the Andaman sea, and how these minority groups are integrated/integrating into the nation states and affected by globalization as much as nationalism. Another highly relevant field for comparative studies is urbanism and urban dynamics in the Southeast Asian metropolis and regional centres. Further topics which need the comparative perspective are local conflicts, the raise of new ethnicities, and the so-called return of religion, as Martin Riesebrodt from the Chicago fundamentalist project has designated the revival of fundamentalisms.

Such studies can not be conducted individually. Because all these issues are beyond national frameworks cooperation is required. Increasingly, NGOs construct their networks on different levels, and it might be useful for researchers to learn from them. In our understanding, the result of such an endeavour might be that the study of Southeast Asia is not just a special field of regional sociology or anthropology, but itself an integral part of global discourses regardless of the identity in terms of ID-cards of the scientist doing research.

3

Research Method and Design

RESEARCH

Research can be defined as the search for knowledge, or as any systematic investigation, with an open mind, to establish novel facts, usually using a scientific method. The primary purpose for applied research is discovering, interpreting, and the development of methods and systems for the advancement of human knowledge on a wide variety of scientific matters of our world and the universe.

Scientific research relies on the application of the scientific method, a harnessing of curiosity. This research provides scientific information and theories for the explanation of the nature and the properties of the world around us. It makes practical applications possible.

Scientific research is funded by public authorities, by charitable organizations and by private groups, including many companies. Scientific research can be subdivided into different classifications just as to their academic and application disciplines. Artistic research can take form when creative works are considered both the research and the object of research itself. It is the debatable body of thought which offers an alternative to purely scientific methods in research in its search for knowledge and truth. Historical research is embodied in the scientific method. The phrase my research is also used loosely to describe a person's entire collection of information about a particular subject.

SOCIAL WORK RESEARCH

Social work is a professional and academic discipline committed to the pursuit of social welfare, social change and social justice. The field works towards research and practice to improve the quality of life and to the development of the potential of each individual, group and community of a society. Social workers perform interventions through research, policy, community organizing, direct practice and teaching.

Research is often focused on areas such as human development, social policy, public administration, programme evaluation and international and community development. Social workers are organized into local, national, continental and international professional bodies.

Social work, an interdisciplinary field, includes theories from economics, education, sociology, medicine, philosophy, politics, psychology, and as well as anti-oppressive and anti-racist discourse.

Social work has its roots in the struggle of society to deal with poverty and the resultant problems. Therefore, social work is intricately linked with the idea of charity work; but must be understood in broader terms. The concept of charity goes back to ancient times, and the practice of providing for the poor has roots in many major ancient civilizations and world religions.

Contemporary Professional Development

The International Federation of Social Workers states, of social work today, that:

- "social work bases its methodology on a systematic body of evidence-based knowledge derived from research and practice evaluation, including local and indigenous knowledge specific to its context. It recognizes the complexity of interactions between human beings and their environment, and the capacity of people both to be affected by and to alter the multiple influences upon them including bio-psychosocial factors. The social work profession draws on theories of human development, social theory and social systems to analyse complex situations and to facilitate individual, organizational, social and cultural changes."

Qualifications

Professional social workers are generally considered those who hold a degree in social work. Often these practitioners must also obtain a license or be professionally registered. The education of social workers begins with a Bachelor's degree or diploma in Social Work.

Some countries offer Postgraduate degrees in Social Work like Master's or Ph.D. More and more graduates of social work continue to post-doctoral studies. It has been argued that social work education is supposed to be a lifelong process.

In a number of countries and jurisdictions, registration or licensure of people working as social workers is required and there are mandated qualifications.

In other places, a professional association sets academic and experiential requirements for admission to membership.

The success of these professional bodies' efforts is demonstrated in the fact that these same requirements are recognized by employers as necessary for employment.

Professional Associations

There are a number of associations for social workers, which exist to provide ethical guidance and other forms of support for their members and social work in general. These associations/organizations are distinguished in international, continental or semi-continental, national and regional. The main international ones are the International Federation of Social Workers (IFSW), International Association of Schools of Social Work (IASSW) and the British Association of Social Workers (BASW)

Role of the Professional

The main tasks of professional social workers can include a variety of services such as case management, clinical social work, human services management, social welfare policy analysis, policy and practice development, community organizing, international, social and community development, advocacy, teaching and social and political research.

QUALITATIVE RESEARCH

Qualitative research seeks out the 'why', not the 'how' of its topic through the analysis of unstructured information - things like interview transcripts, open ended survey responses, e-mails, notes, feedback forms, photos and videos. It doesn't just rely on statistics or numbers, which are the domain of quantitative researchers. Qualitative research is used to gain insight into people's attitudes, behaviours, value systems, concerns, motivations, aspirations, culture or lifestyles. It's used to inform business decisions, policy formation, communication and research.

Focus groups, in-depth interviews, content analysis, ethnography, evaluation and semiotics are among the many formal approaches that are used, but qualitative research also involves the analysis of any unstructured material, including customer feedback forms, reports or media clips. Collecting and analyzing this unstructured information can be messy and time consuming using manual methods. When faced with volumes of materials, finding themes and extracting meaning can be a daunting task.

QUALITATIVE, QUANTITATIVE AND MIXED-METHOD RESEARCH

There are two overarching ways of gathering data, or fields of research. These are qualitative research methods and quantitative research methods.

Qualitative research is concerned with developing knowledge where little or none exists and uses words, observations, and descriptions to develop this knowledge. Quantitative research is concerned with expanding knowledge that already exists and using numerical data to report the findings from the research. But, perhaps you want to use both qualitative and quantitative methods, or a mixed-method design, in your research. A mixed-method design allows researchers to design a study using both qualitative and quantitative methods by using numerical and textual data.

Qualitative Research

Social work is a profession that owes a large debt of gratitude to many other disciplines. Anthropology, psychology, sociology, and medicine have all contributed to the development of our profession. One of the areas in which this becomes exceedingly clear is the field of qualitative research. Qualitative research has deep roots in the fields of anthropology and sociology, where the development of rigorous and exact methods for fieldwork has long been fostered.

The use of qualitative research methods is debated among social work practitioners, faculty, researchers, and other professionals. It is generally agreed that qualitative research is employed when little or nothing is known about a subject, or when the researcher wants to gain an in-depth understanding of a person's experience. Some may argue that qualitative methods are better suited for studies on complicated topics such as a person's comfort level with death, how it feels to be unemployed, or how a child views the drinking habits of an alcoholic parent.

Qualitative research primarily relies on information generated from observations of the researcher and discussions and interviews with study participants. However, researchers engaged in qualitative research might also gather some descriptive information such as the demographics of participants and their settings in order to place their experiences within a context.

In their simplest form, qualitative research methods are used to help us understand the characteristics of a phenomenon. Often this type of research uncovers these characteristics by focusing on the ideas of the people involved.

As an example, let us imagine for a moment that you are a case manager at a homeless shelter and the year is 1982. You have noticed that a large number of your consumers who report being intravenous drug users are also suffering from a strange new illness that seems to impair their immune system.

You may be aware that AIDS was a relatively unknown disease in 1982 and that scientists were just beginning to understand the causes of the transmission of this disease. As a case manager, you may want to design a qualitative study that will help you explore the experiences of those who are suffering from this disease by interviewing people living with AIDS (recording their own words). You may also want to collect some demographic information such as sex, age, race, and length of illness to describe their experiences within the context of the research population.

Quantitative Research

Advocates of quantitative research argue that it is only through the use of methods that report numerical representation that the social sciences can become truly valid. Quantitative research seeks to explain relationships between two or more factors. The aim of quantitative research is to determine how one thing (a variable) affects another in a population. A variable is any attribute or characteristic that changes or assumes different values. Variables can represent subject characteristics (e.g., age, race, sex) or the things you are really interested in (e.g., agency performance; rate of relapse in addiction treatment; physiological, psychological, or sociological causes of child maltreatment). Variables can also represent the effect of any intervention that subjects receive, such as a cultural sensitivity training.

Mixed-Method Research

Mixed-method research uses both qualitative and quantitative research designs. Using more than one research method while collecting and analysing data in a study is called *concurrent mixed-method research*. When data collected through the use of one type of research design provides a basis for the collection of data using the other type, this is called *sequential mixed-method research*. When data are analyzed one way and then analysed again in another way, it is called *conversion mixed-method research*.

There are several reasons to use a mixed-method design. Among these are that it can test the consistency of findings obtained through different forms of data collection.

This is referred to as *triangulation*; this means that the findings from the methods used are consistent and support each other. Or a researcher might use a mixed-method design because it allows him or her to use qualitative methods to add richness and detail to the results obtained from the use of quantitative methods.

Researchers may also choose a mixed-method design so they can use results from one method to shape subsequent methods or steps in the research process. This is frequently seen when a qualitative study is used to shape a quantitative study. In addition, mixed-method research can be used as a means to develop new research questions or to use one method to challenge results obtained through another method.

Developing Your Research Questions

You may be asking yourself at this point, "Where do research questions originate?" Research questions may arise from your personal experience. Thus, a person who was adopted may feel compelled to study the factors that make adoptions work well for children.

Research questions may develop out of research articles or theories you are studying. A theory is a statement or set of statements designed to explain a phenomenon based upon observations and experiments and often agreed upon by most experts in a particular field. For example, you may want to test the credibility of the claims put forth by a developmental theory on aging that you learned about in one of your human behavior classes. Research questions may arise out of your own practice experience. Regardless of the source, most questions are born out of the researcher's personal interest in a subject.

To illustrate this process, we may begin with an observation ("This person smiles at me and goes out of her way to help me"), then we have an idea ("This person would make a good friend"), and then we develop a question ("Does this person like me?"). We can examine this question by drawing from our past experiences, by consulting others, or by asking the person directly.

When you are developing research questions, there are some issues to keep in mind. The first thing to consider is whether the question is empirical. This means the researcher must decide whether it can be quantified. For example, a question such as "What is the best religion?" is both value laden and subjective ("the best"). As a researcher, you need to be careful to remember that we can study values in order to understand what others think, but we cannot conduct research on values in order to evaluate them. Therefore, we can approach value-laden issues through qualitative methods that are meant to deal with the subjective questions that we have—this eliminates any objectivity from the research. "How many people cheat on their partner?" or "Has having an abortion prevented further unwanted pregnancies?" are both examples of questions that attempt to quantify issues of moral worth and can be measured through quantitative methods.

What is a Hypothesis?

A hypothesis is a research statement about relationships between variables that is testable and that can be accepted or rejected based on the evidence. Therefore, you can only develop hypotheses that are quantifiable. To design a study to test your hypothesis, you use quantitative research methods. Hypotheses are divided into two categories: research hypotheses and null hypotheses. The research hypothesis asserts that there is a relationship between the variables, and the null hypothesis claims that the relationship between the variables can be rejected. In other words, the null hypothesis is what the researcher is attempting to reject. For example, we may have a null hypothesis that no difference exists between a treatment group and a nontreatment group after intervention. If this is rejected, then the research hypothesis that the treatment group will be different from the nontreatment group after intervention (e.g., less sick or more educated) is supported. Hypotheses are typically abbreviated as Ho (null hypothesis), Ha (research hypothesis), and H1, H2, H3 (a number is used when there is more than one research hypothesis).

Imagine that you are working at an emergency shelter with a consumer named Joe. Joe is in need of permanent housing (he has been living on the streets for the past two years). While you are collecting assessment history with Joe, he discloses that he has a long history of drug abuse. One initial hypothesis may be "A history of substance abuse is related to not having stable housing." In further discussions with Joe, you explore this hypothesis with him, and he confirms that his substance abuse has interfered with his ability to seek and keep a job—a strong factor in his being homeless. You then decide to design a research study to determine if this relationship between substance abuse and homelessness exists beyond your client. You can also test a second hypothesis that looks at the relationship between substance abuse and unemployment.

Data Collection

Qualitative researchers may use different approaches in collecting data, such as the grounded theory practice, narratology, storytelling, classical ethnography, or shadowing. Qualitative methods are also loosely present in other methodological approaches, such as action research or actor-network theory. Forms of the data collected can include interviews and group discussions, observation and reflection field notes, various texts, pictures, and other materials.

Qualitative research often categorizes data into patterns as the primary basis for organizing and reporting results. Qualitative researchers typically rely on the following methods for gathering information: *Participant Observation, Non-participant Observation, Field Notes, Reflexive Journals, Structured Interview, Semi-structured Interview, Unstructured Interview, and Analysis of documents and materials*.

The ways of participating and observing can vary widely from setting to setting. Participant observation is a strategy of reflexive learning, not a single method of observing In participant observation researchers typically become members of a culture, group, or setting, and adopt roles to conform to that setting. In doing so, the aim is for the researcher to gain a closer insight into the culture's practices, motivations and emotions. It is argued that the researchers' ability to understand the experiences of the culture may be inhibited if they observe without participating.

Some distinctive qualitative methods are the use of focus groups and key informant interviews. The focus group technique involves a moderator facilitating a small group discussion between selected individuals on a particular topic. This is a particularly popular method in market research and testing new initiatives with users/workers.

One traditional and specialized form of qualitative research is called cognitive testing or pilot testing which is used in the development of quantitative survey items. Survey items are piloted on study participants to test the reliability and validity of the items.

In the academic social sciences the most frequently used qualitative research approaches include the following:

1. Ethnographic Research, used for investigating cultures by collecting and describing data that is intended to help in the development of a theory. This method is also called "ethnomethodology" or "methodology of the people". An example of applied ethnographic research, is the study of a particular culture and their understanding of the role of a particular disease in their cultural framework.
2. Critical Social Research, used by a researcher to understand how people communicate and develop symbolic meanings.
3. Ethical Inquiry, an intellectual analysis of ethical problems. It includes the study of ethics as related to obligation, rights, duty, right and wrong, choice etc.
4. Foundational Research, examines the foundations for a science, analyses the beliefs and develops ways to specify how a knowledge base should change in light of new information.
5. Historical Research, allows one to discuss past and present events in the context of the present condition, and allows one to reflect and provide possible answers to current issues and problems. Historical research helps us in answering questions such as: Where have we come from, where are we, who are we now and where are we going?
6. Grounded Theory, is an inductive type of research, based or "grounded" in the observations or data from which it was developed; it uses a variety of data sources, including quantitative data, review of records, interviews, observation and surveys.
7. Phenomenology, describes the "subjective reality" of an event, as perceived by the study population; it is the study of a phenomenon.
8. Philosophical Research, is conducted by field experts within the boundaries of a specific field of study or profession, the best qualified

individual in any field of study to use an intellectual analyses, in order to clarify definitions, identify ethics, or make a value judgment concerning an issue in their field of study.

GROUNDED THEORY

Grounded theory (GT) is a systematic methodology in the social sciences involving the generation of theory from data. It is mainly used in qualitative research, but is also applicable to quantitative data.

Grounded theory is a research method that operates almost in a reverse fashion from traditional research and at first may appear to be in contradiction to the scientific method.

Rather than beginning with a hypothesis, the first step is data collection, through a variety of methods. From the data collected, the key points are marked with a series of *codes,* which are extracted from the text.

The codes are grouped into similar *concepts* in order to make them more workable. From these concepts, *categories* are formed, which are the basis for the creation of a *theory*, or a reverse engineered hypothesis. This contradicts the traditional model of research, where the researcher chooses a theoretical framework, and only then applies this model to the phenomenon to be studied.

Four Stages of Analysis

Stage	*Purpose*
Codes	Identifying anchors that allow the key points of the data to be gathered
Concepts	Collections of codes of similar content that allows the data to be grouped
Categories	Broad groups of similar concepts that are used to generate a *theory*
Theory	A collection of explanations that explain the subject of the research

Development

Grounded theory was developed by two sociologists, Barney Glaser and Anselm Strauss. Their collaboration in research on dying hospital patients led them to write the book Awareness of Dying. In this research they developed the constant comparative method, later known as Grounded Theory.

Split in Methodology

Since their original publication in 1967, Glaser and Strauss have disagreed on how to conduct grounded theory, resulting in a split in the theory between Straussian and Glaserian paradigms. This split occurred most obviously after Strauss published *Qualitative Analysis for Social Scientists* (1987). Thereafter Strauss, together with Juliet Corbin, published *Basics of Qualitative Research:*

Grounded Theory Procedures and Techniques in 1990. This was followed by a rebuke by Glaser (1992) who set out, chapter by chapter, to highlight the differences in what he argued was original grounded theory and why, according to Glaser, what Strauss and Corbin had written was not grounded theory in its "intended form". This divergence in methodology is a subject of much academic debate, which Glaser (1998) calls a "rhetorical wrestle".

According to Kelle (2005), "the controversy between Glaser and Strauss boils down to the question of whether the researcher uses a well defined 'coding paradigm' and always looks systematically for 'causal conditions,' 'phenomena/context, intervening conditions, action strategies' and 'consequences' in the data, or whether theoretical codes are employed as they emerge in the same way as substantive codes emerge, but drawing on a huge fund of 'coding families.'

Both strategies have their pros and cons. Novices who wish to get clear advice on how to structure data material may be satisfied with the use of the coding paradigm. Since the paradigm consists of theoretical terms which carry only limited empirical content the risk is not very high that data are forced by its application. However, it must not be forgotten that it is linked to a certain micro-sociological perspective. Many researchers may concur with that approach especially since qualitative research always had a relation to micro-sociological action theory, but others who want to employ a macro-sociological and system theory perspective may feel that the use of the coding paradigm would lead them astray."

Glaser's Approach

The first book, *The Discovery of Grounded Theory*, published in 1967, was "developed in close and equal collaboration" by Glaser and Strauss. Glaser wrote a methodology "Theoretical Sensitivity" in 1978 and has since written five more books on the method and edited five readers with a collection of grounded theory articles and dissertations.

The Glaserian strategy is not a qualitative research method, but claims the dictum "all is data". This means that not only interview or observational data but also surveys or statistical analyses or "whatever comes the researcher's way while studying a substantive area" (Glaser quote) can be used in the comparative process as well as literature data from science or media or even fiction. Thus the method according to Glaser is not limited to the realm of qualitative research, which he calls "QDA" (Qualitative Data Analysis). QDA is devoted to descriptive accuracy while the Glaserian method emphasizes conceptualization abstract of time, place and people. A grounded theory concept should be easy to use outside of the substantive area where it was generated.

Goals of Grounded Theory

Grounded theory is a systematic generation of theory from data that contains both inductive and deductive thinking. One goal is to formulate hypotheses based on conceptual ideas. Others may try to verify the hypotheses that are generated by constantly comparing conceptualized data on different levels of abstraction, and these comparisons contain deductive steps. Another goal of a grounded theory study is to discover the participants' main concern and how they continually try to resolve it. The questions the researcher repeatedly asks in grounded theory are "What's going on?" and "What is the main problem of the participants and how are they trying to solve it?" These questions will be answered by the core variable and its subcores and properties in due course.

Grounded theory does not aim for the "truth" but to conceptualize what's going on by using empirical data. In a way grounded theory resembles what many researchers do when retrospectively formulating new hypotheses to fit data. However, in grounded theory the researcher does not formulate the hypotheses in advance since preformed hypotheses are prohibited.

If the researcher's goal is accurate description, then another method should be chosen since grounded theory is not a descriptive method. Instead it has the goal of generating concepts that explain people's actions regardless of time and place. The descriptive parts of grounded theory are there mainly to illustrate the concepts. In most behavioral research endeavors persons or patients are units of analysis, whereas in GT the unit of analysis is the incident. There are typically at least several hundred incidents analyzed in a grounded theory study since usually every participant reports many incidents.

When comparing many incidents in a certain area, the emerging concepts and their relationships are in reality probability statements. Consequently, GT is not a qualitative method but a general method that can use any kind of data even if qualitative at the moment are most popular (Glaser, 2001, 2003). However, although working with probabilities, most GT studies are considered as qualitative since statistical methods are not used, and figures not presented. The results of GT are not a reporting of statistically significant probabilities but a set of probability statements about the relationship between concepts, or an integrated set of conceptual hypotheses developed from empirical data (Glaser 1998). Validity in its traditional sense is consequently not an issue in GT, which instead should be judged by fit, relevance, workability, and modifiability.

Fit has to do with how closely concepts fit with the incidents they are representing, and this is related to how thoroughly the constant comparison of incidents to concepts was done.

Relevance. A relevant study deals with the real concern of participants, evokes "grab" (captures the attention) and is not only of academic interest.

Workability. The theory works when it explains how the problem is being solved with much variation.

Modifiability. A modifiable theory can be altered when new relevant data is compared to existing data. A GT is never right or wrong, it just has more or less fit, relevance, workability and modifiability.

GT Nomenclature

A concept is the overall element and includes the categories which are conceptual elements standing by themselves, and properties of categories, which are conceptual aspects of categories. The core variable explains most of the participants' main concern with as much variation as possible. It has the most powerful properties to picture what's going on, but with as few properties as possible needed to do so. A popular type of core variable can be theoretically modeled as a basic social process that accounts for most of the variation in change over time, context, and behavior in the studied area. "GT is multivariate. It happens sequentially, subsequently, simultaneously, serendipitously, and scheduled" (Glaser, 1998).

All is data is a fundamental property of GT which means that everything that gets in the researcher's way when studying a certain area is data. Not only interviews or observations but anything is data that helps the researcher generating concepts for the emerging theory. Field notes can come from informal interviews, lectures, seminars, expert group meetings, newspaper articles, Internet mail lists, even television shows, conversations with friends etc. It is even possible, and sometimes a good idea, for a researcher with much knowledge in the studied area to interview herself, treating that interview like any other data, coding and comparing it to other data and generating concepts from it. This may sound silly since you don't have to interview yourself to know what you know, but you don't know it on the conceptual level! And GT deals with conceptual level data.

Open coding or substantive coding is conceptualizing on the first level of abstraction. Written data from field notes or transcripts are conceptualized line by line. In the beginning of a study everything is coded in order to find out about the problem and how it is being resolved. The coding is often done in the margin of the field notes. This phase is often tedious since you are conceptualizing all incidents in the data, which yields many concepts. These are compared as you code more data, and merged into new concepts, and eventually renamed and modified. The GT researcher goes back and forth while comparing data, constantly modifying, and sharpening the growing theory at the same time as she follows the build-up schedule of GT's different steps. Strauss and Corbin (1990, 1998) also proposed the axial coding and defined it in 1990 as "a set of procedures whereby data are put back together in new ways after open coding, by making connections between categories." They proposed a "coding paradigm" (also discussed, among others, by Kelle, 2005) that involved "conditions, context, action/interactional strategies and consequences."

Selective coding is done after having found the core variable or what is thought to be the core, the tentative core. The core explains the behavior of the participants in resolving their main concern. The tentative core is never wrong. It just more or less fits with the data. After chosen your core variable you selectively code data with the core guiding your coding, not bothering about concepts with little importance to the core and its subcores. Also, you now selectively sample new data with the core in mind, which is called theoretical sampling – a deductive part of GT. Selective coding delimits the study, which makes it move fast. This is indeed encouraged while doing GT (Glaser, 1998) since GT is not concerned with data accuracy as in descriptive research but is about generating concepts that are abstract of time, place and people. Selective coding could be done by going over old field notes or memos which are already coded once at an earlier stage or by coding newly gathered data.

Theoretical codes integrate the theory by weaving the fractured concepts into hypotheses that work together in a theory explaining the main concern of the participants. Theoretical coding means that the researcher applies a theoretical model to the data. It is important that this model is not forced beforehand but has emerged during the comparative process of GT. So the theoretical codes just as substantives codes should emerge from the process of constantly comparing the data in field notes and memos.

Memoing

Theoretical memoing is "the core stage of grounded theory methodology" (Glaser 1998). "Memos are the theorizing write-up of ideas about substantive codes and their theoretically coded relationships as they emerge during coding, collecting and analyzing data, and during memoing" (Glaser 1998).

Memoing is also important in the early phase of a GT study such as open coding. The researcher is then conceptualizing incidents, and memoing helps this process. Theoretical memos can be anything written or drawn in the constant comparison that makes up a GT. Memos are important tools to both refine and keep track of ideas that develop when you compare incidents to incidents and then concepts to concepts in the evolving theory. In memos you develop ideas about naming concepts and relating them to each other. In memos you try the relationships between concepts in two-by-two tables, in diagrams or figures or whatever makes the ideas flow, and generates comparative power. Without memoing the theory is superficial and the concepts generated not very original. Memoing works as an accumulation of written ideas into a bank of ideas about concepts and how they relate to each other. This bank contains rich parts of what will later be the written theory. Memoing is total creative freedom without rules of writing, grammar or style (Glaser 1998). The writing must be an instrument for outflow of ideas, and nothing else. When you write memos the ideas become more realistic, being converted from thoughts in your mind to words, and thus ideas communicable to the afterworld. In GT the preconscious processing that occurs when coding and comparing is recognized. The researcher is encouraged to register ideas about the ongoing study that eventually pop up in everyday situations, and awareness of the serendipity of the method is also necessary to achieve good results.

Sorting

In the next step memos are sorted, which is the key to formulate the theory for presentation to others. Sorting puts fractured data back together. During sorting lots of new ideas emerge, which in turn are recorded in new memos giving the memo-on-memos phenomenon. Sorting memos generates theory that explains the main action in the studied area. A theory written from unsorted memos may be rich in ideas but the connection between concepts is weak.

Writing

Writing up the sorted memo piles follows after sorting, and at this stage the theory is close to the written GT product. The different categories are now related to each other and the core variable. The theoretical density should be dosed so concepts are mixed with description in words, tables, or figures to optimize readability. In the later rewriting the relevant literature is woven in to put the theory in a scholarly context. Finally, the GT is edited for style and language and eventually submitted for publication.

No Pre-research Literature Review, No Taping and no Talk

GT according to Glaser gives the researcher freedom to generate new concepts explaining human behavior. This freedom is optimal when the researcher refrains from taping interviews, doing a pre research literature review, and talking about the research before it is written up. These rules makes GT different from most other methods using qualitative data.

No pre-research literature review. Studying the literature of the area under study gives preconceptions about what to find and the researcher gets desensitized by borrowed concepts. Instead, grounded theories in other areas, and GT method books increase theoretical sensitivity. The literature should instead be read in the sorting stage being treated as more data to code and compare with what has already been coded and generated.

No taping. Taping and transcribing interviews is common in qualitative research, but is counterproductive and a waste of time in GT which moves fast when the researcher delimits his data by field-noting interviews and soon after generates concepts that fit with data, are relevant and work in explaining what participants are doing to resolve their main concern.

No talk. Talking about the theory before it is written up drains the researcher of motivational energy. Talking can either render praise or criticism, and both diminish the motivational drive to write memos that develop and refine the concepts and the theory (Glaser 1998). Positive feedback makes you content with what you've got and negative feedback hampers your self-confidence. Talking about the GT should be restricted to persons capable of helping the researcher without influencing his final judgments.

The Grounded Theory Institute

Glaser founded the Grounded Theory Institute in 1999 as a non-profit web-based organization, which describes itself on its webpage as "dedicated to the evolving methodology of Dr.Barney G. Glaser, Ph.D.". The Institute provides an online forum for the discussion of grounded theory, and publishes the journal, "The Grounded Theory Review." The Institute also includes the Sociology Press, which Dr. Glaser founded in 1970.

Strauss's Approach

Generally speaking, grounded theory is an approach for looking systematically at (mostly) qualitative data (like transcripts of interviews or protocols of observations) aiming at the generation of theory. Sometimes, grounded theory is seen as a qualitative method, but grounded theory reaches farther: it combines a specific style of research (or a paradigm) with pragmatic theory of action and with some methodological guidelines.

This approach was written down and systematized in the 1960s by Anselm Strauss (himself a student of Herbert Blumer) and Barney Glaser (a student of Paul Lazarsfeld), while working together in studying the sociology of illness at the University of California, San Francisco. For and with their studies, they developed a methodology, which was then made explicit and became the foundation stone for an important branch of qualitative sociology.

Important concepts of grounded theory are categories, codes and codings. The research principle behind grounded theory is neither inductive nor deductive, but combines both in a way of abductive reasoning (coming from the works of Charles Sanders Peirce). This leads to a research practice where data sampling, data analysis and theory development are not seen as distinct and disjunct, but as different steps to be repeated until one can describe and explain the phenomenon that is to be researched. This stopping point is reached when new data does not change the emerging theory anymore. In an interview that was conducted shortly before Strauss' death (1994), he named three basic elements every grounded theory approach should include (Legewie/Schervier-Legewie (2004)). These three elements are:

- *Theoretical sensitive coding*, that is, generating theoretical strong concepts from the data to explain the phenomenon researched;
- *theoretical sampling*, that is, deciding whom to interview or what to observe next according to the state of theory generation, and that implies starting data analysis with the first interview, and writing down memos and hypotheses early;
- the need to *compare* between phenomena and contexts to make the theory strong.

Differences

Grounded theory according to Glaser emphasizes induction or emergence, and the individual researcher's creativity within a clear frame of stages, while Strauss is more interested in validation criteria and a systematic approach.

Criticism

Critiques of grounded theory have focused on its status as theory (is what is produced really 'theory'?), on the notion of 'ground' (why is an idea of 'grounding' one's findings important in qualitative inquiry—what are they 'grounded' *in*?) and on the claim to use and develop inductive knowledge. These criticisms are summed up by Thomas and James.

These authors also suggest that it is impossible to free oneself of preconceptions in the collection and analysis of data in the way that Glaser and Strauss say is necessary. They also point to the formulaic nature of grounded theory and the lack of congruence of this with open and creative interpretation-which ought to be the hallmark of qualitative inquiry. They suggest that the one element of grounded theory worth keeping is constant comparative method.

Grounded theory was developed in a period when other qualitative methods were often considered unscientific. Of all qualitative methods it achieved the widest acceptance of its academic rigor. Thus, especially in American academia, qualitative research is often equated to grounded theory. This equation is sometimes criticized by qualitative researchers using other methodologies (for example, traditional ethnography, narratology, and storytelling).

STRENGTHS AND LIMITATIONS OF RESEARCH

Research Limitations

Every study, no matter how well it is conducted, has some limitations. This is why it does not seem reasonable to use the words "prove" and "disprove" with respect to research findings. It is always possible that future research may cast doubt on the validity of any hypothesis or the conclusions from a study.

Limitations of Case Studies

Case studies may be viewed as having the most limitations. You cannot make causal conclusions from case studies. This is true because we cannot rule out alternative explanations. It is always unclear about the generality of the findings of a case study. A case study involves the behaviour of one person. The behaviour of one person may not reflect the behaviour of most people. Thus, we do not know how others may behave.

Limitations of Correlational Studies

Correlational research also has the same limitations as case studies. Correlational research merely demonstrates that we can predict a variable from another variable. It is demonstrating that two variables are associated. However, two variables can be associated without there being a causal relationship between the variables. We cannot make causal conclusions from correlational findings because we cannot rule out all alternative explanations for correlational findings. Thus, making causal conclusions from correlational findings is a logical error. If we find that A is associated with B, it could mean that A caused B, B caused A, or some third variable caused both A and B without there being any causal relationship between A and B. Even if we could rule out one of the possible relationships, we cannot rule out all alternative explanations from correlational studies. For every correlational study, there is the possibility that some third variable caused the two variables without there being a causal relationship between the variables. Correlational research may also have limitations with respect to the generality of the findings. Perhaps the study involved a specific group of people, or the relation between the variables were only investigated in some situations. Thus, it may be uncertain whether the correlational findings may generalize to other people or situations.

Limitations of Randomized Experiments

Experiments involving the random assignment of participants to conditions may allow us to make causal conclusions if the variables that are manipulated are not confounded with other variables. However, there still may be limitations with respect to the generality of the findings. The experiment may have involved a specific group of people, certain situations, and only some of the possible conceptualizations of variables. Thus, we may not know whether the findings will generalized to other people, situations, or conceptualizations of the variables.

RESEARCH DESIGN

Research can be defined as the search for knowledge, or as any systematic investigation, to establish novel facts, solve new or existing problems, prove new ideas, or develop new theories, usually using a scientific method. The primary purpose for basic research (as opposed to applied research) is discovering, interpreting, and the development of methods and systems for the advancement of human knowledge on a wide variety of scientific matters of our world and the universe.

Scientific research relies on the application of the scientific method, a harnessing of curiosity. This research provides scientific information and theories for the explanation of the nature and the properties of the world around us.

It makes practical applications possible. Scientific research is funded by public authorities, by charitable organizations and by private groups, including many companies. Scientific research can be subdivided into different classifications according to their academic and application disciplines.

Artistic research, also seen as 'practice-based research', can take form when creative works are considered both the research and the object of research itself.

It is the debatable body of thought which offers an alternative to purely scientific methods in research in its search for knowledge and truth.

Historical research is embodied in the historical method. Historians use primary sources and other evidence to systematically investigate a topic, and then to write histories in the form of accounts of the past. The phrase *my research* is also used loosely to describe a person's entire collection of information about a particular subject.

Etymology

As per the Merriam-Webster Online Dictionary, the word *research* is derived from the Middle French *"recerche"*, which means "to go about seeking", the term itself being derived from the Old French term *"recerchier"* a compound word from "re-" + "cerchier", or "sercher", meaning 'search'. The earliest recorded use of the term was in 1577.

Definitions

Research has been defined in a number of different ways.

A broad definition of research is given by Martin Shuttleworth-"In the broadest sense of the word, the definition of research includes any gathering of data, information and facts for the advancement of knowledge."

The Merriam-Webster Online Dictionary defines research in more detail as "a studious inquiry or examination; especially : investigation or experimentation aimed at the discovery and interpretation of facts, revision of accepted theories or laws in the light of new facts, or practical application of such new or revised theories or laws".

Scientific Research

Generally, research is understood to follow a certain structural process. Though step order may vary depending on the subject matter and researcher, the following steps are usually part of most formal research, both basic and applied:

1. Observations and Formation of the topic
2. Hypothesis
3. Conceptual definitions
4. Operational definition
5. Gathering of data
6. Analysis of data
7. Test, revising of hypothesis
8. Conclusion, reiteration if necessary.

A common misunderstanding is that by this method a hypothesis could be proven or tested. Generally a hypothesis is used to make predictions that can be tested by observing the outcome of an experiment. If the outcome is inconsistent with the hypothesis, then the hypothesis is rejected. However, if the outcome is consistent with the hypothesis, the experiment is said to support the hypothesis. This careful language is used because researchers recognize that alternative hypotheses may also be consistent with the observations.

In this sense, a hypothesis can never be proven, but rather only supported by surviving rounds of scientific testing and, eventually, becoming widely thought of as true. A useful hypothesis allows prediction and within the accuracy of observation of the time, the prediction will be verified. As the accuracy of observation improves with time, the hypothesis may no longer provide an accurate prediction. In this case a new hypothesis will arise to challenge the old, and to the extent that the new hypothesis makes more accurate predictions than the old, the new will supplant it.

Exploratory Research Designs

An exploratory research design is a type of research design that allows us to use our powers of observation, inquiry, and assessment to form tentative theories about what we are seeing and experiencing. It is generally used to explore understudied topics. In essence, we need to find out about a phenomenon. By asking an open-ended question (that is, a question that is worded in a way that allows the respondent to answer in his or her own words as opposed to merely soliciting a yes-or-no response) and observing the environment, we can begin to identify common themes from the information we gather. For instance, imagine you are a crisis call worker shortly after the 9/11 terrorist attacks. You are receiving a high volume of calls from rescue workers involved in the recovery of human remains. You have little or no knowledge about this experience; therefore, you explore the callers' experiences with them by asking questions such as "What is it like for you?" After listening to several workers, you might discover evidence of a common theme, for example, that the callers have been experiencing periods of tearfulness. Based on this evidence, you can then tell other callers that this experience appears to be common among rescue workers.

Explanatory Research Designs

An explanatory research design is a type of research design that focuses on examining the relationships between two or more factors and attempts to determine if they are related, and if so, in what ways and how strongly they are related.

For example, you may believe there is a relationship between the amount of time students spend studying for their research methods class and their final course grade in that class. Your hypothesis might be "The more students study research methods, the better their grades in that course will be." In fact, you would be able to find studies that have provided evidence that a relationship exists. If you were so inclined, it would be possible to design a study to examine just how strong the relationship is between hours spent studying and final course grades.

Descriptive Research Designs

In a sense, all research is descriptive by nature, as it describes how and/ or why a phenomenon occurs. Qualitative research methods do this using words, and quantitative research methods using numbers. A descriptive research design is a method that can be used to seek information that uses numeric language (how many, how much, etc.) to describe a population or phenomenon. This can be used in both qualitative and quantitative methods of research. For example, if you were conducting a quantitative study of victims of domestic violence, you may want to collect information on certain characteristics, such as their average age, what percentage of them have children, and the type of abuse and how frequently it occurs. You might also ask them to interpret the severity of the last abuse episode, using a scale from 1 to 5. It is important to note here that although this type of research looks at patterns such as how often an event occurs or ways that responses develop in relation to each other, it does not try to address why these patterns exist.

Descriptive information is also collected during qualitative studies to help put the experiences into context with the population reporting them. For example, while conducting interviews with 9/11 rescue workers, you might also collect information on how many of these individuals are firefighters, police officers, health professionals, volunteer civilians, and so forth. By using this mixed-method design, you may also be reporting how frequently the rescue workers reported similar textual information—for example, "Six out of ten volunteers stated they would volunteer again, regardless of the difficulties they are experiencing now."

Evaluative Research Designs

Evaluative designs can also draw from both fields of research. An evaluative research design draws from qualitative research methods when statements made in interviews and focus groups and written comments are used to describe outcomes. For instance, positive comments from a survey may be included in a program evaluation to demonstrate consumer satisfaction. Evaluative designs can also draw from the quantitative field of research. For instance, an evaluative design might examine how many and what type of residents were serviced at an agency over the last month.

Single-Subject Designs

Finally, a single-subject design uses systematic methodology to measure an individual's progress over time and measures whether a relationship exists between an intervention and a specific outcome. These designs can also draw from either or both methods of research. In a study using qualitative methods, the consumer's own statement that he or she is suicidal might be used to justify an extension for mental health treatment from an insurance company.

The Context of Design

Before examining types of research designs it is important to be clear about the role and purpose of research design. We need to understand what research design is and what it is not. We need to know where design fits into the whole research process from framing a question to finally analysing and reporting data.

Description and Explanation

Social researchers ask two fundamental types of research questions:

1. What is going on?
2. Why is it going on?

Descriptive Research

Although some people dismiss descriptive research as 'mere description', good description is fundamental to the research enterprise and it has added immeasurably to our knowledge of the shape and nature of our society. Descriptive research encompasses much government sponsored research including the population census, the collection of a wide range of social indicators and economic information such as household expenditure patterns, time use studies, employment and crime statistics and the like.

Descriptions can be concrete or abstract. A relatively concrete description might describe the ethnic mix of a community, the changing age profile of a population or the gender mix of a workplace. Alternatively the description might ask more abstract questions such as 'Is the level of social inequality increasing or declining?', 'How secular is society?' or 'How much poverty is there in this community?'

Accurate descriptions of the level of unemployment or poverty have historically played a key role in social policy reforms. By demonstrating the existence of social problems, competent description can challenge accepted assumptions about the way things are and can provoke action. Good description provokes the 'why' questions of explanatory research. If we detect greater social polarization over the last 20 years we are forced to ask 'Why is this happening?' But before asking 'why?' we must be sure about the fact and dimensions of the phenomenon of increasing polarization. It is all very well to develop elaborate theories as to why society might be more polarized now than in the recent past, but if the basic premise is wrong then attempts to explain a non-existent phenomenon are silly. Of course description can degenerate to mindless fact gathering or what C.W. Mills called 'abstracted empiricism'. There are plenty of examples of unfocused surveys and case studies that report trivial information and fail to provoke any 'why' questions or provide any basis for generalization. However, this is a function of inconsequential descriptions rather than an indictment of descriptive research itself.

Explanatory Research

Explanatory research focuses on why questions. For example, it is one thing to describe the crime rate in a country, to examine trends over time or to compare the rates in different countries. It is quite a different thing to develop explanations about why the crime rate is as high as it is, why some types of crime are increasing or why the rate is higher in some countries than in others. The way in which researchers develop research designs is fundamentally affected by whether the research question is descriptive or explanatory. It affects what information is collected.

For example, if we want to explain why some people are more likely to be apprehended and convicted of crimes we need to have hunches about why this is so. We may have many possibly incompatible hunches and will need to collect information that enables us to see which hunches work best empirically. Answering the 'why' questions involves developing causal explanations. Causal explanations argue that phenomenon Y is affected by factor X.

Some causal explanations will be simple while others will be more complex. For example, we might argue that there is a direct effect of gender on income. We might argue for a causal chain, such as that gender affects choice of field of training which in turn affects occupational options, which are linked to opportunities for promotion, which in turn affect income level. Or we could posit a more complex model involving a number of interrelated causal chains.

Prediction, Correlation and Causation

People often confuse correlation with causation. Simply because one event follows another, or two factors co-vary, does not mean that one causes the other. The link between two events may be coincidental rather than causal. There is a correlation between the number of fire engines at a fire and the amount of damage caused by the fire. Is it therefore reasonable to conclude that the number of fire engines causes the amount of damage? Clearly the number of fire engines and the amount of damage will both be due to some third factor ± such as the seriousness of the fire.

Similarly, as the divorce rate changed over the twentieth century the crime rate increased a few years later. But this does not mean that divorce causes crime. Rather than divorce causing crime, divorce and crime rates might both be due to other social processes such as secularization, greater individualism or poverty. Students at fee paying private schools typically perform better in their final year of schooling than those at government funded schools. But this need not be because private schools produce better performance. It may be that attending a private school and better final-year performance are both the outcome of some other cause. Confusing causation with correlation also confuses prediction with causation and prediction with explanation. Where two events or characteristics are correlated we can predict one from the other. Knowing the type of school attended improves our capacity to predict academic achievement. But this does not mean that the school type affects academic achievement. Predicting performance on the basis of school type does not tell us why private school students do better.

Good prediction does not depend on causal relationships. Nor does the ability to predict accurately demonstrate anything about causality. Recognizing that causation is more than correlation highlights a problem. While we can observe correlation we cannot observe cause. We have to infer cause. These inferences however are 'necessarily fallible... [they] are only indirectly linked to observables'. Because our inferences are fallible we must minimize the chances of incorrectly saying that a relationship is causal when in fact it is not. One of the fundamental purposes of research design in explanatory research is to avoid invalid inferences.

Deterministic and Probabilistic Concepts of Causation

There are two ways of thinking about causes: deterministically and probabilistically. The smoker who denies that tobacco causes cancer because he smokes heavily but has not contracted cancer shows deterministic causation. Probabilistic causation is illustrated by health authorities who point to the increased chances of cancer among smokers. Deterministic causation is where variable X is said to cause Y if, and only if, X invariably produces Y.

That is, when X is present then Y will 'necessarily, inevitably and infallibly' occur. This approach seeks to establish causal laws such as: whenever water is heated to 100¾C it always boils. In reality laws are never this simple. They will always specify particular conditions under which that law operates. Indeed a great deal of scientific investigation involves specifying the conditions under which particular laws operate. Thus, we might say that at sea level heating pure water to 100 ¾C will always cause water to boil. Alternatively, the law might be stated in the form of 'other things being equal' then X will always produce Y. A deterministic version of the relationship between race and income level would say that other things being equal then a white person will [always] earn a higher income than a black person. That is, race (X) causes income level (Y).

Stated like this the notion of deterministic causation in the social sciences sounds odd. It is hard to conceive of a characteristic or event that will invariably result in a given outcome even if a fairly tight set of conditions is specified. The complexity of human social behaviour and the subjective, meaningful and voluntaristic components of human behaviour mean that it will never be possible to arrive at causal statements of the type 'If X, and A and B, then Y will always follow.' Most causal thinking in the social sciences is probabilistic rather than deterministic. That is, we work at the level that a given factor increases the probability of a particular outcome, for example: being female increases the probability of working part time; race affects the probability of having a high status job. We can improve probabilistic explanations by specifying conditions under which X is less likely and more likely to affect Y.

But as suggested, never achieve complete or deterministic explanations. Human behaviour is both willed and caused: there is a double-sided character to human social behaviour. People construct their social world and there are creative aspects to human action but this freedom and agency will always be constrained by the structures within which people live. Because behaviour is not simply determined we cannot achieve deterministic explanations. However, because behaviour is constrained we can achieve probabilistic explanations. We can say that a given factor will increase the likelihood of a given outcome but there will never be certainty about outcomes.

Despite the probabilistic nature of causal statements in the social sciences, much popular, ideological and political discourse translates these into deterministic statements. Findings about the causal effects of class, gender or ethnicity, for example, are often read as if these factors invariably and completely produce particular outcomes. One could be forgiven for thinking that social science has demonstrated that gender completely and invariably determines position in society, roles in families, values and ways of relating to other people.

Theory Testing and Theory Construction

Attempts to answer the 'why' questions in social science are theories. These theories vary in their complexity, abstraction and scope. To understand the role of theory in empirical research it is useful to distinguish between two different styles of research: theory testing and theory building.

Theory Building

Theory building is a process in which research begins with observations and uses inductive reasoning to derive a theory from these observations. These theories attempt to make sense of observations. Because the theory is produced after observations are made it is often called post factum theory or ex post facto theorizing. This form of theory building entails asking whether the observation is a particular case of a more general factor, or how the observation fits into a pattern or a story. For example, Durkheim observed that the suicide rate was higher among Protestants than Catholics.

But is religious affiliation a particular case of something more general? Of what more general phenomenon might it be an indicator? Are there other observations that shed light on this? He also observed that men were more suicidal than women, urban dwellers more than rural dwellers and the socially mobile more than the socially stable.

He argued that the common factor behind all these observations was that those groups who were most suicidal were also less well socially integrated and experienced greater ambiguity about how to behave and what is right and wrong. He theorized that one of the explanations for suicidal behaviour was a sense of normlessness ± a disconnectedness of individuals from their social world. Of course, there may have been other ways of accounting for these observations but at least Durkheim's explanation was consistent with the facts.

Theory Testing

In contrast, a theory testing approach begins with a theory and uses theory to guide which observations to make: it moves from the general to the particular. The observations should provide a test of the worth of the theory. Using deductive reasoning to derive a set of propositions from the theory does this. We need to develop these propositions so that if the theory is true then certain things should follow in the real world. We then assess whether these predictions are correct. If they are correct the theory is supported.

If they do not hold up then the theory needs to be either rejected or modified. For example, we may wish to test the theory that it is not divorce itself that affects the wellbeing of children but the level of conflict between parents.

To test this idea we can make predictions about the wellbeing of children under different family conditions. For the simple theory that it is parental conflict rather than divorce that affects a child's wellbeing there are four basic 'conditions'. For each 'condition' the theory would make different predictions about the level of children's wellbeing that we can examine. If the theory that it is parental conflict rather than parental divorce is correct the following propositions should be supported:

- *Proposition* 1: children in situations (a) and (b) would be equally well off That is, where parental conflict is low, children with divorced parents will do just as well as those whose parents are married.
- *Proposition* 2: children in situations (c) and (d) should be equally poorly off That is, children in conflictual couple families will do just as badly as children in post-divorce families where parents sustain high conflict.
- *Proposition* 3: children in situation (c) will do worse than those in situation (a) That is, those with married parents in high conflict will do worse than those who have married parents who are not in conflict.
- *Proposition* 4: children in situation (d) will do worse than those in situation (b) That is, those with divorced parents in high conflict will do worse than those who have divorced parents who are not in conflict.

- *Proposition* 5: children in situation (b) will do better than those in situation (c) That is, children with divorced parents who are not in conflict will do better than those with married parents who are in conflict.
- *Proposition* 6: children in situation (a) will do better than those in situation (d) That is, children with married parents who are not in conflict will do better than those with divorced parents who are in conflict.

No single proposition would provide a compelling test of the original theory. Indeed, taken on its own proposition 3, for example, would reveal nothing about the impact of divorce. However, taken as a package, the set of propositions provides a stronger test of the theory than any single proposition. Although theory testing and theory building are often presented as alternative modes of research they should be part of one ongoing process. Typically, theory building will produce a plausible account or explanation of a set of observations. However, such explanations are frequently just one of a number of possible explanations that fit the data. While plausible they are not necessarily compelling. They require systematic testing where data are collected to specifically evaluate how well the explanation holds when subjected to a range of crucial tests.

What is Research Design

How is the term 'research design' to be used in this book? An analogy might help. When constructing a building there is no point ordering materials or setting critical dates for completion of project stages until we know what sort of building is being constructed. The first decision is whether we need a high rise office building, a factory for manufacturing machinery, a school, a residential home or an apartment block. Until this is done we cannot sketch a plan, obtain permits, work out a work schedule or order materials. Similarly, social research needs a design or a structure before data collection or analysis can commence.

A research design is not just a work plan. A work plan details what has to be done to complete the project but the work plan will flow from the project's research design. The function of a research design is to ensure that the evidence obtained enables us to answer the initial question as unambiguously as possible. Obtaining relevant evidence entails specifying the type of evidence needed to answer the research question, to test a theory, to evaluate a programme or to accurately describe some phenomenon. In other words, when designing research we need to ask: given this research question, what type of evidence is needed to answer the question in a convincing way? Research design 'deals with a logical problem and not a logistical problem'. Before a builder or architect can develop a work plan or order materials they must first establish the type of building required, its uses and the needs of the occupants. The work plan flows from this. Similarly, in social research the issues of sampling, method of data collection, design of questions are all subsidiary to the matter of 'What evidence do I need to collect?' Too often researchers design questionnaires or begin interviewing far too early ± before thinking through what information they require to answer their research questions. Without attending to these research design matters at the beginning, the conclusions drawn will normally be weak and unconvincing and fail to answer the research question.

Design Versus Method

Research design is different from the method by which data are collected. Many research methods texts confuse research designs with methods. It is not uncommon to see research design treated as a mode of data collection rather than as a logical structure of the inquiry. But there is nothing intrinsic about any research design that requires a particular method of data collection. Although cross-sectional surveys are frequently equated with questionnaires and case studies are often equated with participant observation data for any design can be collected with any data collection method.

How the data are collected is irrelevant to the logic of the design. Failing to distinguish between design and method leads to poor evaluation of designs.

Equating cross-sectional designs with questionnaires, or case studies with participant observation, means that the designs are often evaluated against the strengths and weaknesses of the method rather than their ability to draw relatively unambiguous conclusions or to select between rival plausible hypotheses.

Quantitative and Qualitative Research

Similarly, designs are often equated with qualitative and quantitative research methods.

Social surveys and experiments are frequently viewed as prime examples of quantitative research and are evaluated against the strengths and weaknesses of statistical, quantitative research methods and analysis.

Case studies, on the other hand, are often seen as prime examples of qualitative research ± which adopts an interpretive approach to data, studies 'things' within their context and considers the subjective meanings that people bring to their situation. It is erroneous to equate a particular research design with either quantitative or qualitative methods. Yin, a respected authority on case study design, has stressed the irrelevance of the quantitative/ qualitative distinction for case studies. He points out that:

- A point of confusion... has been the unfortunate linking between the case study method and certain types of data collection ± for example those focusing on qualitative methods, ethnography, or participant observation. People have thought that the case study method required them to embrace these data collection methods... On the contrary, the method does not imply any particular form of data collection ± which can be qualitative or quantitative.

Similarly, Marsh argues that quantitative surveys can provide information and explanations that are 'adequate at the level of meaning'. While recognizing that survey research has not always been good at tapping the subjective dimension of behaviour, she argues that:

- Making sense of social action... is... hard and surveys have not traditionally been very good at it. The earliest survey researchers started a tradition... of bringing the meaning from outside, either by making use of the researcher's stock of plausible explanations... or by bringing it from subsidiary in-depth interviews sprinkling quotes... liberally on the raw correlations derived from the survey. Survey research became much more exciting... when it began including meaningful dimensions in the study design. [This has been done in] two ways, firstly [by] asking the actor either for her reasons directly, or to supply information about the central values in her life around which we may assume she is orienting her life. [This] involves collecting a sufficiently complete picture of the context in which an actor finds herself that a team of outsiders may read off the meaningful dimensions.

Adopting a Sceptical Approach to Explanations

The need for research design stems from a sceptical approach to research and a view that scientific knowledge must always be provisional. The purpose of research design is to reduce the ambiguity of much research evidence. We can always find some evidence consistent with almost any theory. However, we should be sceptical of the evidence, and rather than seeking evidence that is consistent with our theory we should seek evidence that provides a compelling test of the theory. There are two related strategies for doing this: eliminating rival explanations of the evidence and deliberately seeking evidence that could disprove the theory.

Plausible Rival Hypotheses

A fundamental strategy of social research involves evaluating 'plausible rival hypotheses'. We need to examine and evaluate alternative ways of explaining a particular phenomenon. This applies regardless of whether the data are quantitative or qualitative; regardless of the particular research design;

and regardless of the method of data collection. Our mindset needs to anticipate alternative ways of interpreting findings and to regard any interpretation of these findings as provisional ± subject to further testing. The idea of evaluating plausible rival hypotheses can be illustrated using the example of the correlation between type of school attended and academic achievement.

Many parents accept the causal proposition that attendance at fee paying private schools improves a child's academic performance. Schools themselves promote the same notion by prominently advertising their pass rates and comparing them with those of other schools or with national averages. By implication they propose a causal connection: 'Send your child to our school and they will pass.'

The data they provide are consistent with their proposition that these schools produce better results. But these data are not compelling. There are at least three other ways of accounting for this correlation without accepting the causal link between school type and achievement. There is the selectivity explanation: the more able students may be sent to fee paying private schools in the first place.

There is the family resources explanation: parents who can afford to send their children to fee paying private schools can also afford other help. It is this help rather than the type of school that produces the better performance of private school students. Finally, there is the family values explanation: parents who value education most are prepared to send their children to fee paying private schools and it is this family emphasis on education, not the schools themselves, that produces the better academic performance. All these explanations are equally consistent with the observation that private school students do better than government school students.

Without collecting further evidence we cannot choose between these explanations and therefore must remain open minded about which one makes most empirical sense. There might also be methodological explanations for the finding that private school students perform better academically. These methodological issues might undermine any argument that a causal connection exists. Are the results due to questionable ways of measuring achievement? From what range and number of schools were the data obtained? On how many cases are the conclusions based? Could the pattern simply be a function of chance? These are all possible alternative explanations for the finding that private school students perform better.

Good research design will anticipate competing explanations before collecting data so that relevant information for evaluating the relative merits of these competing explanations is obtained. In this example of schools and academic achievement, thinking about alternative plausible hypotheses beforehand would lead us to find out about the parents' financial resources, the study resources available in the home, the parents' and child's attitudes about education and the child's academic abilities before entering the school.

SOCIAL WORK RESEARCH

Social work has long been concerned with strengthening the extent to which its research is capable of informing and guiding practice. Over the years increasing attention has been directed toward this purpose. This attention resulted in the founding in the 1970s of the first two journals dedicated to publishing research and the founding about 20 years later of a journal dedicated to research on practice. These advances notwithstanding, concern persists that social work researchers are not meeting the needs of practitioners. Such concern was reflected in the convening of a symposium in 1996 on psychosocial intervention research, cosponsored by the Institute for the Advancement of Social Work Research and the Office of Behavioral and Social Sciences Research at the National Institutes of Health, as well as in the publication of a special issue on intervention research in the journal Social Work Research (September 1997).

Emanating from similar concerns, this article reviews current publications in social work and assesses their potential in contributing to a body of knowledge of effective interventions. This review is based on the premise that social work practice must adhere to and be guided by effectiveness criteria. That is, interventions should be selected and used on the basis of their empirically demonstrated effectiveness. Because journal publications are a major vehicle for accumulating and disseminating professional knowledge, they constitute a primary source of guidance for practice. Accordingly, we examined the current research published in social work journals in relation to its potential for contributing to effective practice.

Purpose of Professional Knowledge

The premise that intervention should be based on relevant and valid knowledge is at the core of professional practice. Rosen (1978, 1996) has conceptualized the knowledge needs of practice as related to the purposes for which knowledge is used and its function in practice. Three types of knowledge were distinguished: descriptive, explanatory, and control. Descriptive knowledge guides practitioners in classifying phenomena they encounter into meaningful conceptual categories. Often it is used by practitioners in deciding whether and to what extent a particular manifestation or event should be of concern-that is, considered a problem. Descriptive knowledge includes information on the characteristics, indicators, or incidences of phenomena of professional concern (for example, poverty, child abuse, maladaptive behavior, mental disorders, and community violence).

Descriptive knowledge, in articulation with its values, also helps to formulate social work's objectives (Rosen, 1978), informs policy decisions about which services are needed by which client groups, and aids practitioners in assessing and classifying clients and problems into professionally meaningful categories. Explanatory knowledge is knowledge that provides insight into and understanding of the phenomena of concern—their dynamics, factors influencing their variability, and their consequences. It alerts practitioners to factors that probably contribute to the development and persistence of problems, and most important it provides practitioners with the basis for predicting the type and extent of other undesirable conditions likely associated with problems. Understanding of such dynamics guides practitioners' decisions about whether intervention is needed and toward which outcomes it is indicated. The third purpose for which knowledge is used in practice is to enhance practitioners' ability to control a phenomenon of concern—that is, the ability to change it (ameliorative function) or maintain its desired course preventive function). Knowledge fulfils its control functions when it is capable of guiding practitioners in the selection and implementation of interventions that successfully attain the desired outcomes.

To discharge their responsibility fully with regard to any case or client, practitioners must rely on knowledge that has been tested and validated in relation to the function it serves—descriptive, explanatory, or control. Descriptive and explanatory knowledge are required for practice tasks of assessing, explaining, or anticipating the course of naturally occurring events (including those viewed as problems)—that is, providing ex post facto explanations regarding antecedent factors or predicting the naturally occurring consequences of the events. Performing these practice tasks involves passive predictions: The practitioner's role is a passive one in relation to the occurrence of the predicted event (Rosen, 1993). A critical junction in knowledge needs occurs when, based on passive prediction, a practitioner decides that intervention toward some outcome is indicated. At that point the practitioner must rely on control-capable knowledge to guide the selection of interventions and their implementation. Practitioners also change their mode of operation from passive to active prediction at that point. They no longer predict the natural consequence of an event or process, but rather predict the consequences (outcomes) of their own interventions, and their activities are deliberately designed to confirm the prediction. The attainment of desired outcomes, then, is a consequence of practitioners' action. To bring a practice episode (treatment) to a successful conclusion, practitioners must have and use valid knowledge capable of guiding both passive and active predictions.

An example from the field of mental health may further illustrate the functions of descriptive, explanatory, and control knowledge in practice, as well as underscore the distinction between passive and active prediction. A recently divorced client seeks help for insomnia, irritability, and loss of appetite. Based on these complaints and the client's Beck Depression Inventory score, the social worker concludes that the client is depressed. In making this diagnosis the social worker was using descriptive knowledge that guided the classification of the client by professionally meaningful concepts (diagnosis) by viewing the client's characteristics in relation to population base rates and norms. Using explanatory knowledge the social worker formulated a hypothesis that the divorce likely precipitated the client's depression and that the client's condition would deteriorate unless treated (passive predictions). Thus, the social worker used descriptive knowledge for diagnosis and explanatory knowledge in assessment and for deciding that treatment was indicated. The social worker is in need of control knowledge to undertake treatment. Control knowledge would guide the social worker in the choice of an effective intervention (for example, cognitive-behavioral intervention) as well as in the implementation of the intervention's specific activities. Unlike explanatory knowledge, control knowledge deals with active prediction: The social worker's deliberate activities will bring about the predicted outcomes.

Unfortunately, the distinction between and different knowledge requirements of passive and active prediction tasks in practice often are overlooked. Failing to make such distinctions also may be coupled with the assumption (often implicit) that the ability to explain a phenomenon (passive prediction) is sufficient for being able to control it. These failures and assumptions, in turn, are likely to result in a disproportionate emphasis by social work researchers on research aimed at descriptive and explanatory knowledge at the expense of research directed specifically to production of control-capable knowledge (Rosen, 1996).

An appreciable part of the descriptive and explanatory knowledge essential for practice has been produced by the social sciences, in which explanation is the ultimate knowledge objective. In contrast, production of control knowledge aimed at influencing and changing events traditionally has been the domain and responsibility of the professions, as it is in social work. A report of the Task Force on Social Work Research (1991) similarly observed, "There is a substantial body of social, behavioral, and biological research on many of the underlying causes of the human problems social workers address. But there are many gaps in our knowledge about `what works'—that is, about the most effective... means of helping". Social work's disproportionate emphasis on descriptive and explanatory knowledge perhaps is sustained further by unwitting and indiscriminate adherence to the knowledge purposes and priorities of the social sciences, which occurs as a gratuitous appendage to social work's necessary use of social science's substantive and methodological contributions. Ours have been among the voices that for some time urged social work researchers to intensify efforts toward the production of control-capable knowledge, and we also conceptualized the treatment process to facilitate such research. Now it is our intent to examine research produced in social work in terms of the relative emphasis on descriptive, explanatory, and control knowledge and to assess the adequacy of control knowledge in informing practitioners' active predictions and guiding of interventions.

EXPLORATORY RESEARCH

Exploratory research is a type of research conducted for a problem that has not been clearly defined. Exploratory research helps determine the best research design, data collection method and selection of subjects. It should draw definitive conclusions only with extreme caution. Given its fundamental nature, exploratory research often concludes that a perceived problem does not actually exist.

Exploratory research often relies on secondary research such as reviewing available literature and/or data, or qualitative approaches such as informal discussions with consumers, employees, management or competitors, and more formal approaches through in-depth interviews, focus groups, projective methods, case studies or pilot studies. The Internet allows for research methods that are more interactive in nature. For example, RSS feeds efficiently supply researchers with up-to-date information; major search engine search results may be sent by email to researchers by services such as Google Alerts; comprehensive search results are tracked over lengthy periods of time by services such as Google Trends; and websites may be created to attract worldwide feedback on any subject.

The results of exploratory research are not usually useful for decision-making by themselves, but they can provide significant insight into a given situation. Although the results of qualitative research can give some indication as to the "why", "how" and "when" something occurs, it cannot tell us "how often" or "how many".

Exploratory research is not typically generalizable to the population at large.

Social exploratory research "seeks to find out how people get along in the setting under question, what meanings they give to their actions, and what issues concern them. The goal is to learn 'what is going on here?' and to investigate social phenomena without explicit expectations." (Russell K. Schutt, "Investigating the Social World," 5th ed.). This methodology is also at times referred to as a grounded theory approach to qualitative research or interpretive research, and is an attempt to unearth a theory from the data itself rather than from a predisposed hypothesis. Earl Babbie identifies three purposes of social science research. The purposes are exploratory, descriptive and explanatory. Exploratory research is used when problems are in a preliminary stage. Exploratory research is used when the topic or issue is new and when data is difficult to collect. Exploratory research is flexible and can address research questions of all types (what, why, how). Exploratory research is often used to generate formal hypotheses. Shields and Tajalli link exploratory research with the conceptual framework working hypothesis.

Applied Research

Applied research in administration is often exploratory because there is need for flexibility in approaching the problem. In addition there are often data limitations and a need to make a decision within a short time period. Qualitative research methods such as case study or field research are often used in exploratory research.

There are three types of objectives in a marketing research project.

- Exploratory research or formulative research
- Descriptive research
- Causal research.

Exploratory research or formulative research: The objective of exploratory research is to gather preliminary information that will help define problems and suggest hypotheses.'

Descriptive Research: The objective of descriptive research is to describe things, such as the market potential for a product or the demographics and attitudes of consumers who buy the product.'

Causal research: The objective of causal research is to test hypotheses about cause-and-effect relationships.

CONSTRUCTIVE RESEARCH

Constructive research is perhaps the most common computer science research method. This type of approach demands a form of validation that doesn't need to be quite as empirically based as in other types of research like exploratory research. Nevertheless the conclusions have to be objectively argued and defined. This may involve evaluating the "construct" being developed analytically against some predefined criteria or performing some benchmark tests with the prototype.

The term "construct" is often used in this context to refer to the new contribution being developed. Construct can be a new theory, algorithm, model, software, or a framework. The "fuzzy info from many sources" tab refers to different info sources like training materials, processes, literature, articles, working experience etc. In the "solution" tab, "theoretical framework" represents a tool to be used in the problem solving.

The "practical relevance" tab it refers to empirical knowledge creation that offers final benefits.

The "theoretical relevance" tab it gives the new theoretical knowledge that needs scientific acceptance: the back arrow to "theoretical body of knowledge" tab.

Steps to be followed in "practical utility" tab (a):

- set objectives and tasks
- identify process model
- select case execution
- interview case organization
- prepare simulation
- run simulation
- interpret simulation results
- give feedback.

Steps to be followed in "epistemic utility" tab (b):

- constructive research
- case research
- surveys
- qualitative and quantitative methods
- theory creating
- theory testing.

RESEARCH AND DEVELOPMENT

The phrase research and development (also R and D or, more often, R&D), according to the Organization for Economic Co-operation and Development, refers to "creative work undertaken on a systematic basis in order to increase the stock of knowledge, including knowledge of man, culture and society, and the use of this stock of knowledge to devise new applications".

Research and development is often scientific or towards developing particular technologies and is frequently carried out as corporate or governmental activity.

Overview

New product design and development is more often than not a crucial factor in the survival of a company. In an industry that is changing fast, firms must continually revise their design and range of products. This is necessary due to continuous technology change and development as well as other competitors and the changing preference of customers. Without an R&D

program, a firm must rely on strategic alliances, acquisitions, and networks to tap into the innovations of others.

A system driven by marketing is one that puts the customer needs first, and only produces goods that are known to sell. Market research is carried out, which establishes what is needed. If the development is technology driven then it is a matter of selling what it is possible to make. The product range is developed so that production processes are as efficient as possible and the products are technically superior, hence possessing a natural advantage in the market place.

R&D has a special economic significance apart from its conventional association with scientific and technological development. R&D investment generally reflects a government's or organization's willingness to forgo current operations or profit to improve future performance or returns, and its abilities to conduct research and development. The top eight spenders in terms of percentage of GDP were Israel (4.53%), Sweden (3.73%), Finland (3.45%) Japan (3.39%), South Korea (3.23%), Switzerland (2.9%), Iceland (2.78%) and United States (2.62%). The Commitment to Development Index ranks these countries, rewarding them for research and development that support the creation and dissemination of innovations of value to developing countries.

In general, R&D activities are conducted by specialized units or centers belonging to companies, universities and state agencies. In the context of commerce, "research and development" normally refers to future-oriented, longer-term activities in science or technology, using similar techniques to scientific research without predetermined outcomes and with broad forecasts of commercial yield.

Statistics on organizations devoted to "R&D" may express the state of an industry, the degree of competition or the lure of progress. Some common measures include: budgets, numbers of patents or on rates of peer-reviewed publications. Bank ratios are one of the best measures, because they are continuously maintained, public and reflect risk.

In the U.S., a typical ratio of research and development for an industrial company is about 3.5% of revenues. A high technology company such as a computer manufacturer might spend 7%. Although Allergan (a biotech company) tops the spending table with 43.4% investment, anything over 15% is remarkable and usually gains a reputation for being a high technology company. Companies in this category include pharmaceutical companies such as Merck & Co. (14.1%) or Novartis (15.1%), and engineering companies like Ericsson (24.9%). Such companies are often seen as credit risks because their spending ratios are so unusual.

Generally such firms prosper only in markets whose customers have extreme needs, such as medicine, scientific instruments, safety-critical mechanisms (aircraft) or high technology military armaments. The extreme needs justify the high risk of failure and consequently high gross margins from 60% to 90% of revenues. That is, gross profits will be as much as 90% of the sales cost, with manufacturing costing only 10% of the product price, because so many individual projects yield no exploitable product. Most industrial companies get only 40% revenues.

On a technical level, high tech organizations explore ways to re-purpose and repackage advanced technologies as a way of amortizing the high overhead. They often reuse advanced manufacturing processes, expensive safety certifications, specialized embedded software, computer-aided design software, electronic designs and mechanical subsystems.

Research has shown that firms with a persistent R&D strategy outperform those with an irregular or no R&D investment programme.

Pharmaceuticals

Research often refers to basic experimental research; development refers to the exploitation of discoveries. Research involves the identification of possible chemical compounds or theoretical mechanisms. In the United States, universities are the main provider of research level products. In the United States, corporations buy licences from universities or hire scientists directly when economically solid research level products emerge and the development phase of drug delivery is almost entirely managed by private enterprise. Development is concerned with proof of concept, safety testing, and determining ideal levels and delivery mechanisms. Development often occurs in phases that are defined by drug safety regulators in the country of interest. In the United States, the development phase can cost between $10 to $200 million and approximately one in ten compounds identified by basic research pass all development phases and reach market. Pharmaceuticals market, however are extremely complex in many respects. Large public sector investment in biomedical R & D influence private companies' choices about what to work and how intensively to invest in research and development. The returns on private sector R & D are attractive, on average but they vary considerably from one drug to the next. Consumer demand for prescription drug is often indirect, mediated by doctors and health insurers. New drug must undergo costly and time consuming testing before they sold.

Business

Research and development is nowadays of great importance in business as the level of competition, production processes and methods are rapidly increasing. It is of special importance in the field of marketing where companies keep an eagle eye on competitors and customers in order to keep pace with modern trends and analyse the needs, demands and desires of their customers. Unfortunately, research and development are very difficult to manage, since the defining feature of research is that the researchers do not know in advance exactly how to accomplish the desired result. As a result, higher R&D spending does not guarantee "more creativity, higher profit or a greater market share".

R&D Alliance

An R&D alliance is a mutually beneficial formal relationship between two or more parties to pursue a set of agreed goals while remaining independent organisations, where acquiring new knowledge is a goal by itself. The different parties agree to combine their knowledge to create new innovative products. Thanks to funding from government organizations, like the European Union's Seventh Framework Programme (FP7), and modern advances in technology, R&D alliances have now become more efficient. Every company has their own research and develop department.

R&D Reorientation

Industrial sector is transforming from vertical integration to horizontal structure. So far this transformation has taken place in manufacturing, but now it's the turn for R&D to make a paradigm shift. The restructuring trends of manufacturing predict the future of R&D to be focused, financially independent, universally expanded and distributed.

In 2003 on July the 25th with their article titled Reorienting R&D for a Horizontal Future Downey, Greenberg and Kapur illustrated that a horizontal structure of development in all industrial disciplines is required because of emerging markets, cost cutting needs and globalization. Collaborative networks in a decentralized environment are producing better results because of flexibility and cost reduction. R&D is spreading across the globe for faster development and unique innovations. Building block structure is getting popular in R&D because it is more manageable and focused.

In a challenging market environment after manufacturing now companies are eyeing to reduce the development cost where R&D needs to justify its existence as an independent profit centre with increased productivity and reduced operational costs. This can only be achieved through collaboration and trade-offs. Formation of horizontal collaborative network is challenging because it incorporates the issues of adaptability, security, cultural differences, varying standards, trust and ownership. Globalization is pushing R&D to concentrate on global design approach with the design flexibility where products can be tailored as per different geographic markets.

Innovating products in response to market requirements will keep organizations in business whereas knowing their own productivity and capacity will enable them to operate more effectively. Firms can make better investment decisions if they can predict their development cost. This will directly add to the bottom line of the business. In a race to improve the productivity, lower the cost and save time, firms should not forget to retain the expertise of their core competencies. The proper synchronization of global resources must be addressed in order to save time and money. Companies must support the development of innovation management system for future growth.

Companies are decentralizing their R&D units across the globe to extract the time and diversity benefits. Customer centric orientation is most profitable approach for any firm to operate in a competitive environment. R&D is an area where 'The World is Flat' theory applies perfectly. World is shrinking with the increasing pace of information technology, and the same time decentralization is making our days longer. In this fast pace environment managing intellectual property is more critical for businesses to keep themselves in the race. Never ending attempts should be made to optimize the development with minimal resources. Flattening the innovation process will result in technological development with greater profits and efficiency.

DESIGNING DESIGNS FOR RESEARCH

Much contemporary social research is devoted to examining whether a program, treatment, or manipulation causes some outcome or result. For example, we might wish to know whether a new educational program causes subsequent achievement score gains, whether a special work release program for prisoners causes lower recidivism rates, whether a novel drug causes a reduction in symptoms, and so on. Cook and Campbell (1979) argue that three conditions must be met before we can infer that such a cause-effect relation exists:

1. Covariation. Changes in the presumed cause must be related to changes in the presumed effect. Thus, if we introduce, remove, or change the level of a treatment or program, we should observe some change in the outcome measures.
2. Temporal Precedence. The presumed cause must occur prior to the presumed effect.
3. No Plausible Alternative Explanations. The presumed cause must be the only reasonable explanation for changes in the outcome measures. If there are other factors which could be responsible for changes in the outcome measures we cannot be confident that the presumed cause-effect relationship is correct.

In most social research the third condition is the most difficult to meet. Any number of factors other than the treatment or program could cause changes in outcome measures. Campbell and Stanley (1966) and later, Cook and Campbell (1979) list a number of common plausible alternative explanations (or, threats to internal validity). For example, it may be that some historical event which occurs at the same time that the program or treatment is instituted was responsible for the change in the outcome measures; or, changes in record keeping or measurement systems which occur at the same time as the program might be falsely attributed to the program. The reader is referred to standard research methods texts for more detailed discussions of threats to validity.

This paper is primarily heuristic in purpose. Standard social science methodology textbooks (Cook and Campbell 1979; Judd and Kenny, 1981) typically present an array of research designs and the alternative explanations which these designs rule out or minimize. This tends to foster a "cookbook" approach to research design - an emphasis on the selection of an available design rather than on the construction of an appropriate research strategy. While standard designs may sometimes fit real-life situations, it will often be necessary to "tailor" a research design to minimize specific threats to validity. Furthermore, even if standard textbook designs are used, an understanding of the logic of design construction in general will improve the comprehension of these standard approaches. This paper takes a structural approach to research design. While this is by no means the only strategy for constructing research designs, it helps to clarify some of the basic principles of design logic.

Minimizing Threats to Validity

Good research designs minimize the plausible alternative explanations for the hypothesized cause-effect relationship. But such explanations may be ruled out or minimized in a number of ways other than by design. The discussion which follows outlines five ways to minimize threats to validity, one of which is by research design:

1. By Argument. The most straightforward way to rule out a potential threat to validity is to simply argue that the threat in question is not a reasonable one. Such an argument may be made either *a priori* or *a posteriori*, although the former will usually be more convincing than the latter. For example, depending on the situation, one might argue that an instrumentation threat is not likely because the same test is used for pre and post test measurements and did not involve observers who might improve, or other such factors. In most cases, ruling out a potential threat to validity by argument alone will be weaker than the other approaches listed below. As a result, the most plausible threats in a study should not, except in unusual cases, be ruled out by argument only.

2. By Measurement or Observation. In some cases it will be possible to rule out a threat by measuring it and demonstrating that either it does not occur at all or occurs so minimally as to not be a strong alternative explanation for the cause-effect relationship. Consider, for example, a study of the effects of an advertising campaign on subsequent sales of a particular product. In such a study, history (i.e., the occurrence of other events which might lead to an increased desire to purchase the product) would be a plausible alternative explanation. For example, a change in the local economy, the removal of a competing product from the market, or similar events could cause an increase in product sales. One might attempt to minimize such threats by measuring local economic indicators and the availability and sales of competing products. If there is no change in these measures coincident with the onset of the advertising campaign, these threats would be considerably minimized. Similarly, if one is studying the effects of special mathematics training on math achievement scores of children, it might be useful to observe everyday classroom behavior in order to verify that students were not receiving any additional math training to that provided in the study.
3. By Design. Here, the major emphasis is on ruling out alternative explanations by adding treatment or control groups, waves of measurement, and the like. This topic will be discussed in more detail below.
4. By Analysis. There are a number of ways to rule out alternative explanations using statistical analysis. One interesting example is provided by Jurs and Glass (1971). They suggest that one could study the plausibility of an attrition or mortality threat by conducting a two-way analysis of variance. One factor in this study would be the original treatment group designations (i.e., program vs. comparison group), while the other factor would be attrition (i.e., dropout vs. non-dropout group). The dependent measure could be the pretest or other available pre-program measures. A main effect on the attrition factor would be indicative of a threat to external validity or generalizability, while an interaction between group and attrition factors would point to a possible threat to internal validity. Where both effects occur, it is reasonable to infer that there is a threat to both internal and external validity.

   The plausibility of alternative explanations might also be minimized using covariance analysis. For example, in a study of the effects of "workfare" programs on social welfare case loads, one plausible alternative explanation might be the status of local economic conditions. Here, it might be possible to construct a measure of economic conditions and include that measure as a covariate in the statistical analysis. One must be careful when using covariance adjustments of this type — "perfect" covariates do not exist in most social research and the use of imperfect covariates will not completely adjust for potential alternative explanations. Nevertheless causal assertions are likely to be strengthened by demonstrating that treatment effects occur even after adjusting on a number of good covariates.

5. By Preventive Action. When potential threats are anticipated they can often be ruled out by some type of preventive action. For example, if the program is a desirable one, it is likely that the comparison group would feel jealous or demoralized. Several actions can be taken to minimize the effects of these attitudes including offering the program to the comparison group upon completion of the study or using program and comparison groups which have little opportunity for contact and communication. In addition, auditing methods and quality control can be used to track potential experimental dropouts or to insure the standardization of measurement.

The five categories listed above should not be considered mutually exclusive. The inclusion of measurements designed to minimize threats to validity will obviously be related to the design structure and is likely to be a factor in the analysis.

A good research plan should, where possible. make use of multiple methods for reducing threats. In general, reducing a particular threat by design or preventive action will probably be stronger than by using one of the other three approaches. The choice of which strategy to use for any particular threat is complex and depends at least on the cost of the strategy and on the potential seriousness of the threat.

Design Construction

Basic Design Elements. Most research designs can be constructed from four basic elements:

1. Time. A causal relationship, by its very nature, implies that some time has elapsed between the occurrence of the cause and the consequent effect. While for some phenomena the elapsed time might be measured in microseconds and therefore might be unnoticeable to a casual observer, we normally assume that the cause and effect in social science arenas do not occur simultaneously, In design notation we indicate this temporal element horizontally - whatever symbol is used to indicate the presumed cause would be placed to the left of the symbol indicating measurement of the effect. Thus, as we read from left to right in design notation we are reading across time. Complex designs might involve

a lengthy sequence of observations and programs or treatments across time.

2. Program(s) or Treatment(s). The presumed cause may be a program or treatment under the explicit control of the researcher or the occurrence of some natural event or program not explicitly controlled. In design notation we usually depict a presumed cause with the symbol "X". When multiple programs or treatments are being studied using the same design, we can keep the programs distinct by using subscripts such as "X_1" or "X_2". For a comparison group (i.e., one which does not receive the program under study) no "X" is used.
3. Observation(s) or Measure(s). Measurements are typically depicted in design notation with the symbol "O". If the same measurement or observation is taken at every point in time in a design, then this "O" will be sufficient. Similarly, if the same set of measures is given at every point in time in this study, the "O" can be used to depict the entire set of measures. However, if different measures are given at different times it is useful to subscript the "O" to indicate which measurement is being given at which point in time.
4. Groups or Individuals. The final design element consists of the intact groups or the individuals who participate in various conditions. Typically, there will be one or more program and comparison groups. In design notation, each group is indicated on a separate line. Furthermore, the manner in which groups are assigned to the conditions can be indicated by an appropriate symbol at the beginning of each line. Here, "R" will represent a group which was randomly assigned, "N" will depict a group which was nonrandomly assigned (i.e.; a nonequivalent group or cohort) and a "C" will indicate that the group was assigned using a cutoff score on a measurement.

Perhaps the easiest way to understand how these four basic elements become integrated into a design structure is to give several examples. One of the most commonly used designs in social research is the two-group pre-post design which can be depicted as:

There are two lines in the design indicating that the study was comprised of two groups. The two groups were nonrandomly assigned as indicated by the "N". Both groups were measured before the program or treatment occurred as indicated by the first "O" in each line. Following this preobservation, the group in the first line received a program or treatment while the group in the second line did not. Finally, both groups were measured subsequent to the program. Another common design is the posttest-only randomized experiment. The design can be depicted as:

Here, two groups are randomly selected with one group receiving the program and one acting as a comparison. Both groups are measured after the program is administered.

Expanding a Design. We can combine the four basic design elements in a number of ways in order to arrive at a specific design which is appropriate for the setting at hand. One strategy for doing so begins with the basic causal relationship:

This is the most simple design in causal research and serves as a starting point for the development of better strategies. When we add to this basic design we are essentially expanding one of the four basic elements described above. Each possible expansion has implications both for the cost of the study and for the threats which might be ruled out.

Expanding Across Time. We can add to the basic design by including additional observations either before or after the program or, by adding or removing the program or different programs. For example, we might add one or more pre-program measurements and achieve the following design:

The addition of such pretests provides a "baseline" which, for instance, helps to assess the potential of a maturation or testing threat. If a change occurs between the first and second pre-program measures, it is reasonable to expect that similar change might be seen between the second pretest and the posttest even in the absence of the program. However, if no change occurs between the two pretests, one might be more confident in assuming that maturation or testing is not a likely alternative explanation for the cause-effect relationship which was hypothesized. Similarly, additional postprogram measures could be added. This would be useful for determining whether an immediate program effect decays over time, or whether there is a lag in time between the initiation of the program and the occurrence of an effect. We might also add and remove the program over time:

This is one form of the ABAB design which is frequently used in clinical psychology and psychiatry. The design is particularly strong against a history threat. When the program is repeated it is less likely that unique historical events can be responsible for replicated outcome patterns.

Expanding Across Programs. We have just seen that we can expand the program by adding it or removing it across time. Another way to expand the program would be to partition it into different levels of treatment. For example, in a study of the effect of a novel drug on subsequent behavior. we might use more than one dosage of the drug:

This design is an example of a simple factorial design with one factor having two levels. Notice that group assignment is not specified indicating that any type of assignment might have been used. This is a common strategy in a "sensitivity" or "parametric" study where the primary focus is one the effects obtained at various program levels. In a similar manner, one might expand the program by varying specific components of it across groups. This might be useful if one wishes to study different modes of the delivery of the program, different sets of program materials and the like. Finally, we can expand the program by using theoretically polarized or "opposite" treatments. A comparison group can be considered one example of such a polarization. Another might involve use of a second program which is expected to have an opposite effect on the outcome measures. A strategy of this sort provides evidence that the outcome measure is sensitive enough to differentiate between different programs.

Expanding Across Observations. At any point in time in a research design it is usually desirable to collect multiple measurements. For example, we might add a number of similar measures in order to determine whether the results of these converge. Or, we might wish to add measurements which theoretically should not be affected by the program in question in order to demonstrate that the program discriminates between effects. Strategies of this type are useful for achieving convergent and discriminant validity of measures as discussed in Campbell and Fiske (1959).

Another way to expand the observations is by proxy measurements. Assume that we wish to study a new educational program but neglected to take pre-program measurements. We might use a standardized achievement test for the posttest and grade point average records as a proxy measure of student achievement prior to the initiation of the program. Finally, we might also expand the observations through the use of "recollected" measures. Again, if we were conducting a study and had neglected to administer a pretest or desired information in addition to the pretest information, we might ask participants to recall how they felt or behaved prior to the study and use this information as an additional measure. Different measurement approaches obviously yield data of different quality. What is advocated here is the use of multiple measurements rather than reliance on only a single strategy.

Expanding Across Groups. Often, it will be to our advantage to add additional groups to a design in order to rule out specific threats to validity. For example, consider the following pre-post two-group randomized experimental design:

If this design were implemented within a single institution where members of the two groups were in contact with each other one might expect that intergroup communication, group rivalry, or demoralization of a group which gets denied a desirable treatment or gains an undesirable one might pose threats to the validity of the causal inference. In such a case. one might add an additional nonequivalent group from a similar institution which consists of persons unaware of the original two groups:

In a similar manner, whenever nonequivalent groups are used in a study it will usually be advantageous to have multiple replications of each group. The use of many nonequivalent groups helps to minimize the potential of a particular selection bias affecting the results. In some cases it may be desirable to include the norm group as an additional group in the design. Norming group averages are available for most standardized achievement tests for example, and might comprise an additional nonequivalent control group. Cohort groups might also be used in a number of ways. For example, one might use a single measure of a cohort group to help rule out a testing threat:

In this design, the randomized groups might be sixth graders from the same school year while the cohort might be the entire sixth grade from the previous academic year. This cohort group did not take the pretest and, if they are similar to the randomly selected control group, would provide evidence for or against the notion that taking the pretest had an effect on posttest scores. We might also use pre-post cohort groups:

Here, the treatment group consists of sixth graders, the first comparison group of seventh graders in the same year, and the second comparison group consists of the following year's sixth graders (i.e., the fifth graders during the study year). Strategies of this sort are particularly useful in nonequivalent designs where selection bias is a potential problem and where routinely-collected institutional data is available. Finally, one other approach for expanding the groups involves partitioning groups with different assignment strategies. For example, one might randomly divide nonequivalent groups, or select nonequivalent subgroups from randomly assigned groups. An example of this sort involving the combination of random assignment and assignment by a cutoff is discussed in detail below.

A SIMPLE STRATEGY FOR DESIGN CONSTRUCTION

Considering the basic elements of a research design or the possibilities for expansion are not alone sufficient. We need to be able to integrate these elements with an overall strategy. Furthermore we need to decide which potential threats are best handled by design rather than by argument, measurement, analysis, or preventive action.

While no definitive approach for designing designs exists, we might suggest a tentative strategy based on the notion of expansion discussed above. First, we begin the designing task by setting forth a design which depicts the simple hypothesized causal relationship. Second, we deliberately over-expand this basic design by expanding across time, program. observations, and groups.

At this step, the emphasis is on accounting for as many likely alternative explanations as possible using the design. Finally, we then scale back this over-expanded version considering the effect of eliminating each design component. It is at this point that we face the difficult decisions concerning the costs of each design component and the advantages of ruling out specific threats using other approaches.

There are several advantages which result from using this type of approach to design construction. First, we are forced to be explicit about the decisions which are made. Second. the approach is "conservative" in nature. The strategy minimizes the chance of our overlooking a major threat to validity in constructing our design. Third, we arrive at a design which is "tailored" to the situation at hand. Finally, the strategy is cost-efficient. Threats which can be accounted for by some other, less costly, approach need not be accounted for in the design itself.

An Example of a Hybrid Design

Some of the ideas discussed above can be illustrated in an example. The design in question is drawn from an earlier discussion by Boruch (1975). To our knowledge, this design has never been used, although it has strong features to commend it.

Let us assume that we wish to study the effects of a new compensatory education program on subsequent student achievement. The program is designed to help students who are poor in reading to improve in those skills. We can begin then with the simple hypothesized cause-effect relationship:

Here, the "X" represents the reading program and the "O" stands for a reading achievement test. We decide that it is desirable to add a pre-program measure so that we might investigate whether the program "improves" reading test scores. We also decide to expand across groups by adding a comparison group. At this point we have the typical:

The next problem concerns how the two groups will be assigned. Since the program is specifically designed to help students who need special assistance in reading, we rule out random assignment because it would require denying the program to students in need. We had considered the possibility of offering the program to one randomly assigned group in the first year and to the control group in the second, but ruled that out on the grounds that it would require two years of program expenses and the denial of a potentially helpful program for half of the students for a period of a year. Instead we decide to assign students by means of a cutoff score on the pretest. All students scoring below a preselected percentile on the reading pretest would be given the program while those above that percentile would act as controls (i.e., the regression-discontinuity design). However, previous experience with this strategy (Trochim, 1994) has shown us that it is difficult to adhere to a single cutoff score for assignment to group. We are especially concerned that teachers or administrators will allow students who score slightly above the cutoff point into the program because they have little confidence in the ability of the achievement test to make fine distinctions in reading skills for children who score very close to the cutoff. To deal with this potential problem, we decide to partition the groups using a particular combination of assignment by a cutoff and random assignment:

In this design we have set up two cutoff points. All those scoring below a certain percentile are assigned to the treatment group automatically by this cutoff, All those scoring above another higher percentile are automatically assigned to the comparison group by this cutoff. Finally, all those who fall in the interval between the cutoffs on the pretest are randomly assigned to either the treatment or comparison groups.

There are several advantages to this strategy. It directly addresses the concern to teachers and administrators that the test may not be able to discriminate well between students who score immediately above or below a cutoff point. For example, a student whose true ability in reading would place him near the cutoff might have a bad day and therefore might be placed into the treatment or comparison group by chance factors. The design outlined above is defensible. We can agree with the teachers and administrators that the test is fallible. Nevertheless, since we need some criterion to assign students to the program, we can argue that the fairest approach would be to assign borderline cases by lottery. In addition, by combining two excellent strategies (i.e., the randomized experiment and the regression-discontinuity) we can analyze results separately for each and address the possibility that design factors might bias results.

4

Hypothesis

An hypothesis is a proposed explanation for an observable phenomenon. The term derives from the Greek, meaning "to put under" or "to suppose." For a hypothesis to be put forward as a scientific hypothesis, the scientific method requires that one can test it. Scientists generally base scientific hypotheses on previous observations that cannot satisfactorily be explained with the available scientific theories.

Even though the words "hypothesis" and "theory" are often used synonymously in common and informal usage, a scientific hypothesis is not the same as a scientific theory. A working hypothesis is a provisionally accepted hypothesis. In a related but distinguishable usage, the term hypothesis is used for the antecedent of a proposition; thus in proposition "If P, then Q", P denotes the hypothesis; Q can be called a consequent. P is the assumption in a What If question. The adjective hypothetical, meaning "having the nature of a hypothesis," or "being assumed to exist as an immediate consequence of a hypothesis," can refer to any of these meanings of the term "hypothesis."

Uses

In its ancient usage, hypothesis also refers to a summary of the plot of a classical drama. In Plato's Meno, Socrates dissects virtue with a method used by mathematicians, that of "investigating from a hypothesis." In this sense, 'hypothesis' refers to a clever idea or to a convenient mathematical approach that simplifies cumbersome calculations. Cardinal Bellarmine gave a famous example of this usage in the warning issued to Galileo in the early 17th century: that he must not treat the motion of the Earth as a reality, but merely as a hypothesis. In common usage in the 21st century, a hypothesis refers to a provisional idea whose merit requires evaluation. For proper evaluation, the framer of a hypothesis needs to define specifics in operational terms. A hypothesis requires more work by the researcher in order to either confirm or disprove it. In due course, a confirmed hypothesis may become part of a theory or occasionally may grow to become a theory itself. Normally, scientific hypotheses have the form of a mathematical model.

Sometimes, but not always, one can also formulate them as existential statements, stating that some particular instance of the phenomenon under examination has some characteristic and causal explanations, which have the general form of universal statements, stating that every instance of the phenomenon has a particular characteristic. Any useful hypothesis will enable predictions by reasoning. It might predict the outcome of an experiment in a laboratory setting or the observation of a phenomenon in nature. The prediction may also invoke statistics and only talk about probabilities. Karl Popper, following others, has argued that a hypothesis must be falsifiable, and that one cannot regard a proposition or theory as scientific if it does not admit the possibility of being shown false. Other philosophers of science have rejected the criterion of falsifiability or supplemented it with other criteria, such as verifiability or coherence.

The scientific method involves experimentation on the basis of hypotheses to answer questions and explore observations. In framing a hypothesis, the investigator must not currently know the outcome of a test or that it remains reasonably under continuing investigation. Only in such cases does the experiment, test or study potentially increase the probability of showing the truth of a hypothesis. If the researcher already knows the outcome, it counts as a "consequence" — and the researcher should have already considered this while formulating the hypothesis. If one cannot assess the predictions by observation or by experience, the hypothesis classes as not yet useful, and must wait for others who might come afterward to make possible the needed observations. For example, a new technology or theory might make the necessary experiments feasible.

Scientific Hypothesis

People refer to a trial solution to a problem as a hypothesis — often called an "educated guess" — because it provides a suggested solution based on the evidence. Experimenters may test and reject several hypotheses before solving the problem. Schick and Vaughn, researchers weighing up alternative hypotheses may take into consideration:

- Testability
- Simplicity
- *Scope*: The apparent application of the hypothesis to multiple cases of phenomena
- *Fruitfulness*: The prospect that a hypothesis may explain further phenomena in the future

- *Conservatism*: The degree of "fit" with existing recognized knowledge-systems.

Evaluating Hypotheses

Karl Popper's formulation of hypothetico-deductive method, which he called the method of "conjectures and refutations", demands falsifiable hypotheses, framed in such a manner that the scientific community can prove them false. This view, a hypothesis cannot be "confirmed", because there is always the possibility that a future experiment will show that it is false. Hence, failing to falsify a hypothesis does not prove that hypothesis: it remains provisional.

However, a hypothesis that has been rigorously tested and not falsified can form a reasonable basis for action, *i.e,* we can act as if it were true, until such time as it is falsified. Just because we've never observed rain falling upward, doesn't mean that we never will—however improbable, our theory of gravity may be falsified some day. Popper's view is not the only view on evaluating hypotheses.

For example, some forms of empiricism hold that under a well-crafted, well-controlled experiment, a lack of falsification does count as verification, since such an experiment ranges over the full scope of possibilities in the problem domain. Should we ever discover some place where gravity did not function, and rain fell upward, this would not falsify our current theory of gravity– it would rather suggest an expansion of our theory to encompass some new force or previously undiscovered interaction of forces.

In other words, our initial theory as it stands is verified but incomplete. This situation shows the importance of having well-crafted, well-controlled experiments that range over the full scope of possibilities for applying the theory. In recent years philosophers of science have tried to integrate the various approaches to evaluating hypotheses, and the scientific method in general, to form a more complete system that integrates the individual concerns of each approach. Notably, Imre Lakatos and Paul Feyerabend, both former students of Popper, have produced novel attempts at such a synthesis.

Hypotheses, Concepts and Measurement

Concepts, as abstract units of meaning, play a key role in the development and testing of hypotheses. Concepts are the basic components of hypotheses. Most formal hypotheses connect concepts by specifying the expected relationships between concepts. For example, a simple relational hypothesis such as "education increases income" specifies a positive relationship between the concepts "education" and "income." This abstract or conceptual hypothesis cannot be tested. First, it must be operationalized or situated in the real world by rules of interpretation. Consider again the simple hypothesis "Education increases Income." To test the hypothesis the abstract meaning of education and income must be derived or operationalized.

The concepts should be measured. Education could be measured by "years of school completed" or "highest degree completed" etc. Income could be measured by "hourly rate of pay" or "yearly salary" etc. When a set of hypotheses are grouped together they become a type of conceptual framework. When a conceptual framework is complex and incorporates causality or explanation it is generally referred to as a theory. A philosopher of science Carl Gustav Hempel "An adequate empirical interpretation turns a theoretical system into a testable theory: The hypothesis whose constituent terms have been interpreted become capable of test by reference to observable phenomena. Frequently the interpreted hypothesis will be derivative hypotheses of the theory; but their confirmation or disconfirmation by empirical data will then immediately strengthen or weaken also the primitive hypotheses from which they were derived."

Hempel provides a useful metaphor that describes the relationship between a conceptual framework and the framework as it is observed and perhaps tested. "The whole system floats, as it were, the plane of observation and is anchored to it by rules of interpretation.

These might be viewed as strings which are not part of the network but link certain points of the latter with specific places in the plane of observation. By virtue of those interpretative connections, the network can function as a scientific theory" Hypotheses with concepts anchored in the plane of observation are ready to be tested. In "actual scientific practice the process of framing a theoretical structure and of interpreting it are not always sharply separated, since the intended interpretation usually guides the construction of the theoretician." It is, however, "possible and indeed desirable, for the purposes of logical clarification, to separate the two steps conceptually."

Statistical Hypothesis Testing

When a possible correlation or similar relation between phenomena is investigated, such as, for example, whether a proposed remedy is effective in treating a disease, that is, at least to some extent and for some patients, the hypothesis that a relation exists cannot be examined the same way one might examine a proposed new law of nature: in such an investigation a few cases in which the tested remedy shows no effect do not falsify the hypothesis. Instead, statistical tests are used to determine how likely it is that the overall effect would be observed if no real relation as hypothesized exists. If that likelihood is sufficiently small, the existence of a relation may be assumed. Otherwise, any observed effect may as well be due to pure chance. In statistical hypothesis testing two hypotheses are compared, which are called the null hypothesis and the alternative hypothesis.

The null hypothesis is the hypothesis that states that there is no relation between the phenomena whose relation is under investigation, or at least not of the form given by the alternative hypothesis. The alternative hypothesis, as the name suggests, is the alternative to the null hypothesis: it states that there is some kind of relation. The alternative hypothesis may take several forms, depending on the nature of the hypothesized relation; in particular, it can be two-sided or one-sided. Conventional significance levels for testing the hypotheses are.10.05, and.01.

Whether the null hypothesis is rejected and the alternative hypothesis is accepted, all must be determined in advance, before the observations are collected or inspected. If these criteria are determined later, when the data to be tested is already known, the test is invalid. It is important to mention that the procedure is actually dependent on the number of the participants that is included in the study. For instance, the sample size may be too small to reject a null hypothesis and, therefore, is recommended to specify the sample size from the beginning. It is advisible to define a small, medium and large effect size for each of a number of the important statistical tests which are used to test the hypotheses.

WORKING HYPOTHESIS

A working hypothesis is a hypothesis that is provisionally accepted as a basis for further research in the hope that a tenable theory will be produced, even if the hypothesis ultimately fails. Like all hypotheses, a working hypothesis is constructed as a statement of expectations, which can be linked to the exploratory research purpose in empirical investigation and are often used as a conceptual framework in qualitative research.

History

Use of the phrase "working hypothesis" goes back at least two centuries.

Charles Sanders Peirce came to hold that an explanatory hypothesis is not only justifiable as a tentative conclusion by its plausibility (by which he meant its naturalness and economy of explanation), but also justifiable as a starting point by the broader promise that the hypothesis holds for research. This idea of justifying a hypothesis as potentially fruitful (at the level of research method), not merely as plausible (at the level of logical conclusions), is essential for the idea of a working hypothesis, as later elaborated by Peirce's fellow pragmatist John Dewey.

Peirce held that, as a matter of research method, an explanatory hypothesis is judged and selected for research because it offers to economize and expedite the process of inquiry, by being testable and by further factors in the economy of hypotheses: low cost, intrinsic value (instinctive naturalness and reasoned likelihood), and relations (caution, breadth, and incomplexity) among hypotheses, inquiries, etc. (as in the game of Twenty Questions). The *Century Dictionary Supplement* definition of "working hypothesis" reflects that perspective; Peirce may or may not have written it. Peirce seldom used the phrase "working hypothesis," but he once commented about a related kind of a hypothesis that it was "a hypothesis, which like the working hypothesis of a scientific inquiry, we may not believe to be altogether true, but which is useful in enabling us to conceive of what takes place." For Peirce the pragmatist, conceiving pragmatically of something meant conceiving of its effects in their conceivable implications as to informed practice in general including research.

John Dewey used the concept of the working hypothesis as a pivotal feature in his theory of inquiry. Contrary to the principles of verification and falsifiability, used in formal hypothesis testing found within dominant paradigms of 'normal' science, working hypotheses were conceived by Dewey as neither true nor false but "provisional, working means of advancing investigation," which lead to the discovery of other unforeseen but "relevant" facts. Dewey's development of the concept of the working hypothesis emerged from his contextualist epistemology in which absolute truth is unobtainable and replaced by "warranted assertability". Thus, Dewey noted:

The history of science also shows that when hypotheses have been taken to be finally *true* and hence unquestionable, they have obstructed inquiry and kept science committed to doctrines that later turned out to be invalid.

In Dewey's view, the working hypothesis is generated, not directly as a testable statement of expectation, but instead in order to "direct inquiry into channels in which new material, factual and conceptual, is disclosed, material which is more relevant, more weighted and confirmed, more fruitful, than were the initial facts and conceptions which served as the point of departure".

Abraham Kaplan later described the working hypothesis as "provisional or loosely formatted" theory or constructs.

Design

Working hypotheses are constructed to facilitate inquiry; however, formal hypotheses can often be constructed based on the results of the inquiry, which in turn allows for the design of specific experiments whose data will either support or fail to support the formal hypotheses. In *Unity of Science as a Working Hypothesis* Oppenheim and Putnam argued that unitary science, in which laws from one branch could be equally useful by others, could only be accepted tentatively without further empirical testing. Thus they argued:

We therefore think the assumption that unitary science can be attained through cumulative micro-reduction recommends itself as a working hypothesis. That is, we believe that it is in accord with the standards of reasonable scientific judgment to tentatively accept this hypothesis and to work on the assumption that further progress can be made in this direction.

For Putnam, the working hypothesis, therefore, represents a practical starting point in the design of an empirical research exploration. A contrasting example of this conception of the working hypothesis is illustrated by the brain-in-a-vat thought experiment. This experiment involves confronting the global skeptic position that we, in fact, are all just brains in vats being stimulated by a mad scientist to believe that our reality is real. Putnam argued that this proposition, however, rests on a "magical theory of reference" in which the existential evidence necessary to validate it is assumed. Thus, the brain-in-a-vat proposition does not make for much of a hypothesis at all since there is no means to verify its truth. It does, however, provide a contrast for what a good working hypothesis would look like: one suited to culling potential existential evidence of the subject at hand.

A more concrete example would be that of conjectures in mathematics – propositions which appear to be true but which are formally unproven. Very often, conjectures will be provisionally accepted as working hypotheses in order to investigate its consequences and formulate conditional proofs.

HYPOTHESES, CONCEPTS AND MEASUREMENT

Concepts, as abstract units of meaning, play a key role in the development and testing of hypotheses. Concepts are the basic components of hypotheses. Most formal hypotheses connect concepts by specifying the expected relationships between concepts. For example, a simple relational hypothesis such as "education increases income" specifies a positive relationship between the concepts "education" and "income." This abstract or conceptual hypothesis cannot be tested. First, it must be operationalized or situated in the real world by rules of interpretation. Consider again the simple hypothesis "Education increases Income." To test the hypothesis the abstract meaning of education and income must be derived or operationalized. The concepts should be measured. Education could be measured by "years of school completed" or "highest degree completed" etc. Income could be measured by "hourly rate of pay" or "yearly salary" etc.

When a set of hypotheses are grouped together they become a type of conceptual framework. When a conceptual framework is complex and incorporates causality or explanation it is generally referred to as a theory. According to noted philosopher of science Carl Gustav Hempel "An adequate empirical interpretation turns a theoretical system into a testable theory: The hypothesis whose constituent terms have been interpreted become capable of test by reference to observable phenomena. Frequently the interpreted hypothesis will be derivative hypotheses of the theory; but their confirmation or disconfirmation by empirical data will then immediately strengthen or weaken also the primitive hypotheses from which they were derived."

Hempel provides a useful metaphor that describes the relationship between a conceptual framework and the framework as it is observed and perhaps tested (interpreted framework). "The whole system floats, as it were, above the plane of observation and is anchored to it by rules of interpretation. These might be viewed as strings which are not part of the network but link certain points of the latter with specific places in the plane of observation. By virtue of those interpretative connections, the network can function as a scientific theory" Hypotheses with concepts anchored in the plane of observation are ready to be tested. In "actual scientific practice the process of framing a theoretical structure and of interpreting it are not always sharply separated, since the intended interpretation usually guides the construction of the theoretician." It is, however, "possible and indeed desirable, for the purposes of logical clarification, to separate the two steps conceptually."

STATISTICAL HYPOTHESIS TESTING

A statistical hypothesis test is a method of making decisions using data, whether from a controlled experiment or an observational study (not controlled). In statistics, a result is called statistically significant if it is unlikely to have occurred by chance alone, according to a pre-determined threshold probability, the significance level. The phrase "*test of significance*" was coined by Ronald Fisher: "Critical tests of this kind may be called tests of significance, and when such tests are available we may discover whether a second sample is or is not significantly different from the first."

Hypothesis testing is sometimes called confirmatory data analysis, in contrast to exploratory data analysis. In frequency probability, these decisions are almost always made using null-hypothesis tests (i.e., tests that answer the question *Assuming that the null hypothesis is true, what is the probability of observing a value for the test statistic that is at least as extreme as the value that was actually observed?*) One use of hypothesis testing is deciding whether experimental results contain enough information to cast doubt on conventional wisdom.

A result that was found to be statistically significant is also called a positive result; conversely, a result that is not unlikely under the null hypothesis is called a negative result or a null result.

Statistical hypothesis testing is a key technique of frequentist statistical inference. The Bayesian approach to hypothesis testing is to base rejection of the hypothesis on the posterior probability. Other approaches to reaching a decision based on data are available via decision theory and optimal decisions.

The *critical region* of a hypothesis test is the set of all outcomes which, if they occur, will lead us to decide that there is a difference. That is, cause the null hypothesis to be rejected in favor of the alternative hypothesis. The critical region is usually denoted by the letter *C*.

The Testing Process

In the statistical literature, statistical hypothesis testing plays a fundamental role. The usual line of reasoning is as follows:

1. We start with a research hypothesis of which the truth is unknown.
2. The first step is to state the relevant null and alternative hypotheses. This is important as mis-stating the hypotheses will muddy the rest of the process. Specifically, the null hypothesis allows to attach an attribute: it should be chosen in such a way that it allows us to conclude whether the alternative hypothesis can either be accepted or stays undecided as it was before the test.
3. The second step is to consider the statistical assumptions being made about the sample in doing the test; for example, assumptions about the statistical independence or about the form of the distributions of the observations. This is equally important as invalid assumptions will mean that the results of the test are invalid.
4. Decide which test is appropriate, and stating the relevant test statistic T.
5. Derive the distribution of the test statistic under the null hypothesis from the assumptions. In standard cases this will be a well-known result. For example the test statistics may follow a Student's t distribution or a normal distribution.
6. The distribution of the test statistic partitions the possible values of T into those for which the null-hypothesis is rejected, the so called critical region, and those for which it is not.
7. Compute from the observations the observed value t_{obs} of the test statistic T.
8. Decide to either fail to reject the null hypothesis or reject it in favor of the alternative. The decision rule is to reject the null hypothesis H_0 if the observed value t_{obs} is in the critical region, and to accept or "fail to reject" the hypothesis otherwise.

It is important to note the philosophical difference between accepting the null hypothesis and simply failing to reject it. The "fail to reject" terminology highlights the fact that the null hypothesis is assumed to be true from the start of the test; if there is a lack of evidence against it, it simply continues to be assumed true. The phrase "accept the null hypothesis" may suggest it has been proved simply because it has not been disproved, a logical fallacy known as the argument from ignorance. Unless a test with particularly high power is used, the idea of "accepting" the null hypothesis may be dangerous. Nonetheless the terminology is prevalent throughout statistics, where its meaning is well understood. Alternatively, if the testing procedure forces us to reject the null hypothesis (H-null), we can accept the alternative hypothesis (H-alt) and we conclude that the research hypothesis is supported by the data. This fact expresses that our procedure is based on probabilistic considerations in the sense we accept that using another set could lead us to a different conclusion.

5

Methods and Research in Qualitative Approaches

There are a wide variety of methods that are common in qualitative measurement. In fact, the methods are largely limited by the imagination of the researcher.

Participant Observation

One of the most common methods for qualitative data collection, participant observation is also one of the most demanding. It requires that the researcher become a participant in the culture or context being observed. The literature on participant observation discusses how to enter the context, the role of the researcher as a participant, the collection and storage of field notes, and the analysis of field data. Participant observation often requires months or years of intensive work because the researcher needs to become accepted as a natural part of the culture in order to assure that the observations are of the natural phenomenon.

Direct Observation

Direct observation is distinguished from participant observation in a number of ways. First, a direct observer doesn't typically try to become a participant in the context. However, the direct observer does strive to be as unobtrusive as possible so as not to bias the observations. Second, direct observation suggests a more detached perspective. The researcher is watching rather than taking part. Consequently, technology can be a useful part of direct observation. For instance, one can videotape the phenomenon or observe from behind one-way mirrors. Third, direct observation tends to be more focused than participant observation. The researcher is observing certain sampled situations or people rather than trying to become immersed in the entire context. Finally, direct observation tends not to take as long as participant observation. For instance, one might observe child-mother interactions under specific circumstances in a laboratory setting from behind a one-way mirror, looking especially for the nonverbal cues being used.

Unstructured Interviewing

Unstructured interviewing involves direct interaction between the researcher and a respondent or group. It differs from traditional structured interviewing in several important ways. First, although the researcher may have some initial guiding questions or core concepts to ask about, there is no formal structured instrument or protocol. Second, the interviewer is free to move the conversation in any direction of interest that may come up. Consequently, unstructured interviewing is particularly useful for exploring a topic broadly. However, there is a price for this lack of structure. Because each interview tends to be unique with no predetermined set of questions asked of all respondents, it is usually more difficult to analyse unstructured interview data, especially when synthesizing across respondents.

Dependability

The traditional quantitative view of reliability is based on the assumption of replicability or repeatability. Essentially it is concerned with whether we would obtain the same results if we could observe the same thing twice. But we can't actually measure the same thing twice — by definition if we are measuring twice, we are measuring two different things. In order to estimate reliability, quantitative researchers construct various hypothetical notions (e.g., true score theory) to try to get around this fact.

The idea of dependability, on the other hand, emphasizes the need for the researcher to account for the ever-changing context within which research occurs. The research is responsible for describing the changes that occur in the setting and how these changes affected the way the research approached the study.

Confirmability

Qualitative research tends to assume that each researcher brings a unique perspective to the study. Confirmability refers to the degree to which the results could be confirmed or corroborated by others. There are a number of strategies for enhancing confirmability. The researcher can document the procedures for checking and rechecking the data throughout the study. Another researcher can take a "devil's advocate" role with respect to the results, and this process can be documented. The researcher can actively search for and describe and *negative instances* that contradict prior observations. And, after he study, one can conduct a *data audit* that examines the data collection and analysis procedures and makes judgements about the potential for bias or distortion. There has been considerable debate among methodologists about the value and legitimacy of this alternative set of standards for judging qualitative research.

On the one hand, many quantitative researchers see the alternative criteria as just a relabeling of the very successful quantitative criteria in order to accrue greater legitimacy for qualitative research. They suggest that a correct reading of the quantitative criteria would show that they are not limited to quantitative research alone and can be applied equally well to qualitative data. They argue that the alternative criteria represent a different philosophical perspective that is subjectivist rather than realist in nature. They claim that research inherently assumes that there is some reality that is being observed and can be observed with greater or less accuracy or validity. if you don't make this assumption, they would contend, you simply are not engaged in research (although that doesn't mean that what you are doing is not valuable or useful).

Perhaps there is some legitimacy to this counter argument. Certainly a broad reading of the traditional quantitative criteria might make them appropriate to the qualitative realm as well. But historically the traditional quantitative criteria have been described almost exclusively in terms of quantitative research. No one has yet done a thorough job of translating how the same criteria might apply in qualitative research contexts. For instance, the discussions of external validity have been dominated by the idea of statistical sampling as the basis for generalizing. And, considerations of reliability have traditionally been inextricably linked to the notion of true score theory.

But qualitative researchers do have a point about the irrelevance of traditional quantitative criteria. How could we judge the external validity of a qualitative study that does not use formalized sampling methods? And, how can we judge the reliability of qualitative data when there is no mechanism for estimating the true score?

No one has adequately explained how the operational procedures used to assess validity and reliability in quantitative research can be translated into legitimate corresponding operations for qualitative research.

While alternative criteria may not in the end be necessary (and I personally hope that more work is done on broadening the "traditional" criteria so that they legitimately apply across the entire spectrum of research approaches), and they certainly can be confusing for students and newcomers to this discussion, these alternatives do serve to remind us that qualitative research cannot easily be considered only an extension of the quantitative paradigm into the realm of nonnumeric data.

SAMPLING IN QUALITATIVE RESEARCH

Even if it were possible, it is not necessary to collect data from everyone in a community in order to get valid findings. In qualitative research, only a sample (that is, a subset) of a population is selected for any given study. The study's research objectives and the characteristics of the study population (such as size and diversity) determine which and how many people to select.

We briefly describe three of the most common sampling methods used in qualitative research: purposive sampling, quota sampling, and snowball sampling. As data collectors, you will not be responsible for selecting the sampling method. The explanations below are meant to help you understand the reasons for using each method.

Purposive Sampling

Purposive sampling, one of the most common sampling strategies, groups participants according to preselected criteria relevant to a particular research question (for example, HIV-positive women in Capital City). Sample sizes, which may or may not be fixed prior to data collection, depend on the resources and time available, as well as the study's objectives. Purposive sample sizes are often determined on the basis of theoretical saturation (the point in data collection when new data no longer bring additional insights to the research questions). Purposive sampling is therefore most successful when data review and analysis are done in conjunction with data collection.

Quota Sampling

Quota sampling, sometimes considered a type of purposive sampling, is also common. In quota sampling, we decide while designing the study how many people with which characteristics to include as participants. Characteristics might include age, place of residence, gender, class, profession, marital status, use of a particular contraceptive method, HIV status, etc. The criteria we choose allow us to focus on people we think would be most likely to experience, know about, or have insights into the research topic. Then we go into the community and – using recruitment strategies appropriate to the location, culture, and study population – find people who fit these criteria, until we meet the prescribed quotas.

Purposive and Quota Sampling Differ

Purposive and quota sampling are similar in that they both seek to identify participants based on selected criteria. However, quota sampling is more specific with respect to sizes and proportions of subsamples, with subgroups chosen to reflect corresponding proportions in the population. If, for example, gender is a variable of interest in how people experience HIV infection, a quota sample would seek an equal balance of HIV-positive men and HIV-positive women in a given city, assuming a 1:1 gender ratio in the population. Studies employ purposive rather than quota sampling when the number of participants is more of a target than a steadfast requirement – that is, an approximate rather than a strict quota.

Snowball Sampling

A third type of sampling, snowballing – also known as chain referral sampling – is considered a type of purposive sampling. In this method, participants or informants with whom contact has already been made use their social networks to refer the researcher to other people who could potentially participate in or contribute to the study. Snowball sampling is often used to find and recruit "hidden populations," that is, groups not easily accessible to researchers through other sampling strategies.

RECRUITMENT IN QUALITATIVE RESEARCH

A recruitment strategy is a project-specific plan for identifying and enrolling people to participate in a research study. The plan should specify criteria for screening potential participants, the number of people to be recruited, the location, and the approach to be used. We address some of the questions that may come up during the recruitment of participants.

Recruitment Strategies Decided

Ideally, the local principal investigator and qualitative research team members work together, in close consultation with community leaders and gatekeepers (that is, community members in positions of official or unofficial authority), to develop a plan to identify and recruit potential participants for each site.

Recruitment strategies are determined by the type and number of data collection activities in the study and by the characteristics of the study population. They are typically flexible and can be modified if new topics, research questions, or subpopulations emerge as important to the study, or if initial strategies do not result in the desired number of recruits. The criteria for selection can also be changed if certain data collection activities or subpopulations of people prove not to be useful in answering the research questions, as discussed in greater detail below.

Disagree with Recommendations from Local Leaders'

It is important for the research team to be respectful of and responsive to the guidance and advice of local experts and community leaders. Remember that they have had more opportunity to establish rapport with the local community and they will also have to maintain that rapport after the study is complete. Remember also that community members may hold community leaders and local organizations accountable for any misunderstandings or other problems resulting from the behaviour of the field staff.

People when We try to Recruit

Each research team develops guidelines for the introductory comments staff make to potential participants at each site. These guidelines need to be sensitive to the social and cultural contexts from which participants will be recruited.

They should also reflect the researchers' awareness that willingness to participate in an interview or focus group will depend on how well the participants understand what the study is about, what will be expected of them if they participate, and how their privacy will be respected.

In developing recruitment guidelines, it is important to take special care to avoid saying anything that could be interpreted as coercive. The voluntary nature of participation in research studies should always be emphasized.

Recruit People who are Legally

Yes, you may recruit minors, but in most cases you must obtain informed consent from the parent or guardian, as well as from the potential participant.

Exceptions to the parental consent requirement include pregnant adolescents and homeless minors, but you should always consult the guidelines of the relevant ethics review boards before proceeding with recruitment. Moreover, recruitment of minors must be specifically approved by all relevant ethics review boards. Because they are considered a vulnerable population, recruiting minors for research studies is a highly sensitive issue, and extra measures are required to ensure their protection.

Always Need to Obtain Informed Consent

The ethics committee that reviews and approves the study protocol determines whether informed consent needs to be obtained for each data collection activity. Typically, formal informed consent is necessary for all qualitative research methods except participant observation, regardless of the sampling method used to identify potential participants and the strategies used to recruit them.

Whether this informed consent is oral or written depends on a number of project-specific factors and ultimately upon approval by the ethics committee. During recruitment, obtaining informed consent for qualitative research involves clearly explaining the project to potential study participants.

Recruitment Strategy is not Working

After data collection is under way, the local principal investigator and field staff may find that the recruitment strategy is not working as well as anticipated. Because qualitative research is an iterative process, it is permissible to change the recruitment strategy, as long as the proper approvals are obtained. For example, it may be necessary to develop a new recruitment strategy because following the original plan has resulted in inadequate enrollment or because researchers determine that they need participants who meet a different set of criteria. After meeting to discuss alternatives, the research team should write down reasons why the strategy was not working or needs to be changed and outline how they would like to change it.

Proposed changes in the recruitment strategy must be submitted to the sponsoring organization, and some will require submission of a protocol amendment for approval by the ethics committees that initially approved the research. If new criteria for participation are proposed, for instance, they must be approved by relevant ethics committees before the new phase of recruitment can begin. Similarly, increasing the number of recruits would also require ethics committee approval. Because of the limited time frame for data collection, it is important that the field staff work closely with the site principal investigator and community gatekeepers to identify and recruit the new set of research participants.

THE INCOMPLETENESS OF STATISTICAL MODELS

How to interpret this graph and how to bring narrative evidence to bear? A first potential concern is that the predicted probabilities from the model are typically very small. Indeed, some 90% of the predicted probabilities fall between.0004 and .05. This is probably as it should be – or as it has to be – for two reasons. First, measured by year of onset, civil war starts are extremely rare. We have only about 127 onsets in nearly seven thousand country years. So, not conditioning on any other factors, the probability of a civil war starting in a randomly selected country year in this period was only about .017. Predicting civil war onset in a given country year from factors that can be coded across a large sample of countries and years is a bit like trying to find a needle in a haystack.

Second, it is virtually impossible to identify factors that are codable for a broad cross-section of countries and that can do an excellent job of predicting in *which year* a civil war will break out, if any. The random narratives reinforced our prior belief that a great deal of essentially random historical contingency is involved in determining whether and exactly when a country will "get" a civil war. Bad luck, idiosyncratic choices by leaders, complicated and ex ante unpredictable political and social interactions may all factor into explaining why a particular civil war started at a particular time, or even at all, in a particular country. It is a historian's project, and an admirable project at that, to try to understand such particularities and idiosyncrasies for particular cases. Our social science project, implausible though it may be, is to try to identify some factors and mechanisms that do "travel" across countries and years, raising the risk of civil war onset in a consistent and appreciable manner. This is a difficult task and we do not expect that even in the best case it will be possible to come anywhere close to perfect ex ante prediction. (Arguably, we could only do this if the participants themselves could do even better, given that they always have access to much more relevant case-specific information. But many examples suggest that it is quite rare for people and even politicians in a country to be able to forecast with confidence, a full year in advance, that a civil war will begin.)

Several of the key explanatory variables in our statistical model do not change much over time within countries. These variables are mountainousness, per capita income, population, and to some extent oil production. This means that while they may contribute a lot to explaining variation in the propensity for civil war outbreaks *across* countries, they are seriously handicapped for explaining in which year a war will start. The four variables that do (or can) change sharply from year to year – Prior war, New state, Instability, and Anocracy – are all quite crude measures. They are relatively easily coded across a broad cross-section of countries and years, but they do not condition in any sophisticated way on political circumstances or events occurring in the country. While they are statistically and substantively significant as predictors of onset, none of them is diagnostic in the sense that they have empirically been followed by onset with a near certainty. Thus, even when several of these time-varying variables are "on," the predicted probability of civil war breaking out in the very next year may only reach .2 or .3.

So, if one had to bet on civil war starting in a particular year using the model's predicted probabilities, even the country years with some of the highest estimated chances of onset are more likely than not to remain peaceful. The highest probability in the dataset is .51 for Indonesia in 1949 and 1950. After that is Pakistan in 1947 and 1948, with a probability of onset at .35. For all but two cases in the entire dataset, for any given country/year, a betting person should bet against a civil war onset occurring that year.

Changes in Predicted Probabilities

How then to interpret year-to-year changes in predicted probabilities for a given country? Relatively large jumps or falls in the graph correspond to changes on one or more of the sharply time varying explanatory factors. For each such case we can ask (1) if the change coincides with or shortly precedes a civil war onset, do we see a causal link from the independent variable to the outcome?; (2) if there is no onset, do we see signs of strife or other indications of increased conflict that might have become a civil war (and which appear causally related to the change on the independent variable)? And if so, why didn't the violence escalate to the level of civil war?; and (3) if there is no onset and no sign of increased violent conflict, why not? For all these cases we can and should also ask if we have miscoded (measured) the dependent variable or an independent variable, giving too much or too little credit to the model and the theory.

Similarly, for years in which we see an onset but no change in predicted probabilities, what occasioned the onset? Is there some new explanatory factor evident that could be coded across cases? Are there miscodings of variables in the model? If the predicted probability of conflict from the model is high on average (relative to the mean for the region or the world), do we see evidence linking any of the slow-moving variables like income or population and the outcome?

In more statistical terms, one way to interpret the graph of predicted onset probabilities for a given country is to interpret the statistical model as a model of an underlying, unobserved *propensity* for civil war in a given country year. The logit transformation scales the estimated propensity index into the [0, 1] interval as predicted probabilities. With narrative analysis we can try to go beyond assessing the fit of the model by looking at 0/1 outcome predictions, as in the standard quantitative approach to binary outcomes. Instead, to some extent we may be able to assess the model's fit by comparing changes in the predicted propensity of civil war to changes in the actual propensity as judged from the narrative evidence.

Despite difficulties in interpreting blunt variables in case analysis, our narratives of particular countries provide a useful complement and comparison to the statistical model. Before summarizing why they are useful, we will draw from the Algerian narrative to give a specific example of this approach.

Learning from the Narratives

In the case of Algeria's two civil wars, practitioners in the field of comparative politics committed only to the statistical approach might see the nice fit between model and the real world would and then let sleeping dogs lie. Algeria, with its poverty, its oil, its large population, and its mountains was a likely candidate for civil war. This was especially the case for two periods, 1962-63 and 1991-1992, when political factors (being a new state in 1962; political instability and the movement toward anocracy beginning in 1990) pushed the expected probability of civil war well above the world average. And in fact, the onsets of civil war took place precisely when our models showed that Algeria was especially prone to such violence.

Why examine with a fine-toothed comb cases for which no explanation is needed? In our method, however, Algeria was chosen through random selection, and so we could not let this sleeping dog lie. Waking him up proved rewarding. The civil war onset when Algeria was a new state indeed involved a commitment problem like that we theorized in proposing why the variable New State associates with civil war. Berbers who had prospered under French rule feared a loss of status to Arabs who would be the majority group in the new Algerian state. Furthermore, the local guerrilla units that bore the greatest brunt of the fighting for independence feared marginalization once the regular army entered Algeria from Morocco and Tunisia. If these regional militias did not fight for power in the summer of 1962, they feared marginalization as they did not trust the new leadership to give them as much as they might be able to take by fighting. Indeed some of these units and at least one from the Berber region took part in the 1962 rebellion.

The narrative also made clear that this "weak state" commitment problem stemmed as well from a factor not previously considered, namely, the ineffectiveness of France's transfer of power. France left the scene when the independence movement was divided in several ways, with no clearly dominant force and no general commitment to any constitutional mechanism to decide among them or guarantee future, peaceful chances at power. Independence to a new state without a credible commitment by the former metropole to support the leadership to which it transfers power yielded a vacuum that drew in insurgents. It was France's inability to commit to Prime Minister Ben Bella rather than just Ben Bella's inability to commit to the future security of minorities that accounted for post-independence violence in 1962.

The civil war coded as beginning in 1992, as our theoretical arguments concerning anocracy and political instability expected, emerged out of the political opening granted by the authoritarian regime in 1990. The opening indicated division within the governing elite and a general sense of weakening in the face of public dissatisfaction and pressure. Clerics in the FIS (Islamic Salvation Front) were emboldened to exploit an economic crisis to challenge the regime in the name of fundamentalist ideals. The commitment problem again appears as critical in the explanation for why there was violence rather than a negotiated or democratic solution – the military regime feared that the first national election lost to the Islamists would be the last election held anytime soon. This is consistent with our theoretical account linking anocracy and political instability (indicated by changed Polity scores) to civil war.

However, a careful look at the civil war that ensued brought into question our interpretation of the impact of per capita income. We have argued that on average, country poverty proxies for a weak central government administration and coercive apparatus, unable to collect information on its own population or to use information strategically to root out insurgents. In the Algerian case, we find a very strong army, one that that had learned much from the experience in fighting the French during the long war of independence. The army was well taken care of and it had the resources and will to develop sophisticated counter-insurgency units. So Algeria's moderately low per capita income (versus the regional or world averages) is in this case a poor measure of state coercive capabilities, and civil war occurred despite relatively strong coercive capability.

The narrative suggested, however, another quite different mechanism linking low per capita income and civil war. Area experts have pointed to the earlier closing of the migration outlet to Algerian youth as a causal factor in the onset of the war. Indeed, the rebellion came shortly after France cut off the immigration spigot. Instead of further inciting the anti-immigration program of M. Le Pen and his Front National in France, young Algerians that would formerly have been unemployed or sending back remittances from France were being recruited into the FIS. And so, the low GDP and weak economy in Algeria worked through a second mechanism (available recruits) rather than the first (weak military) to translate high likelihood to actual onset (consistent in this case with Collier and Hoeffler's (2004) interpretation of the role of income).

Since the FIS was a religious mobilization, the narrative almost invited us to ask whether the civil war of 1992 can be explained by some religious factor, even if religion played no role in our statistical analysis. There can be little doubt that Islamic symbols had a powerful emotional impact on the population. In the late 1970s, Muslim activists engaged in isolated and relatively small-scale assertions of fundamentalist principles: harassing women whom they felt were inappropriately dressed, smashing establishments that served alcohol, and evicting official imams from their mosques. The Islamists escalated their actions in 1982, when they called for the abrogation of the National Charter and for the formation of an Islamic government. Amidst an increasing number of violent incidents on campuses, Islamists killed one student. After police arrested 400 Islamists, about 100,000 demonstrators thronged to Friday prayers at a university mosque. Islamists were also able to mobilize large numbers of supporters successfully to demand that the government abrogate rights given to women in the colonial period. And of course, the Islamist political party shocked and awed the military authorities in their impressive first round electoral victory in December 1991 (Metz 1993). Fundamentalism was popular!

However, it is not clear why Islamic fundamentalists confronted the FLN. Algerian nationalism, consequent on the French denial of citizenship to Muslims in the 1870 Cremieux Decree, was always "Islamic" in sentiment. The FLN was never considered, as many in the army command considered themselves, secular and perhaps even anti-Islam. Some FLN leaders were Islamists. The FIS did not represent a deep cultural cleavage in Algeria. In fact, there is a popular pun among Algerians, "le FIS est le fils du FLN" (Quandt 1998, 96-7). The trump in the FIS hand was not its religious devotion or its sole identification with Islam.

Furthermore, a careful examination of the FIS reveals little about Islam as the source for the Algerian rebellion. For one, the clerics followed the urban proletariat into war rather than led them. There is evidence that in fact the clerics sought in the late 1980s to calm the riots in the streets instigated by the unemployed youth (Pelletiere 1992, 6). To be sure, the GIA (the leading insurgent militia) relied on fundamentalist ideology in order to finance the war through the "Islamic rent" paid by Middle East states. But this was a strategy of raising funds more than a sign of Islamic devotion.

The narrative suggests that it was not Islamic fundamentalism, but rather state strategies in regard to religion that played a vital role in driving the insurgency. After independence, the Algerian government asserted state control over religious activities for purposes of national consolidation and political control. Islam became the religion of the state in the new constitution and the publicly displayed religion of its leaders. No laws could be enacted that would be contrary to Islamic tenets or that would in any way undermine Islamic beliefs and principles. The state monopolized the building of mosques, and the Ministry of Religious Affairs controlled an estimated 5,000 public mosques by the mid-1980s. Imams were trained, appointed, and paid by the state, and the Friday *khutba*, or sermon, was issued to them by the Ministry of Religious Affairs. That ministry also administered religious property, provided for religious education and training in schools, and created special institutes for Islamic learning.

What is the implication of state control over religion? Our statistical analysis of the whole sample found that religious discrimination could not distinguish countries that experienced civil wars from those that did not. But the narrative suggests a different mechanism. The very act of authorizing and subsidizing religious organizations and leaders automatically politicized religious protest. As religious entrepreneurs sought to capture new audiences for their local mosques, they were in fact challenging state authority. Through its subsidization and promotion of Islam, the Algerian authorities opened themselves up to forms of symbolic attack they could not easily repel. By seeking to suppress religious experimentation, the FLN found itself more vulnerable to attack than if it kept entirely out of religious affairs. In sum, rather than some deep religious message of FIS that articulated with the religious sentiments of the people, it was the situation in which the state, by seeking to co-opt religious opposition, that gave that opposition a chance to articulate a clear anti-regime message through renegade mosques. State sponsorship of religion backfired grievously. The Algerian case thus suggests that state *sponsorship* of religion (rather than *discrimination* against it) raises the probability of a successful insurgency.

QUALITATIVE AND QUANTITATIVE METHODS

Some research techniques don't attempt to measure things, rather they aim to obtain deep insights and understand why people behave and think in the way that they do. These insights cannot be obtained by hundreds or thousands of interviews; they come from loosely structured interviewing by a skilled researcher or from focus groups.

These are flexible research methods that rely heavily on the skills of the researcher or moderator to interact with the respondents and to dig deep into their motivations and experiences. Such methods are *qualitative* and imply that they seek quality over quantity.

Qualitative research is exploratory and involves using unstructured techniques based on small samples. It helps to find out what it is that people like – or dislike – about a product, service or advertisement, and why they feel that way.

The data arising from qualitative research are largely words – the responses from people in the focus groups and depth interviews. Body language may be a further input as this could provide additional clues as to the inner feelings of respondents. Qualitative research is carried out by just one or two researchers who steep themselves in the subject, building their understanding.

COMPARISONS BETWEEN QUALITATIVE AND QUANTITATIVE METHODS

Some authors have chosen to posit qualitative and quantitative research as diametrically opposed constructs. This may confuse a beginning researcher in that it simplistically implies that qualitative research might never use numbers while quantitative research might never use subjects' perceptions.

More useful, perhaps, is the comparison of Borg and Gall (1989) who name the two approaches *positivistic* and *naturalistic* and compare them on the dimensions of the vision of the nature of reality, relationship of the researcher to the research subject, issues of generalizability, discussion of causality, and role of values.

Lincoln and Guba (1985) and Denzin and Lincoln (1994) define the term *paradigm* as a systematic set of beliefs, and their accompanying methods, which provide a view of the nature of reality. They contend that the history of inquiry can be divided into eras based on people's view of the world and how to study it. They argue that scientific inquiry is defined by the positivist paradigm, which has prevailed until recently. They call the earliest era the *prepositivist era,* which included human scientific endeavor about the time of Aristotle to the middle of the 1700s. This was the precursor to a more modern perspective. Lincoln and Guba say that research during this era consisted of passive observation and description. They consider the modern scientific method to have emerged in the positivist era, from about the middle 1700s to the present. Positivism, they note, can be identified by scientific research that involves hypotheses, manipulation, active observation of occurrences, and, thus, testing of hypotheses. These authors argue that the positivist paradigm is limited and is challenged currently by the emerging postpositivist paradigm, which they also call the *naturalistic paradigm.*

This conception of the naturalistic paradigm is echoed by Erlandson, Harris, Skipper, and Allen (1993) who note in their book, *Doing Naturalistic Inquiry,* that naturalistic inquiry is a new paradigm as opposed to the older prevailing positivist one. They say that while naturalistic research may use qualitative research methods, it cannot be equated these methods. They mention the "paradigm wars" raging in research in general. They note that constructivism and naturalistic inquiry have evolved together.

The paradigm debate as it has evolved in educational technology is more recent. The introduction of critical theory issues, the presentation of qualitative m shops at AECT national conferences, and the discussion of alternative research techniques are all indicators of change. One aspect of the paradigm debate is the issue of how one's perspective directs the type of research questions studied and how methods are chosen. Some believe that researchers must declare a paradigm from which they work, and that the paradigm naturally dictates methods and questions. This is a different approach from that taken in this chapter, namely, that methods may be chosen based on questions to be studied.

Other authors, such as Goetz and LeCompte (1984), contend that it is perhaps not useful to build simplistic dichotomies of research models. They argue that dichotomies such as generative verificative, inductive-deductive, subjective-objective, and constructive-enumerative to describe research models must be examined carefully and that "all factors must be balanced in composing a research design". While many of the authors above use the term *naturalistic inquiry,* it is perhaps more useful for that term to be applied to the paradigm as Lincoln and Guba (1985) and Erlandson et al. (1993) apply it. Goetz and

LeCompte use the term *ethnographic* for research using qualitative methods, but ethnography is just one form that qualitative research may take. In this chapter, we will use the term *qualitative research.* This seems to be a less value-laden term and one that has come to the fore recently. (As evidence, one major publisher of textbooks for social science research, Sage Publications, California, publishes an extensive series of references for all aspects of conducting this type of research under the title "qualitative methods.") It remains to be seen whether this is the term that in decades hence will continue to be used.

In sum, we in this chapter agree that forcing a choice between using qualitative or quantitative methods limits and inhibits the quality of research. Our argument is that the questions a researcher strives to answer should drive the choice of methods. Our assumption is that there is no reason data-gathering methods cannot be combined in a study, that a researcher cannot investigate carefully and creatively any questions he or she chooses. Rather than limiting our endeavors in this time of tremendous strides in technology development, this approach should enable researchers to take chances, to make leaps, to enhance development in the field by yielding both "answers" and "understanding." As will be seen in the next section, this approach has a solid tradition in educational communications and technology.

That said, given the tremendous ferment in educational research today, it behooves any researcher using qualitative methods to be aware of the "paradigm war" discussions. A researcher may choose to build a study using qualitative methods to answer certain questions, in a study that blends these methods with experimental or quasi-experimental methods. The researcher may design an entirely qualitative study to come to a deep understanding about what is happening in a setting, or how the participants perceive of their world. This study may stand on its own, or be used as a sort of pilot study to generate questions and hypotheses prior to conducting an experimental study. In any case, the researcher should be specific about how he or she defines the assumptions of the study and why what was done was done — in short, to be able to enter into the current and upcoming discussions as a thoughtful, critical, and creative researcher.

In educational communications and technology research, and in educational research in general, there is similar debate about the definition and purpose of qualitative methods. This can be viewed as a natural consequence of discussion in education about the utility of constructivist as opposed to positivist views of education. This discussion can be enjoyed at national and regional conferences in the field, and in the journals. It can be said that the larger debate regarding naturalistic versus positivistic research is creating a more open arena in which studies can be presented and published. Indeed, the editors of the leading journals in the field have indicated they welcome the submission of well-crafted qualitative studies. While not many such reports have been published, it is hoped that this chapter may positively influence the future. We will therefore, in this chapter, avoid the larger debate and focus on qualitative methods as tools.

It may come as a surprise to some that use of qualitative data collection methods has a long tradition in educational technology research. Early research efforts often used qualitative methods to evaluate and describe the use of media in the classroom. Experimental researchers have often used qualitative methods to collect attitude data, for instance, to yield possible explanations of students' behaviour. These data are typically collected using surveys, but may be collected using interviews. It is not unusual for an experimental researcher to further inform the study by conducting observations of the subjects. Researchers often conduct a case study to unobtrusively learn more about students, teachers, and trainers who use a new technology. Case studies present detailed data that may be used to derive questions later to be investigated in an experiment. Evaluation researchers have long used qualitative methods, in particular surveys, interviews, observations, and historical and document analysis.

While not researchers, per se, instructional systems designers have always used the qualitative methods of surveys, interviews, and observations during the front-end analysis and evaluation phases of development. Markle (1989), for example, contends that even in the early, more "behaviorist" days of instructional design, developers listened to their learners, watched them carefully, and humbly incorporated what learners taught them into their drafts of instructional materials. Similarly, what recent authors, especially computer scientists, are calling testing in "software engineering", "prototype evaluation" (Smith & Wedman, 1988), "prototype testing," "quality assurance" (McLean, 1989), or "quality control is clearly formative evaluation, usually incorporating some qualitative methods. Beyond these basic uses of qualitative methods, however, there have been calls in the field to use these methods to address new research questions. With the increasing use of computer-based interactive technologies in education and industry, opportunities, and at times the responsibility, to explore new questions about the processes of learning and instruction are evolving. Educational technologists have issued the call for the use of more qualitative research methods to explore training and school processes. Driscoll (1995) suggests that educational technologists select research paradigms based on what they perceive as the most critical questions. Noting the debate regarding paradigms, she adds that educational technology is a relatively young field in which "numerous paradigms may vie for acceptability and dominance". Robinson (1995) and Reigeluth (1989) concur, noting the considerable debate within the field regarding suitable research questions and methods. Winn (1989) also calls for more descriptive studies yielding information about learning and instruction. Clark agrees with Winn, calling for reconsideration of how media are studied (1983), and stating that researchers should conduct planned series of studies, selecting methods based on extensive literature reviews (1989). He recommends that prescriptive studies be conducted to determine why instructional development methods work. Qualitative methods can serve these purposes admirably.

The approach taken in this chapter, that choosing qualitative or quantitative methods need not be an either/or proposition, is similar to the approach of Hannafin and his associates in their development of the ROPES guidelines for designing instruction. Their guidelines blend behaviorist with cognitive principles in what they call applied cognitivism.

In our field, new educational technologies are continually being developed. Recent developments have been interactive multimedia, new distance learning systems, information technologies such as hypertext databases and the Internet, interactive learning environments, microworlds, and virtual-reality systems. Many teachers, trainers, administrators, managers, community members, and institutional leaders contend that the evolution of new technologies will continue to change the nature of teaching, training, instruction, and learning.

It is not only new technologies that require new research methods. The more recent developments in critical theory, postmodernism, and philosophical thought presented in this handbook and elsewhere also suggest distinctive changes and additions to our research endeavors and to the questions and problems in education with which technology is involved.

A recent study that used new technologies and combined qualitative and quantitative methods is that of Wiegmann (1996). In her dissertation, she combined techniques to examine preservice teachers' attitudes and perceptions of efficacy regarding instructional technologies. Her quasi-experimental study used a nonequivalent control-group design to investigate the effects of presentation techniques used in a science methods class.

Her data were collected using pre-and postsurveys. She also collected student artifacts in the form of student lesson plans, daily technology-use surveys, and reflective journals focusing on topics pertinent to science education and the use of technology in the classroom. Quantitative data analyses in the form of chi-square and factor analysis were combined with qualitative, more-narrative data about the student journals and lesson plans. Questions included, "Does the method used affect teachers' attitudes toward technology?" and "Does the method used to present preservice teachers with ways to use technology in instruction affect the instructional strategies they incorporate into their lesson plans?"

New technologies also enable researchers to study learners and learning processes in new ways. Computers allow sophisticated tracking of the paths that learners take through a lesson. We can view each decision a learner makes and analyse the relationship among the patterns of those decisions and their performance and attitudes.

New technologies may also require that we ask new questions in new ways. We may need to expand our views of what we should investigate and how. For instance, a qualitative view of how teachers and their students use a new technology may yield a view of "what is really happening" when the technology is used. Developers are well aware that instruction is not always delivered as designed, and this holds true for technology-based instruction. The history of educational technology includes records of the failures of a technological approach, often for reasons stemming from poorly planned implementation. We need to know what is really occurring when technologies or new approaches are used. Newman (1989) holds that learning environments can affect instructional technologies. He writes, "How a new piece of educational technology gets used in a particular environment cannot always be anticipated ahead of time. It can be argued that what the environment does with the technology provides critical information to guide design process". He adds, "It is seldom the case that the technology can be inserted into a classroom without changing other aspects of the environment".

A lucid discussion of the issues related to using qualitative techniques in investigating aspects of the technology of computer-based instruction is presented by Neuman (1989). She presents, for example, her findings on teacher perceptions and behaviors for integrating this type of interactive technological innovation into their classrooms. In another qualitative study of an instructional innovation, Jost (1994) investigated aspects of effective use of calculators in teaching calculus.

Well-designed research is never easy to conduct. Qualitative research studies typically require considerably more time to design, collect, and analyse data and to report the results than do quantitative studies. Yet professors in the field often hear students stating that they plan to do a qualitative study because it will be easier or quicker. Unfortunately, all too often poorly conceived and conducted studies are called qualitative in an effort to avoid defining and describing methods used to collect data, to avoid assumptions of the study, and even to clearly describe results. At conferences, one often hears editors of the leading journals exhorted to publish more qualitative research. Editors reply that they will publish such studies, provided reviewers and editors can determine that the studies are sound and relevant.

It should be noted that there is still some concern regarding the acceptance of qualitative research by journals. Not every editor or reviewer is an expert in identifying well-developed research reports of qualitative studies. Questions of sample size and validity may be inappropriately raised about qualitative studies, indicating that reviewers may need more experience with qualitative methods, or that reviewers with more experience with qualitative methods could be selected.

The concerns with regard to quality of research are not confined to educational technology. Lincoln and Guba (1985) note that "The naturalistic inquirer soon becomes accustomed to hearing charges that naturalistic studies are undisciplined; that he or she is guilty of 'sloppy' research, engaging in 'merely subjective' observations, responding indiscriminately to the 'loudest bangs or brightest lights' ". Methods for evaluating the soundness of a qualitative study, and for conducting a study ethically, will be presented in a later section. However, before discussing the methods qualitative researchers use, it is critical to illustrate the characteristics of good qualitative research. Not all will be present in any one study, as each study is designed differently to investigate different issues. However, it is worth considering what makes a study "qualitative."

In addition to the characteristics described in the earlier definition of qualitative research, in this chapter many of Lincoln and Guba's (1985) characteristics of naturalistic research will be assumed to apply to qualitative research. Qualitative research is done in a natural setting. The main data-gathering instrument is the human researcher. The researcher uses tacit, that is, intuitive or felt, knowledge, as well as propositional knowledge. Qualitative methods are used generally, but not to the exclusion of quantitative methods. Sampling is often purposive or theoretical rather than random or representative. Data analysis is typically inductive rather than deductive, but again, not exclusively. In naturalistic studies, theory is grounded in the data rather than determined a priori, although in qualitative studies theories often do drive the processes used in the investigation.

In contrast to experimental studies, in qualitative studies the design often emerges as the study progresses, with the researcher continually refining the methods and questions. Similarly, the focus of the study determines what data are collected, and the boundaries of what is studied may change during the study as new issues and questions emerge.

In qualitative research, the "reality" or the meaning of a situation and setting are negotiated among the researcher and those studied, with the understanding that multiple realities are always present. Many qualitative studies use a case study approach in the report, rather than a scientific report; some, in fact, describe the results by building a narrative or sort of story. A qualitative researcher tends to interpret results of a study or draw conclusions based on the particulars of that study, rather than in terms of generalizability to other situations and settings. Similarly, such a researcher is likely to be hesitant about advocating broad application of the findings of one study to other settings.

A final assumption of this chapter is that qualitative studies can be evaluated for quality, and rigor is not tossed out because a study is not quantitative in nature. While some of the criteria may be different from those used in quantitative research, many criteria for evaluating what Lincoln and Guba call the "trustworthiness" of a qualitative study will be discussed, many related to the particular methods used in qualitative research.

In summary, we concur with the call of Salomon (1991) that it is time to transcend the debate about qualitative versus quantitative research. In a stronger message, Robinson (1995) suggests that, "The paradigm debate should be declared a draw... [We should] accept the dual perspectives of our paradigm debate, if we are to meet the challenges of the future and be at all helpful in shaping the educational success of the next century". Robinson continues, "All ways of knowing and all social constructs should be equally accepted and represented in our literature... individuals should be encouraged to question and consider how they approach the world, how they understand learning, and how they believe knowledge is achieved".

QUANTITATIVE RESEARCH AND SOCIAL SCIENCES

In the social sciences, quantitative research refers to the systematic empirical investigation of quantitative properties and phenomena and their relationships. The objective of quantitative research is to develop and employ mathematical models, theories and/or hypotheses pertaining to phenomena. The process of measurement is central to quantitative research because it provides the fundamental connection between empirical observation and mathematical expression of quantitative relationships.

Quantitative research is used widely in social sciences such as psychology, sociology, anthropology, and political science. Research in mathematical sciences such as physics is also 'quantitative' by definition, though this use of the term differs in context. In the social sciences, the term relates to empirical methods, originating in both philosophical positivism and the history of statistics, which contrast qualitative research methods.

Qualitative methods produce information only on the particular cases studied, and any more general conclusions are only hypotheses. Quantitative methods can be used to verify, which of such hypotheses are true.

A comprehensive analysis of 1274 articles published in the top two American sociology journals between 1935 and 2005 found that roughly two thirds of these articles used quantitative methods.

Quantitative research is generally made using scientific methods, which can include:

- The generation of models, theories and hypotheses
- The development of instruments and methods for measurement
- Experimental control and manipulation of variables
- Collection of empirical data
- Modeling and analysis of data
- Evaluation of results

In the social sciences particularly, quantitative research is often contrasted with qualitative research which is the examination, analysis and interpretation of observations for the purpose of discovering underlying meanings and patterns of relationships, including classifications of types of phenomena and entities, in a manner that does not involve mathematical models. Approaches to quantitative psychology were first modelled on quantitative approaches in the physical sciences by Gustav Fechner in his work on psychophysics, which built on the work of Ernst Heinrich Weber. Although a distinction is commonly drawn between qualitative and quantitative aspects of scientific investigation, it has been argued that the two go hand in hand. For example, based on analysis of the history of science, Kuhn (1961) concludes that "large amounts of qualitative work have usually been prerequisite to fruitful quantification in the physical sciences". Qualitative research is often used to gain a general sense of phenomena and to form theories that can be tested using further quantitative research. For instance, in the social sciences qualitative research methods are often used to gain better understanding of such things as intentionality (from the speech response of the researchee) and meaning (why did this person/group say something and what did it mean to them?)(Kieron Yeoman).

Although quantitative investigation of the world has existed since people first began to record events or objects that had been counted, the modern idea of quantitative processes have their roots in Auguste Comte's positivist framework.

GROUNDED THEORY

Grounded theory is considered a type of qualitative methodology. Strauss and Corbin (1994), however, in their overview of grounded theory note that it is "a general methodology for developing theory that is grounded in data systematically gathered and analysed', adding that it is sometimes called the constant comparative method and that it is applicable as well to quantitative research. In grounded theory, the data may come from observations, interviews, and videotape or document analysis, and, as in other qualitative research, these data may be considered strictly qualitative or may be quantitative. The purpose of the methodology is to develop theory, through an iterative process of data analysis and theoretical analysis, with verification of hypotheses ongoing throughout the study. A grounded theory perspective leads the researcher to begin a study without completely preconceived notions about what the research questions should be, assuming that the theory on which the study is based will be tested and refined as the research is conducted.

The researcher collects extensive data with an open mind. As the study progresses, he or she continually examines the data for patterns, and the patterns lead the researcher to build the theory. Further data collection leads to further refinement of the questions. The researcher continues collecting and examining data until the patterns continue to repeat and few relatively, or no clearly, new patterns emerge. The researcher builds the theory from the phenomena, from the data, and the theory is thus built on, or "grounded" in, the phenomena. As Borg and Gall (1989) note, even quantitative researchers see the value of grounded theory and might use qualitative techniques in a pilot study without completely a priori notions of theory to develop a more-grounded theory on which to base later experiments.

A recent example of a grounded-theory approach in an educational technology study is that of Oliver's (1992). This research investigated and described the activities used in a university televised distance education system, analysing the use of camera techniques as they related to interaction in class. Oliver videotaped hours of two-way video instruction and analysed the amount and kind of classroom interactions that occurred. She also examined and described the various television shots and transitions used. Outside observers also coded the videotapes. Using grounded-theory techniques, Oliver used the data she transcribed and the emerging categories of data to create a theory of televised instruction. The theory involved the use of close-up camera techniques and the "clean-cut" transition to enhance interaction.

Participant Observation

Participant observation is a qualitative method frequently used in social science research. It is based on a long tradition of ethnographic study in anthropology. In participant observation, the observer becomes "part" of the environment, or the cultural context. The method usually involves the researcher's spending considerable time "in the field," as anthropologists do. Anthropologists typically spend a year or more in a cultural setting in order to really understand the culture in depth, even when they begin the study with a broad overall research question. The hallmark of participant observation is interaction among the researcher and the participants. The main subjects take part in the study to varying degrees, but the researcher interacts with them continually. For instance, the study may involve periodic interviews interspersed with observations so that the researcher can question the subjects and verify perceptions and patterns. These interviews may themselves take many forms, as noted in an upcoming section. For example, a researcher may begin by conducting open-ended unstructured interviews with several teachers to begin to formulate the research questions. This may be followed by a set of structured interviews with a few other teachers, based on results of the first series, forming a sort of oral questionnaire. Results of these interviews may then determine what will initially be recorded during observations. Later, after patterns begin to appear in the observational data, the researcher may conduct interviews asking the teachers about these patterns and why they think they are occurring, or if indeed those are categories of information. Similarly, a researcher might conduct videotaped observations of a set of teachers, analyse the tapes to begin to make taxonomies of behaviors, and then conduct interviews with the teachers, perhaps while they view the tapes together, to determine how the teachers themselves categorize these behaviors. Thus, the researcher becomes a long-term participant in the research setting.

Educational researchers have come under some criticism, at times legitimately so, for observing in educational settings for very brief periods of time, such as once for a few hours, and then making sweeping generalizations about teachers, schools, and students from these brief "slices of time." Yet, educational researchers typically do not have the resources to "live" in the observed settings for such extended periods of time as anthropologists do. There are several exceptions" including, but not limited to, Harry Wolcott's studies of a Kwakiutl village and school (1967) and of one year in the life of a school principal (1973); John Ogbu's (1974) ethnography of urban education; and Hugh Mehan's (1979) collaborative study of social interactions in a classroom, done with Courtney Cazden and her cooperating teacher, LaDonna Coles.

It is reasonable that fine educational technology research can be conducted using participant observation techniques, with somewhat limited research questions. Not every phenomenon can possibly be recorded. Most qualitative observational studies rely on the researcher's writing down what occurs in the form of extensive field notes. The researcher then analyzes these notes soon after observations are carried out, noting patterns of behaviors and events and phenomena to investigate in further observations. Still, the researcher is the instrument in most participant observations and, being human, cannot observe and record everything. Therefore, in most educational research studies, the investigator determines ahead of time what will be observed and recorded, guided but not limited by the research questions.

In an example of a limited participant observation case study, Robinson (1994) observed classes using "Channel One" in a midwestern middle school. While Robinson was not there for more than one semester, she did observe and participate in the class discussions for many hours of classroom instruction, as well as interview about 10% of the students. She did not focus on all school activities, or on all the categories of interaction within the classrooms, but focused her observations and field notes on the use of the televised news show and the reaction to it from students, teachers, administrators, and parents.

It should be noted that novice observers initially think they can avoid the observational limitations by simply videotaping everything that goes on in the setting, such as the classroom. The use of videotape and audiotape in data collection is useful, particularly in nonparticipant observational studies of particular behaviors and phenomena. However, it can be readily seen that videotaping everything is usually not a way to avoid defining or focusing research questions. For instance, without an exceptionally wide-angle lens, no video camera can record all that goes on in one classroom. If such a lens is used, then the wide view will preclude being able to see enough detail to understand much of what is going on. For example, computer screens will not be clearly visible, nor will specific nonverbal behaviours. In addition, if conversations are of interest in order to understand the types of behaviours students are engaged in, no one camera at the back of the room will be able to record all the conversations. Finally, those who have conducted microanalysis of videotaped classroom observations find it is not unusual to require 10 hours to analyse the behaviours and language recorded in I hour of videotape. It can easily be seen that the decision to videotape dozens of hours of classroom behaviours with one camera in the room might result in little useful data being collected, even after hundreds of hours of analysis. Videotape can successfully be used in data collection when the researcher knows what he or she wants to analyse. The preceding note of caution is just a reminder to the qualitative researcher that "shotgun" data collection is no substitute for determining ahead of time what the study is all about.

What can happen with videotape can also happen with written field notes. Trying to glean meaning by sifting through notebook after notebook of descriptions of classroom happenings, especially long after observations were made, is nearly impossible. What is needed is for observations to be at least loosely guided by purposes and questions. Even in studies using a grounded theory approach, observers generally analyse for patterns in observations throughout the entire data collection phase.

Spradley's (1980) book details how to conduct participant observations. He discusses the variety of roles the observer might take, noting that the observer becomes to varying degrees an "insider," in line with what Pelto and

Pelto (1978) call the emic view. Spradley suggests that the research site and setting, of course, be selected to best answer the research questions, but with an eye toward simplicity, accessibility, possibility of remaining relatively unobtrusive, permissibleness, assurance that the activities of interest will occur frequently, and degree to which the researcher can truly become a participant. Spradley (1980) provides specific techniques for conducting observations, for conducting iterative interviews with subjects, and for analysing behaviours, especially language used by informants in interviews. In particular, he notes that cultural domains, or categories of cultural meaning, can be derived from interviews and observations with participants. Finally, he provides advice regarding how to analyse data and write the ethnography.

The stages of participant observation, from an anthropological perspective, have been delineated by Bernard (1988). He describes the excitement, and sometimes fear, of the initial contact period; the next stage, which is often a type of shock as one gets to know the culture in more detail; a period of intense data collection he identifies with discovering the obvious, followed by the need for a real break; a stage in which the study becomes more focused; followed by exhaustion, a break and frantic activity; and finally, carefully taking leave of the field setting.

Spradley (1980) advises that ethical issues be addressed throughout the study. These issues are common to most types of qualitative research methods. For instance, Spradley advises that the researcher consider the welfare and interests of the informants, that is, the collaborating subjects first. He says informants' rights, interests, and sensibilities must be safeguarded; informants should not be exploited. Subjects should be made aware of the purposes of the research study. Their privacy should be protected. Many of these issues are common to all types of research. However, Spradley adds that reports should be made available to informants, so that they too are participants in the study. In some of the interview techniques described later, in fact, verifying analyses and preliminary reports with subjects is one way to ensure the authenticity of the results and to delve deeper into the research questions. Ethical issues in qualitative research, as well as criteria for evaluating the rigor and quality of such research.

Borg and Gall (1979) discuss the types of questions one might address using participant observation techniques. These include such questions as who the participants are; what are their typical and atypical patterns of behaviour; and where, when, how, and why the phenomena occur. In short, participant observation is often successfully used to describe what is happening in a context and why it happens. These are questions that cannot be answered in the standard experiment.

Another example of participant observation is described by Reilly (1994). His use of videotaping and video production instruction as a project in a California high school involved defining a new type of literacy, combining print, video, and computer technologies. Students produced videotapes that were then transferred to disc and made available for others' use. The research involved many hours of in-school data collection and analysis, and was very action oriented, with a product from the students as well as a written report from the researcher.

The work of Higgins and Rice (1991) is another excellent example of a qualitative study with an educational technology focus. These researchers investigated teachers' perceptions of testing. They used triangulation, by using a variety of methods to collect data; however, a key feature of the study was participant observation. Researchers observed six teachers for a sample of 10 hours each. Trained observers recorded instances of classroom behaviours that could be classified as assessment.

Another exemplary study that used multiple methods to triangulate data but that relied primarily on participant observation is that of Moallem (1994). This researcher investigated an experienced teacher's model of teaching and thinking by conducting a series of observations and interviews over a 7-month period. Using a constant comparative style, she analysed the data, which allowed categories of the teacher's frames of reference, knowledge and beliefs, planning and teaching techniques, and reflective thinking to emerge. She then built a model of the teacher's conceptions.

Nonparticipant Observation

Nonparticipant observation is one of several methods for collecting data considered to be relatively unobtrusive. Many recent authors cite the early work of Webb, Campbell, Schwartz, and Sechrest (1966) as laying the groundwork for use of all types of unobtrusive measures. Several types of nonparticipant observation have been identified by Goetz and LeCompte (1984). These include stream-of-behaviour chronicles, recorded in written narratives or using videotape or audiotape; proxemics and kinesics, that is, the study of uses of social space and movement; and interaction analysis protocols, typically in the form of observations of particular types of behaviours, categorized and coded for analysis of patterns. Bernard (1988) describes two types of nonparticipant observation, which he calls disguised field observation and naturalistic field experiments. He cautions in the first case for care to be taken that subjects are not harmfully deceived. Reflecting recent postmodern and constructivist (as well as deconstructionist) trends, Adler and Adler (1994) extend paradigms of observational research to include dramaturgical constructions of reality, and auto-observation, as well as more typical ethnomethodology. In nonparticipant observation, the observer does not interact to a great degree with those he or she is observing [as opposed to what Bernard (1988) calls direct, reactive observation]. The researcher primarily observes and records, and has no specific role as a participant. Usually, of course, the observer is "in" the scene, and thus affects it in some way; this must be taken into account. For instance, observers often work with teachers or instructors to have them explain to students briefly why the observer is there. Care should be taken once more not to bias the study. It is often desirable to explain the observations in general terms rather than to describe the exact behaviours being observed, so that participants do not naturally increase those behaviours. Some increase may occur; if the researcher suspects this, it would be appropriate to note it in the analyses and report.

As with participant observation, nonparticipant observers may or may not use structured observation forms, but are often more likely to. In this type of study, often several trained observers make brief sampled observations over periods of time, and observation forms help to ensure consistency of the data being recorded.

Nonparticipant observation is often used to study focused aspects of a setting, in order to answer specific questions within a study. This method can yield extensive detailed data, over many subjects and settings, if desired, in order to search for patterns, or to test hypotheses developed as a result of using other methods, such as interviews. It can thus be a powerful tool in triangulation. Observational data may be coded into categories, frequencies tabulated, and relationships analysed, yielding quantitative reports of results.

Guidelines for conducting nonparticipant observation are provided by Goetz and LeCompte (1984), among others. They recommend that researchers strive to be as unobtrusive and unbiased as possible. They suggest verification of data by using multiple observers. The units of analysis, thus data to be recorded, should be specified before beginning; recording methods should be developed; strategies for selection and sampling of units should be determined; and finally all processes should be tested and refined, before the study is begun in earnest.

Examples of studies in which observations were conducted that could be considered relatively nonparticipant observation were Savenye and Strand's (1989) in the initial pilot test, and Savenye (1989) in the subsequent larger field test of a science videodisc and computer-based curriculum. Of most concern during implementation was how teachers used the curriculum. Among other questions researchers were interested in are: how much teachers followed the teachers' guide, the types of questions they asked students when the system paused for class discussion, and what teachers added to or didn't use from the curriculum. In the field test (Savenye, 1989), a careful sample of classroom lessons was videotaped and the data coded. For example, teacher questions were coded according to a taxonomy based on Bloom's (1984), and results indicated that teachers typically used the system pauses to ask recall-level rather than higher-level questions.

Analysis of the coded behaviours for what teachers added indicated that most of the teachers in the sample added examples to the lessons which would provide relevance for their own learners, and that almost all of the teachers added reviews of the previous lessons to the beginning of the new lesson. Some teachers seemed to feel they needed to continue to lecture their classes; therefore they duplicated the content presented in the interactive lessons. Developers used the results of the studies to make changes in the curriculum and in the teacher training that accompanied it. Of interest in this study was a comparison of these varied teacher behaviours with the student achievement results. Borich (1989) found that learning achievement among students who used the interactive videodisc curriculum was significantly higher than among control students. Therefore, teachers had a great degree of freedom in using the curriculum, and the students still learned well.

If how students use interactive lessons is the major concern, researchers might videotape samples of students using an interactive lesson in cooperative groups, and code student statements and behaviours, as did Schmidt (1992). In a study conducted in a museum setting, Hirumi, Allen, and Savenye (1994) used qualitative methods to measure what visitors learned from an interactive videodisc-based natural history exhibit.

Nonparticipant observations may be used in studies that are primarily quantitative experimental studies in order to answer focused research questions about what learners do while participating in studies. For instance, a researcher may be interested in what types of choices learners make while they proceed through a lesson. This use of observations to answer a few research questions within experimental studies is exemplified in a series of studies of cooperative learning and learner control in television or computer-delivered instruction by Klein, Sullivan, Savenye, and their colleagues.

Jones, Crooks, and Klein (1995) describe the development of the observational instrument used in several of these studies. Klein and Pridemore (1994), in a study of cooperative learning in a television lesson, observed four sets of behaviours. These were coded as helping behaviours, on-task group behaviours, on-task individual behaviours, and off-task behaviours. In a subsequent experimental study using a computer-based lesson, Crooks, Klein, Jones, and Dwyer (1995) observed students in cooperative dyads, and recorded, coded, and analysed helping, discussion, or off-task behaviours.

In another study of cooperative use of computer-based instruction (Wolf, 1994), only one behaviour was determined to be most related to increased performance, and that was giving elaborated explanations, as defined by Webb (1991, 1983). Instances of this behaviour, then, were recorded and analysed.

An example of using technology to assist in recording and analysing behaviours is shown in Dalton, Hannafin, and Hooper's (1989) study on the achievement effects of individual and cooperative use of computer-based instruction. These researchers audiotaped the conversations of each set of students as they proceeded through the instruction.

A variation on nonparticipant observations represents a blend with trace-behaviour, artifact, or document analysis. This technique, called read-think-aloud protocols, takes the form of asking learners to describe what they do and why they do it, that is, their thoughts about their processes, as they proceed through an activity, such as a lesson. Smith and Wedinan (1988) describe using this technique to analyse learner tracking and choices. Researchers may observe and listen as subjects participate, or researches can use audiotape or videotape to analyse observations later. In either case, the resulting verbal data must be coded and summarized to address the research questions. Techniques for coding are described by Spradley (1980). However, protocol analysis (cf. Ericsson & Simon, 1984) techniques could be used on the resulting verbal data. These techniques also relate to analysis of documentary data, such as journals, discourse, recalled learning measures, and even forms of stories, such as life or career histories.

Many qualitative studies using observational techniques are case studies, and many in educational technology have involved the use of computers in schools. One such study was conducted by Dana (1994), who investigated how the pedagogical beliefs of one first-grade teacher related to her classroom curriculum and teaching practices. The teacher was an experienced and creative computer user who modeled the use of computers for her peers. Many hours of interviews and observations of the classes were made. Classroom videotapes were coded by outside reviewers who were trained to identify examples of the teacher's beliefs, exemplified in classroom practice. Her study provided insights into the methodology and teaching and learning in a computer-rich environment. She suggested changes that schools could make to encourage teachers to become better able to incorporate technology into their classrooms.

Another qualitative case study was conducted by Pitts (1993). He investigated students' organization and activities when they were involved in locating, organizing, and using information in the context of a research project in a biology class. Pitts relied on cognitive theory and information models in developing her theoretical construct. She described how students conducted their research leading to their preparation and use of video to present the results of their research.

Scope. A study using observational techniques may investigate a broad set of research questions, such as how a reorganization has affected an entire institution, or it may be much more narrowly focused. The outcome of the study may take the form of a type of "rich story" that describes an institution or a classroom or another type of cultural setting. A more narrowly focused participant observation study, however, may investigate particular aspects of a setting, such as the use of an educational innovation or its effects on particular classroom behaviours.

While some qualitative researchers might believe that only studies rich in "thick description," as described by Lincoln and Guba (1985) (cf. Geertz, 1973), are legitimate, other researchers might choose to use qualitative techniques to yield quantitative data. This blend of qualitative and quantitative data collection is also being used in anthropological studies. An example of a more narrowly focused relatively nonparticipant observation study is the Savenye and Strand (1989) study described earlier, in which the researchers chose to focus primarily on what types of interactive exchanges occurred between students and teachers while they used an electronic curriculum.

Biases. Educational researchers who choose to do observational studies would do well to remember that although they do not spend years observing the particular instructional community, they may quickly become participants in that community. Their presence may influence results. Similarly, their prior experiences or upbringing may bias them initially toward observing or recording certain phenomena, and later in how they "see" the patterns in the data. In subsequent reports, therefore, this subjectivity should be honestly acknowledged, as is recommended in ethnographic research.

The Observer's Role. In participant observation studies, the researcher is a legitimate member in some way in the community. For instance, in the videodisc-science curriculum study mentioned above, Strand was the senior instructional designer of the materials, Savenye had been an instructional design consultant on the project, and both researchers were known to the teachers through their roles in periodic teacher-training sessions. Observers have limited roles to play in the setting, but they must be careful not to influence the results of the study, that is, to make things happen that they want to happen. This may not seem so difficult, but it may be-for example, if the researcher finds himself or herself drawn to tutoring individuals in a classroom, which may bias the results of the study. Schmidt (1992) describes an example in which she had difficulty not responding to a student in class who turned to her for help in solving a problem; in fact, in that instance, she did assist. More difficult would be a researcher observing illegal behaviours by students who trust the researcher and have asked him or her to keep their activities secret. Potential bias may be handled by simply describing the researcher's role in the research report, but the investigator will want to examine periodically what his or her role is, and what type of influence may result from it.

What Should Be Recorded. What data are recorded should be based on the research questions. For example, in a study of classroom behaviours, every behaviour that instructors and students engage in could potentially be recorded and analysed, but this can be costly in money and time and is often not possible. A researcher using a completely "grounded-theory" approach would spend considerable time in the field recording as much as possible. However, another researcher might legitimately choose to investigate more narrowly defined research questions and primarily collect data related to those questions. Again, what is excluded may be as important as what is included. Therefore, even in a more-focused study, the researcher should be observant about other phenomena occurring and be willing to refine data collection procedures to collect emerging important information, or to change the research questions as the data dictate, even if this necessitates added time collecting data.

Sampling. In observational research, sampling becomes not random but purposive (Borg & Gall, 1989). For the study to be valid, the reader should be able to believe that a representative sample of involved individuals were observed. The "multiple realities" of any cultural context should be represented. The researcher, for instance, who is studying the impact of an educational innovation would never be satisfied with only observing the principals in the schools. Teachers and students using the innovation would obviously need to be observed. What is not so obvious is that it is important in this example to observe novice teachers, more experienced teachers, those who are comfortable with the innovation and those who are not, along with those who are downright hostile to the innovation. Parents might also be observed working with their youngsters or interacting with the teachers. How these various individuals use the innovation becomes the "reality of what is," rather than how only the most enthusiastic teachers or experienced technologists use it.

Multiple Observers. If several observers are used to collect the data, and their data are compared or aggregated, problems with reliability of data may occur. Remember that human beings are the recording instruments, and they tend to see and subsequently interpret the same phenomena in many different ways. It becomes necessary to train the observers and to ensure that observers are recording the same phenomena in the same ways. This is not as easy as it may sound, although it can be accomplished with some effort. A brief description of these efforts should be described in the final research report, as this description will illustrate why the data may be considered consistent.

One successful example of a method to train observers has been used by Klein and his colleagues in several of the studies described earlier. In the study investigating effects of cooperative learning versus individual learning structures, Crooks et al. (1995) determined to observe instances of cooperative behaviours while students worked together in a computer-based lesson. Several observers were trained using a videotape made of a typical cooperative-learning group, with a good-quality audio track and with close views of the computer screens. Observers were told what types of cooperative behaviours to record, such as instances of asking for help, giving help, and providing explanations.

These behaviours were then defined in the context of a computer-based lesson and the observation record form reviewed. Then observers all watched the same videotape and recorded instances of the various cooperative behaviours in the appropriate categories. The trainer and observers next discussed their records, and observers were given feedback regarding any errors.

The following segment of videotape was viewed, and the observers again recorded the behaviours. The training was repeated until observers were recording at a reliability of about 95%. Similarly, Wolf (1994) in her study trained observers to record instances of just one behaviour, providing elaborated explanations.

It should be noted that in studies in which multiple observers are used and behaviours counted or categorized and tallied, it is desirable to calculate and report interrater reliability. This can easily be done by having a number of observers record data in several of the same classroom sessions or in the same segments of tape, and then computing the degree of their agreement in the data.

GUIDELINES IN QUALITATIVE RESEARCH METHOD

Qualitative researchers, like anyone conducting research with people, should undergo formal research ethics training. The material presented here is not a substitute for training on research ethics. *Research ethics* deals primarily with the interaction between researchers and the people they study. *Professional ethics* deals with additional issues such as collaborative relationships among researchers, mentoring relationships, intellectual property, fabrication of data, and plagiarism, among others. While we do not explicitly discuss professional ethics here, they are obviously as important for qualitative research as for any other endeavour. Most professional organizations, such as the American Anthropological Association, the Society for Applied Anthropology, the American Sociological Association, and the American Public Health Association, have developed broad statements of professional ethics that are easily accessible via the Internet.

Why is Research Ethics Important in Qualitative Research?

The history and development of international research ethics guidance is strongly reflective of abuses and mistakes made in the course of biomedical research. This has led some qualitative researchers to conclude that their research is unlikely to benefit from such guidance or even that they are not at risk of perpetrating abuses or making mistakes of real consequence for the people they study. Conversely, biomedical and public health researchers who use qualitative approaches without having the benefit of formal training in the social sciences may attempt to rigidly enforce bioethics practices without considering whether they are appropriate for qualitative research. Between these two extremes lies a balanced approach founded on established principles for ethical research that are appropriately interpreted for and applied to the qualitative research context.

Agreed-upon standards for research ethics help ensure that as researchers we explicitly consider the needs and concerns of the people we study, that appropriate oversight for the conduct of research takes place, and that a basis for trust is established between researchers and study participants.

Whenever we conduct research on people, the well-being of research participants must be our top priority. The research question is always of secondary importance. This means that if a choice must be made between doing harm to a participant and doing harm to the research, it is the research that is sacrificed. Fortunately, choices of that magnitude rarely need to be made in qualitative research! But the principle must not be dismissed as irrelevant, or we can find ourselves making decisions that eventually bring us to the point where our work threatens to disrupt the lives of the people we are researching.

What are the Fundamental Research Ethics Principles?

Three core principles, originally articulated in The Belmont Report,1 form the universally accepted basis for research ethics. *Respect for persons* requires a commitment to ensuring the autonomy of research participants, and, where autonomy may be diminished, to protect people from exploitation of their vulnerability.

The dignity of all research participants must be respected. Adherence to this principle ensures that people will not be used simply as a means to achieve research objectives.

Beneficence requires a commitment to minimizing the risks associated with research, including psychological and social risks, and maximizing the benefits that accrue to research participants.

Researchers must articulate specific ways this will be achieved.

Justice requires a commitment to ensuring a fair distribution of the risks and benefits resulting from research. Those who take on the burdens of research participation should share in the benefits of the knowledge gained. Or, to put it another way, the people who are expected to benefit from the knowledge should be the ones who are asked to participate.

In addition to these established principles, some bioethicists have suggested that a fourth principle, *respect for communities,* should be added. Respect for communities "confers on the researcher an obligation to respect the values and interests of the community in research and, wherever possible, to protect the community from harm." We believe that this principle is, in fact, fundamental for research when community-wide knowledge, values, and relationships are critical to research success and may in turn be affected by the research process or its outcomes.

Informed Consent

Informed consent is a mechanism for ensuring that people understand what it means to participate in a particular research study so they can decide in a conscious, deliberate way whether they want to participate. Informed consent is one of the most important tools for ensuring *respect for persons* during research.

Many people think of informed consent primarily as a *form,* that is, a piece of paper that describes in detail what the research is about, including the risks and benefits. This form generally goes through ethics committee approval procedures, includes legalistic language, and is signed by the participant, the researcher, and possibly a witness. Such informed consent forms are appropriate for biomedical and other research – including qualitative – when the risks faced by participants may be substantial. They may also be necessary for minimal risk research when the foundation for trust between researchers and participants is weak.

But forms are really only one part of an informed consent *process.* In some cases, forms may not be the best way to ensure informed consent. There are also situations where obtaining informed consent from individual participants may not be feasible or necessary. For example, a researcher using participant observation to learn about how transactions occur in a public market would find it very hard to get everyone observed in that setting to sign a consent form and would probably create unwarranted suspicion about her motives in the process of seeking such consent. Yet if people see a stranger hanging around, watching, asking questions, and perhaps taking discreet notes, they may be even more suspicious about why she is there. In these situations, qualitative researchers must use other mechanisms to achieve the goal of informed consent.

Achieve informed Consent

In general, informed consent procedures are based on national and international research ethics guidelines; a review of such guidance is an important part of ethics training. Research organizations and ethics committees often have their own specific guidelines as well.

The first task in achieving informed consent is to inform people about the research in a way they can understand. This can be a multistep process. For example, you may begin by approaching community leaders and explaining the research to them. The leaders may then facilitate a community forum where interested people can learn about the research and ask questions. You might distribute information sheets, advertisements, or brochures, or try to get local newspapers or radio stations to do a report on the research. A community advisory board might be set up. Or the researchers might spend a week or two just talking with people one-on-one. If the researchers will be spending a lot of time in the community setting, or if the research is potentially controversial or sensitive, such efforts can go a long way toward gaining trust as well as understanding.

6

Functions of Quantitative Methods

FUNCTION

In mathematics, a function associates one quantity, the *argument* of the function, also known as the *input*, with another quantity, the *value* of the function, also known as the *output*. A function assigns exactly one output to each input. f(x) is said, "F of X." The argument and the value may be real numbers, but they can also be elements from any given set. An example of a function is $f(x) = 2x$, a function which associates with every number the number twice as large. Thus, with the argument 5 the value 10 is associated, and this is written $f(5) = 10$.

The input to a function need not be a number, it can be any well defined object. For example, a function might associate the letter A with the number 1, the letter B with the number 2, and so on. There are many ways to describe or represent a function, such as a formula or algorithm that computes the output for a given input, a graph that gives a picture of the function, or a table of values that gives the output for certain specified inputs. Tables of values are especially common in statistics, science, and engineering.

The set of all inputs to a particular function is called its domain. The set of all outputs of a particular function is called its image. In modern mathematics functions also have a codomain. For every function, its codomain includes its image. For instance, a codomain of the function squaring real numbers $f(x) = x^2$ usually is defined to be the set of all real numbers. The function f does not have the real numbers – 1, –2, – 3 as outputs, thus they are in its codomain but not in its image. Codomains are useful for function composition. Composition $f \circ g$ (g followed by f) is defined if the codomain of g is the same as the domain of f. Thus the codomain of g defines what functions may follow g. The word range is used in some texts to refer to the image and in others to the codomain, in particular in computing it often refers to the codomain. The domain and codomain are often "understood." Thus for the example given above, $f(x) = 2x$, the domain and codomain were not stated explicitly. They might both be the set of all real numbers, but they might also be the set of integers. If the domain is the set of integers, then image consists of just the even integers.

The set of all the ordered pairs or inputs and outputs $(x, f(x))$ of a function is called its graph. A common way to define a function is as the triple (domain, codomain, graph), that is as the input set, the possible outputs and the mapping for each input to its output.

A function may sometimes be described through its relationship to other functions, for example, as the inverse function of a given function, or as a solution of a differential equation. Functions can be added, multiplied, or combined in other ways to produce new functions.

An important operation on functions, which distinguishes them from numbers, is the composition of functions. There are uncountably many different functions, most of which cannot be expressed with a formula or an algorithm. Collections of functions with certain properties, such as continuous functions and differentiable functions, are called function spaces and are studied as objects in their own right, in such mathematical disciplines as real analysis and complex analysis.

Because functions are so widely used, many traditions have grown up around their use. The symbol for the input to a function is often called the independent variable or argument and is often represented by the letter x or, if the input is a particular time, by the letter t. The symbol for the output is called the dependent variable or value and is often represented by the letter y. The function itself is most often called f, and thus the notation $y = f(x)$ indicates that a function named f has an input named x and an output named y.

Injective and Surjective Functions

Three important kinds of function are the injections (or one-to-one functions), which have the property that if $f(a) = f(b)$ then a must equal b; the surjections (or onto functions), which have the property that for every y in the codomain there is an x in the domain such that $f(x) = y$; and the bijections, which are both one-to-one and onto. This nomenclature was introduced by the Bourbaki group.

When the definition of a function by its graph only is used, since the codomain is not defined, the "surjection" must be accompanied with a statement about the set the function maps onto. For example, we might say f maps onto the set of all real numbers.

Functions with Multiple Inputs and Outputs

The concept of function can be extended to an object that takes a combination of two (or more) argument values to a single result. This intuitive concept is formalized by a function whose domain is the Cartesian product of two or more sets. For example, consider the function that associates two integers to their product: $f(x, y) = x \cdot y$. This function can be defined formally as having domain Z×Z, the set of all integer pairs; codomain Z; and, for graph, the set of all pairs $((x,y), x \cdot y)$. Note that the first component of any such pair is itself a pair (of integers), while the second component is a single integer.

The function value of the pair (x,y) is $f((x,y))$. However, it is customary to drop one set of parentheses and consider $f(x,y)$ a function of two variables, x and y. Functions of two variables may be plotted on the three-dimensional Cartesian as ordered triples of the form $(x,y,f(x,y))$. The concept can still further be extended by considering a function that also produces output that is expressed as several variables. For example, consider the integer divide function, with domain Z×N and codomain Z×N. The resultant (quotient, remainder) pair is a single value in the codomain seen as a Cartesian product.

Currying

An alternative approach to handling functions with multiple arguments is to transform them into a chain of functions that each takes a single argument. For instance, one can interpret Add(3,5) to mean "first produce a function that adds 3 to its argument, and then apply the 'Add 3' function to 5". This transformation is called currying: Add 3 is curry(Add) applied to 3. There is a bijection between the function spaces $C^{A \times B}$ and $(C^B)^A$.

When working with curried functions it is customary to use prefix notation with function application considered left-associative, since juxtaposition of multiple arguments—as in $(f\ x\ y)$—naturally maps to evaluation of a curried function. Conversely, the $\rightarrow$ and $\mapsto$ symbols are considered to be right-associative, so that curried functions may be defined by a notation such as $f\colon Z \rightarrow Z \rightarrow Z = x \mapsto y \mapsto x \cdot y$

Binary Operations

The familiar binary operations of arithmetic, addition and multiplication, can be viewed as functions from R×R to R. This view is generalized in abstract algebra, where n-ary functions are used to model the operations of arbitrary algebraic structures. For example, an abstract group is defined as a set X and a function f from $X \times X$ to X that satisfies certain properties. Traditionally, addition and multiplication are written in the infix notation: $x+y$ and $x \times y$ instead of $+(x, y)$ and $\times(x, y)$.

Specifying a Function

A function can be defined by any mathematical condition relating each argument to the corresponding output value. If the domain is finite, a function f may be defined by simply tabulating all the arguments x and their corresponding function values $f(x)$. More commonly, a function is defined by a formula, or (more generally) an algorithm — a recipe that tells how to compute the value of $f(x)$ given any x in the domain.

There are many other ways of defining functions. Examples include piecewise definitions, induction or recursion, algebraic or analytic closure, limits, analytic continuation, infinite series, and as solutions to integral and differential equations. The lambda calculus provides a powerful and flexible syntax for defining and combining functions of several variables.

Computability

Functions that send integers to integers, or finite strings to finite strings, can sometimes be defined by an algorithm, which gives a precise description of a set of steps for computing the output of the function from its input. Functions definable by an algorithm are called computable functions.

For example, the Euclidean algorithm gives a precise process to compute the greatest common divisor of two positive integers. Many of the functions studied in the context of number theory are computable.

Fundamental results of computability theory show that there are functions that can be precisely defined but are not computable. Moreover, in the sense of cardinality, almost all functions from the integers to integers are not computable.

The number of computable functions from integers to integers is countable, because the number of possible algorithms is. The number of all functions from integers to integers is higher: the same as the cardinality of the real numbers. Thus most functions from integers to integers are not computable. Specific examples of uncomputable functions are known, including the busy beaver function and functions related to the halting problem and other undecidable problems.

DEFINITION OF A FUNCTION AND NOTATION

Definition of Function : *A function from a set A into a set B is a relation from A into B such that each element of A is related to exactly one elements of the set B The set A is called the domain of the function and the set B is called the codomain.*

The definition of a function is the standard one that appears in most texts. The reader should note that a function f is a relation from A into B with two important restrictions :

1. Each elements in the set A the domain of f must be used by the procedure or rule defining f and
2. The phrase "is related to exactly one element of the set B" means that if $(a,b) \in f$ and $(a,c) \in f$ then $b = c$.

Function of Two Variables

If the domain of a function is the Cartesian product of two sets, then our notation and terminology is charged slightly. For example, consider the function $\mathbf{C} : \mathbf{N} \times \mathbf{N} \rightarrow \mathbf{N}$ defined by $c((n_1,n_2)) = n_1^2 + n_2^2 - n_1 n_2 + 10$. For this function we would drop one set of parentheses and write C (4, 2) = 22, not C ((4, 2)) = 22. We call C a function of two variables. From one point of view, this function is no different from any others that we have seen. The elements of the domain happen to be slightly more complicated. On the other hand, we can look at the individual components of the ordered pairs as being separate. If we interpret C as giving us the cost of producing quantities of two products, we can imagine varying n_1, while n_2 is fixed or vice versa.

Pascal Note

The heading of a Pascal function, lists the name, domain, and codomain of the function, in that order. For example, FUNCTION GAUSS (X: REAL): REAL is a heading for a function called gauss with a real domain and codomain.

FUNCTION MAX (FIRST, SECOND: INTEGER): INTEGER describes a function with domain $\mathbf{Z} \times \mathbf{Z}$ and codomain $\mathbf{Z}$.

The analogy mathematical functions and Pascal functions breaks down when a functional value depends on a global variable. An example of this situation is if Y is declared a global integer variable in the main program in which GAUSS is used and if the body of GAUSS is

```
BEGIN
    GAUSS := 2 * X + Y
END
```

Then GAUSS 's domain is actually $\mathbf{R} \times \mathbf{R}$ even though the heading does not indicate it. In most cases, the use of a global variable in a function definition is not considered to be good programming style. Thus, the heading should describe the domain. We close this section with two examples of relations which are not functions.

USE OF STATISTICSIN QUANTITATIVE RESEARCH

Statistics is the most widely used branch of mathematics in quantitative research outside of the physical sciences, and also finds applications within the physical sciences, such as in statistical mechanics. Statistical methods are used extensively within fields such as economics, social sciences and biology.

Quantitative research using statistical methods starts with the collection of data, based on the hypothesis or theory. Usually a big sample of data is collected-this would require verification, validation and recording before the analysis can take place. Software packages such as SPSS and R are typically used for this purpose.

Causal relationships are studied by manipulating factors thought to influence the phenomena of interest while controlling other variables relevant to the experimental outcomes. In the field of health, for example, researchers might measure and study the relationship between dietary intake and measurable physiological effects such as weight loss, controlling for other key variables such as exercise. Quantitatively based opinion surveys are widely used in the media, with statistics such as the proportion of respondents in favor of a position commonly reported. In opinion surveys, respondents are asked a set of structured questions and their responses are tabulated. In the field of climate science, researchers compile and compare statistics such as temperature or atmospheric concentrations of carbon dioxide.

Empirical relationships and associations are also frequently studied by using some form of General linear model, non-linear model, or by using factor analysis. A fundamental principle in quantitative research is that correlation does not imply causation. This principle follows from the fact that it is always possible a spurious relationship exists for variables between which covariance is found in some degree. Associations may be examined between any combination of continuous and categorical variables using methods of statistics.

Measurement

Views regarding the role of measurement in quantitative research are somewhat divergent. Measurement is often regarded as being only a means by which observations are expressed numerically in order to investigate causal relations or associations. However, it has been argued that measurement often plays a more important role in quantitative research. For example, Kuhn argued that within quantitative research, the results that are shown can prove to be strange. This is because accepting a theory based on results of quantitative data could prove to be a natural phenomenon. He argued that such abnormalities are interesting when done during the process of obtaining data, as seen below:

When measurement departs from theory, it is likely to yield mere numbers, and their very neutrality makes them particularly sterile as a source of remedial suggestions. But numbers register the departure from theory with an authority and finesse that no qualitative technique can duplicate, and that departure is often enough to start a search.

In classical physics, the theory and definitions which underpin measurement are generally deterministic in nature. In contrast, probabilistic measurement models known as the Rasch model and Item response theory models are generally employed in the social sciences. Psychometrics is the field of study concerned with the theory and technique for measuring social and psychological attributes and phenomena. This field is central to much quantitative research that is undertaken within the social sciences. Quantitative research may involve the use of *proxies* as stand-ins for other quantities that cannot be directly measured. Tree-ring width, for example, is considered a reliable proxy of ambient environmental conditions such as the warmth of growing seasons or amount of rainfall. Although scientists cannot directly measure the temperature of past years, tree-ring width and other climate proxies have been used to provide a semi-quantitative record of average temperature in the Northern Hemisphere back to 1000 A.D. When used in this way, the proxy record (tree ring width, say) only reconstructs a certain amount of the variance of the original record. The proxy may be calibrated (for example, during the period of the instrumental record) to determine how much variation is captured, including whether both short and long term variation is revealed. In the case of tree-ring width, different species in different places may show more or less sensitivity to, say, rainfall or temperature: when reconstructing a temperature record there is considerable skill in selecting proxies that are well correlated with the desired variable.

QUANTITATIVE METHODS

Quantitative methods are research techniques that are used to gather quantitative data — information dealing with numbers and anything that is measurable. Statistics, tables and graphs, are often used to present the results of these methods. They are therefore to be distinguished from qualitative methods.

In most physical and biological sciences, the use of either quantitative or qualitative methods is uncontroversial, and each is used when appropriate. In the social sciences, particularly in sociology, social anthropology and psychology, the use of one or other type of method has become a matter of controversy and even ideology, with particular schools of thought within each discipline favouring one type of method and pouring scorn on to the other. Advocates of quantitative methods argue that only by using such methods can the social sciences become truly scientific; advocates of qualitative methods argue that quantitative methods tend to obscure the reality of the social phenomena under study because they underestimate or neglect the non-measurable factors, which may be the most important. The modern tendency (and in reality the majority tendency throughout the history of social science) is to use eclectic approaches. Quantitative methods might be used with a global qualitative frame. Qualitative methods might be used to understand the meaning of the numbers produced by quantitative methods. Using quantitative methods, it is possible to give precise and testable expression to qualitative ideas. This combination of quantitative and qualitative data gathering is often referred to as mixed-methods research. The reporting and dissemination of comparative quality information is a relatively new enterprise that has only been possible since reliable and relevant data have become available.

In part because this is such a pioneering set of activities the exploratory discovery-oriented aspects of qualitative methods have made them a critical element of dozens of such efforts.

Focus groups have been used to assess the relevance and comprehensibility of a wide range of quality measures intended to be reported as well as preferences for displaying data graphically. Thus to give just a few examples: (1) the National Committee for Quality Assurance commissioned focus groups to assess candidate indicators for the measures of effectiveness it would include in the third iteration of its Health Employer Data and Information Set (HEDIS®) with Medicaid enrollees and people with Medicare ; (2) the Foundation for Accountability a non-profit organization whose mission is to identify and study ways to disseminate consumer-relevant comparative quality measures commissioned groups to assess whether people without a specific medical condition would or would not respond to condition-specific quality indicators ; while (3) the Centers for Medicare & Medicaid Services (CMS formerly the US Health Care Financing Administration) used focus groups to identify which specific measures on a CAHPS® Medicare survey should be disseminated in its *Medicare & You* handbook. These focus groups have illuminated not only such basic issues as which dimensions of quality are considered important or unimportant by consumers but also subtle and surprising issues such as which quality indicators consumers view as influenced by a health plan as compared with a physician or themselves the relationship between the comprehensibility of an indicator and its perceived salience and the confusion generated by presenting data displays that provide information on both comparative and absolute scores.

In a recent project supported by The Commonwealth Fund and designed to develop and test consumer reports on the quality of Medicare managed care plans in New York City we began by using focus groups to test the overall framework of performance dimensions that was most engaging to consumers. An important learning was that given the current 'mental map' of people with

Medicare a report that limited itself only to comparative quality information and did not prominently include information on premiums and services covered, as well as explaining key differences between managed care plans and fee for service health care delivery would simply not work. The focus groups also clarified our dissemination strategy by demonstrating that the most interested audience for the materials we planned would be relatively low-income people with Medicare who were most likely to view managed care plans as an affordable way to get better service coverage. Participants from higher income levels were negatively disposed toward joining managed care plans and preferred to continue buying a Medigap supplement (an expense that many lower-income participants could ill afford).

We also conducted focus groups of counselors whose responsibility it was to help people deal with Medicare-related problems. These groups helped us to gauge their own exposure to and understanding of quality information (highly limited) and their opinions of the ability of their clients to deal with quality information without personal assistance (also highly limited).

Ultimately these focus groups helped us to develop an innovative strategy for creating materials. Rather than incorporate all the comparative information into one booklet or develop a booklet just on quality we decided to create a set of six related booklets that would cover a variety of managed care plan performance dimensions of interest to consumers. Rather than organize quality information by source (an option since we were providing both CAHPS® scores and scores on HEDIS® indicators) we decided to 'map' different quality measures onto the existing mental map we discerned through the focus groups. For example in focus groups both consumers and counselors confirmed the overwhelming interest of people on Medicare in the prescription benefits available in managed care plans. We therefore created a brief booklet that compared prescription benefits for all Medicare managed care plans in New York City and also included the scores recorded for a number of health care plans on a CAHPS® Medicare Managed Care survey item that asked about members' experiences in getting the prescriptions they needed from their plan. We linked these two kinds of information with a discussion of the use of formularies and the preference for prescribing generic rather than brand name medications among managed care plans. Similarly we learned that consumers were very concerned about access to physicians in managed care plans. This led us to create a booklet titled 'Getting a Plan With Good Doctors', which included a wide range of CAHPS® items that address physician-related issues (ease of finding a good doctor a composite of items on physician communication and the overall rating of all health care providers in the managed care plan).

Cognitive interviewing

The methodology of cognitive interviewing has also been adopted by those developing materials to present comparative quality information. These methods were used in CAHPS® and were also used in our New York City project. Two rounds of cognitive interviews were conducted to test our materials both with people on Medicare and with the kinds of counselor we hoped would help us disseminate and explain the materials. As considerable research demonstrates in reporting the devil is often in the details and it is these details that can best be addressed through cognitive interviews.

The method can and has been used to test both specific elements of reports such as titles labels data displays table layouts fonts colors photographs or other illustrations etc. and broader issues such as how people scan a multi-page document or whether they perceive the purpose of the overall document and actually understand the information correctly. Interviews provide material developers with significant clues to how a reader cognitively processes a document in a manner far more subtle than can be obtained merely by doing a test of its 'readability' or 'literacy level'.

Cognitive tests gave us literally pages of specific ways of improving the materials but also confirmed that for many people with Medicare personal assistance would be essential. We also learned a good deal about what kind of information would have to be provided to counsellors if they were to be effective at providing such assistance.

CONTRIBUTIONS OF QUALITATIVE RESEARCH METHODS

Section one on the logic of relating qualitative and quantitative method begins with a contribution that takes us into the very methodological center of the volume. Combining qualitative and quantitative methods is almost by definition an issue of across-method triangulation. Since it was introduced into the social sciences by DENZIN (1970), the term triangulation has become something of a catchphrase. "Triangulation" is now ubiquitous in the methodological literature of the social sciences—and as it is often the case with such ubiquitous terms, its precise meaning has become lost over time. In his contribution, Udo KELLE proceeds to identify the various meanings in which "triangulation"—which he regards as a metaphor rather than a precise concept—has come to be used and to determine which of these meanings is most appropriate for conceptualising the combination of qualitative and quantitative methods.

He distinguishes three meanings or models of triangulation: (1) triangulation as the mutual validation of results obtained on the basis of different methods (the validity model), (2) triangulation as a means toward obtaining a larger, more complete picture of the phenomenon under study (the complementarity model), and (3) triangulation in its original trigonometrical sense, indicating that a combination of methods is necessary in order to gain any (not necessarily a fuller) picture of the relevant phenomenon at all (the trigonometry model). These three models are in turn brought to bear upon the potential relationships between the results yielded by qualitative and quantitative methods employed in the same study.

In order to determine the applicability of these models to the combination of qualitative and quantitative methods, KELLE goes on to examine the results of three mixed-method studies from life course research, thus tying his methodological considerations back to the actual research process. Judging the applicability of different understandings of triangulation, however, is something which from KELLE's point of view should involve not only methodological and epistemological considerations, but also include theoretical considerations. KELLE's conclusion that it is the trigonometric model of triangulation which holds the greatest promise for conceptualising the combination of qualitative and quantitative methods is thus a qualified conclusion, holding especially for sociological studies with its distinction between micro-and macrolevel descriptions. KELLE thus clarifies the discourse surrounding triangulation by presenting us with a number of models of triangulation to choose from and he adds to the grounds on which to make such a choice by drawing our attention to the relevance of theoretical issues—implicitly raising, of course, the question of what such a choice would look like in other disciplines.

Philipp MAYRING starts out from the observation that the call for the combination of qualitative and quantitative methods has become almost a commonplace in methodology textbooks in the social sciences. This call, reasonable as it may be, MAYRING argues, is nevertheless a long way from actual research practice and does little to tell the researcher how exactly such a combination is to be achieved. By suggesting five levels at which qualitative and quantitative methods can be related—ranging from data to the entire research process—MAYRING alerts us to the details which lie behind the global call for the combination of the two paradigms.

In closing, MAYRING turns to a premise of the inter-relation of the two paradigms which is more often than not left implicit: what are the advantages of such an inter-relation? It is especially in the context of his outline for an integrative documentation of the (qualitative or quantitative) research process that MAYRING shows what the two paradigms stand to gain by no longer ignoring each other. In the case of the quantitative paradigm, this is in particular the greater proximity to the research subject, while the qualitative paradigm will profit most by making the various stages of the research process more transparent and systematic, thus increasing the generalisability of the results. The ontological position of constructivist realism which is at the heart of Gerald CUPCHIK's contribution may strike one—at first sight—as something of a paradox. "Realism" with its implications of a world out there which can be apprehended and known by scientists, is a position which has gone out of fashion in our postmodern times. "Constructivism", on the other hand, carries associations of precisely such a postmodern discourse, suggesting that "the world" is real only to the extent that we make it so, that there are as many worlds, as many "realities" as there are minds to construe them.

In his explication of constructivist realism, CUPCHIK cuts across such dichotomies. His starting point is the assumption that in everyday life, we usually have very little doubt about the reality of events that befall us, our actions and our interactions with others. To the extent that it is precisely these personally and socially relevant realities which constitute the subject matter of the social sciences, the social sciences deal with phenomena which are real—hence "constructivist realism". Yet their reality is not a given, but it is constructed by imbuing the phenomenon in question with meaning—hence "constructivist realism". If this meaning is socially shared, the process of meaning construction will hardly be noticeable; the more discrepant the social realities of two persons, however, the less they will be able to agree upon the reality of a phenomenon. In stressing the importance of the social constitution of meaning, CUPCHIK's position is thus akin to that of social constructionism.

If one starts out from this ontological position, CUPCHIK argues, the competition between qualitative and quantitative research is resolved into complementarity. While researchers from the two paradigms tend to stress either the realist (quantitative) or the constructivist (qualitative) end point, they are in the same position: they both deal with real phenomena in the above sense, with social processes, and they both have to ascribe meaning to their data. Rather than sequencing qualitative and quantitative research in some way, CUPCHIK sees both approaches as essentially inter-related, with quantitative research contributing towards the precise identification of relevant processes, and qualitative research providing the basis for their "thick description".

While most contributors to this volume unanimously advocate the inter-relation of qualitative and quantitative methods, Harald WITT cautions us against the indiscriminate combination of methods from the two paradigms. He points out that a major difference between quantitative and qualitative research is to be seen in their research strategies which he describes as linear and circular respectively. Both research strategies, he argues, are cut out for different research goals, they accomodate different kinds of data and different sample types. WITT goes on to show how combining qualitative and quantitative methods does not necessarily result in getting the best from both worlds. Rather, certain types of method inter-relation may be cumbersome at best; at worst, the results achieved by such an "unhappy" combination will fall far short of what could have been achieved by remaining exclusively within one of the two paradigms. This applies in particular to the use of a qualitative method for data collection in the context of a circular research strategy. WITT thus draws attention to what is easily forgotten in the enthusiasm over transcending the boundaries between the qualitative and the quantitative paradigm: Combining qualitative and quantitative methods is not a good thing at all times, but only provided that such a combination is in line with the overall research goals. WITT also shows that the willingness to combine methods is not enough to make such an informed choice of method or method combination. The researcher who wants to combine methods had better know them all, qualitative and quantitative—no mean feat considering the proliferation of methods both in the quantitative and the qualitative area.

For Gary SHANK, qualitative research is the systematic empirical inquiry into meaning. If, at the broadest level, triangulation is about adopting a sceptical attitude that represents "genuine doubt", and maintaining a receptiveness to any method of inquiry which offers to assuage that doubt, then SHANK is opening up a perspective which prompts researchers to inspect and always keep in mind an awareness of the logical foundations of their inquiries. Logic informs all reasoning, whether it is the hypothetico-deduction we associate with much quantitative inquiry or the inductive efforts often associated with qualitative work. For many researchers, awareness of logic and how it informs the epistemology which supports their empirical work does not get far beyond this distinction. But SHANK alerts us to the several kinds of induction, and to the critical (but widely unremarked) role of abduction in inquiries motivated by an analytic interest in meaning.

SHANK's illustration of the six forms of abduction, or "reasoning to the best explanation", has an affinity with the other, relatively rare, meta-commentaries on the formal properties of qualitative analysis. Its central ground is the logic of inference. When SHANK confronts the relation of quantitative and qualitative methods he first asserts that it is not the method but the question which is important. But, beyond this, he emphasises the effect on the questions we can ask, and answer, if quantitative work were to define research methods. In particular, the valuable fruits of abductive reasoning would be lost.

Drawing on a background in the analysis of political discourse and in the study of Artificial Intelligence, Francisco GUTIERREZ takes our discussion into the issue of how we know what we think we know. Using the case of the famous Turing Test, GUTIERREZ explores the logic by which we establish identity (or any kind of categorical knowledge) more generally. His empirical application is the possibility of discriminating between political actors holding different ideological orientations using only criteria internal to their discourse. Here we are in a central realm of qualitative work, the application and validation of classificatory systems such as typologies. The Artificial Intelligence community, as a result of its efforts to model human reasoning, has developed a close interest in classificatory practices, and the more formal methods of quantitative work can contribute to a better understanding of how people make fundamental distinctions in the course of everyday practical reasoning. Closing his chapter, GUTIERREZ offers an overview of the several points of connection at meta-level between supposedly competing schools of thought, using the notion of paradigm shift to suggest the artificiality of a bipolar contrast between hermeneutic and formal reasoning, "hard" and "soft" methods, and "subjectivity" and "objectivity".

The concluding part of GUTIERREZ's contribution considered inter alia the implications of paradigm shifts in intellectual disciplines, and this serves as the starting point for Dietmar JANETZKO's contribution. He notes that the debate over the status of qualitative and quantitative methods has been subject to its own changes of perspective over time. This fact serves as the basis on which to address a method for analysing conceptual changes (or changes of representation). These changes are amenable to qualitative or quantitative analysis. JANETZKO unfolds an approach to analysing changes of representation on the basis of symbolic, sequential data, which he calls "knowledge tracking", and which allows researchers to investigate both qualitative and quantitative aspects of changes. The approach is embedded in the network representation of cognition and requires the re-casting of the sociologist's or psychologist's theory of the data into the formal terms of a relational structure. JANETZKO argues that, while methods usually are either qualitative or quantitative, knowledge tracking is either or both: used quantitatively, knowledge tracking conducts a data-driven selection between competing theories, while used qualitatively it carries out a data-driven reduction of one theory. In this approach, then, the relationship of quantitative and qualitative can be calibrated to the requirements of the analytic work in hand.

We mentioned that JANETZKO's approach involves a transformation of data and its associated theory into formal terms. In discussing triangulation, the benefits of iterative research designs which develop a programme of research through, for example, a sequence of quantitative inquiry followed by qualitative inquiry followed by further quantitative inquiry have been highlighted. This can be offered as a means of more rigorously and systematically pursuing the object of inquiry. It seems to us that the formalising project represents an alternative to the iterative research design where there is a series of studies alternating quantitative and qualitative approaches. In that the benefit of the latter is a more rigorous understanding of the relationships that have emerged from qualitative and quantitative work separately, JANETZKO's formal manipulation offers the prospect of similar benefit but with an intrinsic gain in efficiency, in that it may reduce the need for further empirical work.

As we outlined above, in our plan for this issue of FQS a central interest was that we should not confine our attention to the established constructions of the relationship between quantitative and qualitative methods, such as the position which sees them as competing and irreconcilable modes of inquiry, or the position which seeks a systematic relationship based on the concept of triangulation. We wanted to stand back a little from these concerns and attend to the contemporary qualitative researcher's perspective on quantitative research, and the contemporary quantitative researcher's perspective on qualitative research. Another point we wanted to pick up was based on the perception that the diffusion of methodological approaches, understandings and practices is never uniform, even within a national community of scholars. When we take a global perspective we see fascinating local developments which feed a distinctive approach into the global social science community (for example, the "participatory research" variant of action research which is strong in Latin America) and we also see backwaters where the penetration of contemporary approaches has been impeded, sometimes reflecting the obstructive influence of political structures or the dominance of approaches associated with perspectives which have in the meantime become outmoded in their culture of origin.

This was one reason for our particular interest in gaining contributions to this issue of FQS from scholars outside the dominant North American/western European social and behavioural science circuit. Jean SALUDADEZ and Primo GARCIA offer us an illuminating glimpse of the perspectives dividing—and relating—the researchers in an applied research institute in the Philippines which speaks directly to our interest in the contemporary relationship of qualitative and quantitative researchers. They profile the quantitative researcher's construction of qualitative research, and the quantitative researcher's understanding of the qualitative researcher's construction of quantitative research. While the study testifies to the continuing reign of quantitative work in such a setting, it also reveals an awareness of the merits and demerits of these modes of inquiry which is a good deal more subtle than a bipolar distinction would permit, thus setting up a framework for viewing the different approaches for interrelating qualitative and quantitative method presented in Section Two.

For these authors, the relationship shows scope to evolve to a more complementary and less conflictual form than has prevailed in the past. Lest it be thought our view of this is as a pretty example of the "maturing" of social science in a post-colonial setting, we might observe that significant developments, such as the withdrawal of a requirement that all doctoral research proposals must be assessed and accepted by a quantitative social scientist or a statistician, are not entirely widespread in the universities of countries such as the United States of America.

Nicole WESTMARLAND addresses the relationship between quantitative and qualitative method from a feminist perspective. She profiles the debate within feminist research over the value of qualitative and quantitative work, where central issues have been the conduct of the research process, the extent to which the two approaches to research adequately capture the reality of women's experiences, and thus the validity of the data upon which quantitative or qualitative researchers base their analyses. This last point means that, of course, the critiques raised by feminists interested in methodology are significant outside the confines of feminist research itself, and are of interest to the wider methodological community. It remains broadly the case that feminist research is drawn largely to qualitative methods, and WESTMARLAND explores the affinities which make this so. However, there is a substantial and important stream in feminist thought on methodology which sees a place for quantitative work in feminist inquiry. WESTMARLAND helps us to see the several ways in which quantitative work is valuable, even necessary, in those approaches to feminist work which prioritise the transformation of the place of women in society. She does so methodologically by contrasting and comparing the role of the survey questionnaire and the semi-structured interview, and empirically by tracing the role of qualitative and quantitative methods in her own researches into the situation of female taxi drivers. For WESTMARLAND, different feminist concerns speak to different research methods, and a dichotomy of qualitative and quantitative based on the claimed superiority of one over the other is a diversion from identifying the best tools for the job.

Annette SCHMITT, Ulrich MEES and Uwe LAUCKEN present and illustrate an approach designed for analysing the structure and the rules underlying everyday social knowledge as it becomes manifest in texts: logographic analysis. Logographic analysis was developed precisely for this purpose; it is informed by the research goal, not by the affinity to either qualitative or quantitative methods (even though the authors are somewhat more at home in the qualitative paradigm), nor was it designed with a view towards combining the two paradigms. The approach thus constitutes a perfect example of the dictum of the priority of the research question over the method.

Considering the research goal and the textual as well as the social character of the data, SCHMITT et al. localise logographic analysis predominantly within the qualitative paradigm. At the same time, however, the analysis also comprises quantitative aspects. In some cases, these are steps which are interleaved with the qualitative ones, such as hypothesis testing and comparative frequency analyses. In other cases, as in assessing the reliability and validity of the initial coding of the texts, qualitative and quantitative aspects of the procedure are so closely linked that it makes little sense to separate the two. Logographic analysis thus evades description in terms of qualitative and quantitative "parts". It is not a combination of qualitative and quantitative methods, but integrates the two and thus transcends the traditional dichotomy.

Numerically aided phenomenology, the approach presented by Don KUIKEN and David MIALL, constitutes another method which, in integrating qualitative and quantitative aspects, succeeds in going beyond the dichotomy between "qualitative" and "quantitative" research. The criterion by which to evaluate research, KUIKEN and MIALL argue, is above all precision in the sense of distinctiveness, coherence, and richness. Where the description of lived experience is concerned, quantitative research is frequently lacking in precision to the extent that it underestimates the complexity of categories of experience, resulting in the reduction of the phenomenon to a few conventional meanings. Qualitative research, on the other hand, lacks precision in that it fails to distinguish between different extents to which a category of experience may be present.

Numerically aided phenomenology, a method for the description of categories of lived experience, is aimed at increasing the precision of qualitative phenomenological research by instituting a quantitative algorithm at the very centre of qualitative data collection. In this, KUIKEN and MIALL regard categories of experience as "polythetic classes", i.e. as arrays of attributes where some attributes will characterise some instances of the category, but presumably no attribute will characterise all instances. Following the identification of relevant attributes by means of an in-depth analysis of the phenomenon, the specification of categories is achieved by drawing upon HUSSERL's concept of "imaginative variation", a kind of thought experiment in which the presence of individual attributes is varied systematically. Within numerically aided phenomenology, this imaginative variation is achieved by means of the quantitative step of cluster analysis. This is again followed by a qualitative procedure, the close inspection of the data on the basis of those clusters which may in turn result in an expansion and further differentiation of the classes or types. Numerical phenomenology may thus be regarded as an approach toward the construction of a typology which combines qualitative and quantitative procedures (while most approaches existing to date are restricted to either of the two paradigms; cf. the overview in KLUGE 1999).

Most contributors to this volume who are in favour of relating qualitative and quantitative methods suggest ways in which such an inter-relation may be actively realised, as in the above numerologically aided phenomenology, in triangulation, etc. Gerhard KLEINING and Harald WITT take a somewhat different approach. The apparent incompatibility of the qualitative and the quantitative paradigm, they argue, is basically just a byproduct of the almost exclusively interpretive orientation of qualitative research in the social sciences. This orientation, however, is thought to imply a number of drawbacks culminating in a "crisis of qualitative research". KLEINING's and WITT's major concern is thus not with the combination of qualitative and quantitative research as such, but with overcoming the interpretive bias of qualitative research. In order to do this, they suggest the reinstatement of heuristic, exploratory methods which are aimed at discovery rather than interpretation. They present their own approach developed along these lines, the Hamburg qualitative heuristic methodology, which combines classic heuristic elements with systematic rules for their application. This methodological orientation toward discovery, the authors argue, can act as a kind of common roof for both qualitative and quantitative designs, thus overcoming the divide between the two paradigms; they go on to demonstrate this by presenting one qualitative and one quantitative example from their own research.

Obviously, an orientation towards discovery as it is advocated by KLEINING and WITT inevitably carries certain implications of a realist ontology and epistemology—which is very much at odds with the ontological stance found, for instance, even in modified versions of postmodernism. By making their ontological assumptions explicit, these authors thus draw attention to the way in which methodological issues relate to the philosophy of science in general, raising the question of the compatibility between our way of combining qualitative and quantitative methods on the one hand and our ontological premises on the other.

Giampietro GOBO argues in accord with the famous dictum that "the devil is in the detail". It is a commonplace that quantitative and qualitative approaches should be integrated, but the prevailing examples of their integration very often revolve around the macro-level comparison of findings from independently-conducted, discrete applications of each type of method. Instead, GOBO argues that our notion of integration needs to become more specific, and he illustrates this by a discussion of how a qualitative research practice can be applied as an integral part of a quantitative inquiry. Survey non-response is a widely-remarked and increasing problem, as GOBO's useful summary of recent methodological research on the matter indicates. This methodological research shows that an important element in non-response to survey interviews is the tactics and persuasive techniques that are used in the first moments of contact between researcher and potential respondent. In the context of telephone interviewing, GOBO demonstrates how an understanding of the communicative process, drawing on discourse analysis, conversation analysis and narrative analysis, can enable researchers to identify analytically the effects of different interviewer tactics, indicate best practice, and thus improve survey techniques.

Section three on innovative applications of methodological inter-relation begins with an example from economics, a discipline we normally do not associate either with an acknowledgement of subjectivity or with the use of qualitative or fieldwork-based methods. There are illuminating exceptions, but the fact remains that the exceptions are occasional and isolated from the mainstream of the discipline.

It follows that triangulation or more broadly, work which integrates quantitative and qualitative method, is a rarity in the economics discipline. At the same time, though, economists are well-aware of the critiques the other social sciences bring to its central convention, the homo economicus or "rational" economic actor, all of whose actions can be modelled, understood and made the basis for prediction precisely because these actors' decisions are wholly and reliably captured by the calculation of costs versus benefits. Since economic models have been known to fail (!), it is plain that there are deficiencies in the cost/benefit heuristic as an exclusive way of understanding those (preponderant) aspects of the social world which relate in one way or another to the allocation of resources (be they material, intellectual or spiritual).

This spurs some economists, at least, to pursue additional means of capturing human decision-making. Stefan MANN provides us with an example, drawing on his research on factors influencing the decision whether to invest in a new agri-business development in a rural region of Germany. It is an example of the classic form of triangulation, with the following twist: MANN argues that the qualitative element of the research exposed only the factors that participants were willing to explicitly articulate (while not being obvious to the researcher), whereas the quantitative element enabled the identification of factors that were effective but not consciously articulated during the research process.

There are different postures towards the integration of quantitative and qualitative methods, only one of which is triangulation. But the established literature might be characterised as being dominated either by approaches which argue that triangulation is possible because, if methods are systematically understood and rigorously used, points of connection can be identified such that both types of methods are addressing the same phenomenon, or by approaches that argue that because the types of method are founded on contrasting epistemologies, their differences are irreconcilable and so triangulation is impossible. During its emergent phase, postmodernist schools of thought have overwhelmingly fallen into the latter category. But as postmodernism has begun to establish its own approach to understanding empirical phenomena (rather than being preoccupied with the need to carve out space for its approach by a backwards-looking critique of what has gone before, in similar fashion to other emergent schools of thought, as can be seen in the stages of the relationship between ethnomethodology and sociology), a more interesting and sophisticated position has emerged. This position naturally acknowledges and even valorises relativism, as a sign of the inevitably multi-perspectival nature of knowledge of the social, but also sees no reason to refrain from quantitative work simply because notions of objectivity have been discarded. Such work must be done alongside, and in articulation with, qualitative work, so as to increase awareness of multiple perspectives and the contingency associated with situated knowledge (rather than to draw quantitative and qualitative findings together into a monolithic framework as in conventional triangulation). Natilene BOWKER offers us a significant example of this approach in a report of her programme of research into online behaviour in Internet Chat Rooms, concluding that multiple methods enable researchers to integrate their, and the research participants', situated knowledge.

In Alexander JAKOB's contribution, the concept of triangulation is applied to the sociological reconstruction of employment biographies of officers in the German army who are about to become civilians. The focus of the study is on the extent to which and the way in which these officers experience uncertainty in facing this substantial change in their life course. JAKOB approaches his topic by means of an across-method triangulation: in a first quantitative phase, a large representative sample is drawn; data are collected by questionnaire and subjected to probabilistic cluster analysis. In a subsequent qualitative phase, a smaller subsample is selected on theoretical grounds and interviewed in depth. The study thus constitutes an example of realising different research phases where the quantitative is followed by a more detailed qualitative step of data collection and analysis (which corresponds to one of the designs for combining qualitative and quantitative research as suggested by MAYRING). Yet JAKOB's study differs from the standard design of this type in that the two phases do not consist of separate studies, but are in fact interdependent and thus complementary. Quantitative data analysis, for instance, is informed by the results of the qualitative phase and in turn allows to draw conclusions concerning the frequency of each of the types in the population. In describing the characteristics of the types, JAKOB also draws upon his analysis of the interviews, aiming for a "thick description". In applying the concept of triangulation, JAKOB is thus not concerned with a mutual validation of "qualitative" and "quantitative" results, but with their complementarity which he employs towards realising a description of the phenomenon under research which is at once more precise and has greater depth than any description he could have obtained by restricting himself to one method only.

UNOBTRUSIVE MEASURES RESEARCH

Unobtrusive measures are measures that don't require the researcher to intrude in the research context. Direct and participant observation require that the researcher be physically present. This can lead the respondents to alter their behaviour in order to look good in the eyes of the researcher. A questionnaire is an interruption in the natural stream of behaviour. Respondents can get tired of filling out a survey or resentful of the questions asked. Unobtrusive measurement presumably reduces the biases that result from the intrusion of the researcher or measurement instrument. However, unobtrusive measures reduce the degree the researcher has control over the type of data collected. For some constructs there may simply not be any available unobtrusive measures.

Indirect Measures

An indirect measure is an unobtrusive measure that occurs naturally in a research context. The researcher is able to collect the data without introducing any formal measurement procedure.

The types of indirect measures that may be available are limited only by the researcher's imagination and inventiveness. For instance, let's say you would like to measure the popularity of various exhibits in a museum. It may be possible to set up some type of mechanical measurement system that is invisible to the museum patrons. In one study, the system was simple. The museum installed new floor tiles in front of each exhibit they wanted a measurement on and, after a period of time, measured the wear-and-tear of the tiles as an indirect measure of patron traffic and interest. We might be able to improve on this approach considerably using electronic measures. We could, for instance, construct an electrical device that senses movement in front of an exhibit. Or we could place hidden cameras and code patron interest based on videotaped evidence.

One of my favourite indirect measures occurred in a study of radio station listening preferences. Rather than conducting an obtrusive survey or interview about favourite radio stations, the researchers went to local auto dealers and garages and checked all cars that were being serviced to see what station the radio was currently tuned to. In a similar manner, if you want to know magazine preferences, you might rummage through the trash of your sample or even stage a door-to-door magazine recycling effort.

These examples illustrate one of the most important points about indirect measures — you have to be very careful about the ethics of this type of measurement. In an indirect measure you are, by definition, collecting information without the respondent's knowledge. In doing so, you may be violating their right to privacy and you are certainly not using informed consent. Of course, some types of information may be public and therefore not involve an invasion of privacy.

There may be times when an indirect measure is appropriate, readily available and ethical. Just as with all measurement, however, you should be sure to attempt to estimate the reliability and validity of the measures. For instance, collecting radio station preferences at two different time periods and correlating the results might be useful for assessing test-retest reliability. Or, you can include the indirect measure along with other direct measures of the same construct (perhaps in a pilot study) to help establish construct validity.

QUANTITATIVE ASSUMPTIONS DATA

To say that qualitative and quantitative data are similar only tells half the story. After all, the intense academic wrangling of the qualitative-quantitative debate must have some basis in reality. My sense is that there are some fundamental differences, but that they lie primarily at the level of assumptions about research (epistemological and ontological assumptions) rather than at the level of the data.

First, let's do away with the most common myths about the differences between qualitative and quantitative research. Many people believe the following:

- Quantitative research is confirmatory and deductive in nature.
- Qualitative research is exploratory and inductive in nature.

I think that while there's a shred of truth in each of these statements, they are not exactly correct. In general, a lot of quantitative research tends to be confirmatory and deductive. But there's lots of quantitative research that can be classified as exploratory as well. And while much qualitative research does tend to be exploratory, it can also be used to confirm very specific deductive hypotheses. The problem I have with these kinds of statements is that they don't acknowledge the richness of both traditions. They don't recognize that both qualitative and quantitative research can be used to address almost any kind of research question. So, if the difference between qualitative and quantitative is not along the exploratory-confirmatory or inductive-deductive dimensions, then where is it?

My belief is that the heart of the quantitative-qualitative debate is philosophical, not methodological. Many qualitative researchers operate under different epistemological assumptions from quantitative researchers. For instance, many qualitative researchers believe that the best way to understand any phenomenon is to view it in its context. They see all quantification as limited in nature, looking only at one small portion of a reality that cannot be split or unitized without losing the importance of the whole phenomenon. For some qualitative researchers, the best way to understand what's going on is to become immersed in it. Move into the culture or organization you are studying and experience what it is like to be a part of it. Be flexible in your inquiry of people in context. Rather than approaching measurement with the idea of constructing a fixed instrument or set of questions, allow the questions to emerge and change as you become familiar with what you are studying.

Many qualitative researchers also operate under different ontological assumptions about the world. They don't assume that there is a single unitary reality apart from our perceptions. Since each of us experiences from our own point of view, each of us experiences a different reality. Conducting research without taking this into account violates their fundamental view of the individual. Consequently, they may be opposed to methods that attempt to aggregate across individuals on the grounds that each individual is unique. They also argue that the researcher is a unique individual and that all research is essentially biased by each researcher's individual perceptions. There is no point in trying to establish "validity" in any external or objective sense. All that we can hope to do is interpret our view of the world as researchers.

Let me end this brief excursion into the qualitative-quantitative debate with a few personal observations. Any researcher steeped in the qualitative tradition would certainly take issue with my comments above about the similarities between quantitative and qualitative data. They would argue (with some correctness I fear) that it is not possible to separate your research assumptions from the data. Some would claim that my perspective on data is based on assumptions common to the quantitative tradition. Others would argue that it doesn't matter if you can code data thematically or quantitatively because they wouldn't do *either* — both forms of analysis impose artificial structure on the phenomena and, consequently, introduce distortions and biases. I have to admit that I would see the point in much of this criticism. In fact, I tend to see the point on both sides of the qualitative-quantitative debate.

QUALITATIVE RESEARCH METHODS

Designing qualitative studies is quite different from designing experimental studies. In fact, designs and methods are continually refined while the researcher conducts a qualitative study. As suggested by Jacobs (1987), the researcher initially chooses methods based on the questions to be addressed; however, the questions, issues, and topics of the study themselves may change as the researcher's conception of the reality of the "world" being studied changes. This may be uncomfortable for those experienced with more quantitative, experimental, or quasi-experimental research. However, most qualitative researchers recommend this process of continual refinement. Goetz and LeCompte (1984), for example, note that methods are "adjusted, expanded, modified, or restricted on the basis of information acquired during the mapping phase of field-work.... Only after final withdrawal from the field can researchers specify the strategies they actually used for a particular study".

Lincoln and Guba (1985) address the contradictory idea of "designing" a naturalistic study completely prior to beginning the study, calling this a "paradox" in that most funding agencies require specificity regarding methods, while methods in a good qualitative study may be expected to change as the study progresses. Erlandson et al. (1993) take the middle road. They say that the answer to whether a naturalistic study should be designed in advance is "Yes-to some extent". They recommend beginning the study by specifying a research problem, selecting a research site, developing working hypotheses, and using interactive processes to refine the research questions. They further suggest that the researcher plan for the stages of conducting the study. These may include negotiating entry to the site, planning for purposive (rather than random) sampling and for data collection, planning for data analysis, determining how quality will be ensured in the study, deciding how the findings of the study will be disseminated, and developing a logistical plan. Erlandson et al. (1993) also recommend reviewing the design of the study regularly. In determining what the research problem is, Bernard (1988) suggests that the researcher ask himself or herself five questions:

1. Does this topic (village — i.e., setting, school, organization, institution- and data collection method) really interest me?
2. Is this a problem that is amenable to scientific inquiry?
3. Are adequate resources available to investigate this topic? (To study this population? To use this particular method?)
4. Will my research question, or the methods I want to use, lead to unresolvable ethical problems?
5. Is the topic (community, method) of theoretical interest?

Once a question or issue has been selected, the choice of qualitative methods falls roughly into the categories of observations, interviews, and document and artifact analysis. Qualitative methods, however, form continua on various dimensions, and researchers espouse many views of how methods may be categorized and conceptualized.

Pelto and Pelto (1978) in their frequently cited text on anthropological research methods remind us that the human investigator is the primary research instrument. These authors categorize methods as either verbal or nonverbal techniques. Verbal techniques include participant observation, questionnaires, and various forms of structured and unstructured interviews. Nonverbal techniques include observations and measures of interactions; proxemics, kinesics, and research involving videotaped observations; use of various types of technical equipment for collecting data; content analysis; and analysis of artifacts and records. Pelto and Pelto (1978) add that methods may be described as having an "emic" or insider's view, as in participant observation, versus an "etic" or outsider's view, as in nonparticipant stream-of-behaviour analyses.

Other researchers use variations of these taxonomies. Goetz and LeCompte (1984) divide methods into interactive (participant observation and several types of interviews) versus noninteractive methods (forms of nonparticipant observation, as well as artifact collection and analysis). Lincoln and Guba (1985) classify methods as those that collect data from human sources (observations and interviews) as opposed to those that collect data from nonhuman sources (documents and records). Other authors, however, note that methods can rarely be classified as simple dichotomies, such as interactive or not, in large part because the researcher is a human being and thus involved, and plays a role even in nonparticipant observation. Bogdan and Biklen (1992) provide the example of the "participant/observer continuum", describing the ways observers who refrain from being overt participants may still interact to varying degrees with those subjects. Researchers who work using an ethnographic perspective consider all methods "doing fieldwork". Similarly, Bernard (1982) calls participant observation the "foundation of anthropological research"; some would say this deep, involved method of interacting with subjects defines qualitative research.

It is assumed that educational technologists will use methods ethically and with a view to doing quality research, but may not always be bound by anthropological tradition. We are in another field with other questions to answer than those in which anthropologists or sociologists may be interested. For instance, it is now possible to design instruction using a multitude of techniques, using many delivery systems. As noted by McNeil and Nelson (1991) and Reeves (1986), many design factors contribute to the success of instruction using new technologies, such as distance education, interactive multimedia, and Internet-based delivery systems. Educational technologists may successfully use and adapt qualitative methods to investigate new and challenging questions.

In this chapter, we will discuss specific methods that may be called observations, interviews, and document and artifact analysis. As in all qualitative research, it is also assumed that educational technology researchers will use and refine methods with the view that these methods vary in their degree of interactiveness with subjects. Each of these methods, in their various forms, along with several research perspectives.

COMPOSITION, IDENTITY, AND INVERSE

Now that we have a good understanding of what a function is, our next step is to consider an important operation on functions. Our purpose is not to develop the algebra of functions as completely as we did for the algebras of logic, matrices, and sets, but the reader should be aware of the similarities between the algebra of functions and that of matrices. We first define equality of functions.

Definition :

Equality. *Let $f, g : A \rightarrow B$; that is, let f and g both be function from the set A into the set B. The function f is equal to the function g, notation $f = g$, if and only if $f(x) = g(x)$ for all $x \in A$.*

Composition

One of the most important operations on functions of composition.

Definition

Composition. *Let $f : A \rightarrow B$ and let $g : B \rightarrow C$. Then the composition of f with g, written gof, is a function from A into C defined by $(gof)(x) = g(f, (x))$, which is read "f followed by g of x is equal to g of f of x."* The reader should note that it is traditional to write the composition of functions from right to left. Thus, in the above definition, the first function performed in computing gof, which is also written gof, is f, on the other hand, for relations, the composition rs is read from left is right, so that the first relation is r.

Theorem 1: Let $f : A \rightarrow B$, $g : B \rightarrow C$, and $h : C \rightarrow D$. Then $h(gf) = (hg)f$.

Proof Technique

In order to prove that two functions are equal, we must use the definition of equality of functions. Assuming that the functions have the same domain, they are equal if, *for each domain element*, the images of that element under the two functions are equal.

Proof : We wish to prove that $(h(gf))(x) = ((hg)f)(x)$ for all $x \in A$.

$h(gf))(x) = h((gf)(x))$ definition of composition of h with $gf = h(g(f(x)))$ definition of composition of g with f.

Similarly,

((hg) f) (x) = (hg) (f (x) definition of composition of hg with f = h (g (f (x))) definition of composition of h with g. Which is the same as the above.

If f is a function from a set A itself, we can find fof, for fof, etc. which we write as f^2, f^3,...This idea can be expressed more elegantly as follows : If $f : A \rightarrow A$, the repeated composition of f with itself is defined recursively a :

1. f^1 (a) = f (a), $a \in A$, and
2. f^{n+1} (a) for $n \geq 1$ and $a \in A$.

Two useful theorems concerning composition are given below. The proofs are left for the exercise.

Theorem 2: *If $f : A \rightarrow B$ and $g : B \rightarrow C$ are injections, then $gf : A \rightarrow C$ is an injection, then $gf : A \rightarrow C$ is an injection.*

Theorem 3: *If $f : A \rightarrow B$ and $g : B \rightarrow C$ are surjections, then $gf : A \rightarrow C$ is a surjection.*

We would now like to define the concepts of identity and inverse for function under the operation of composition. The motivation and descriptions of the definitions of these terms come from the definitions of the terms in the set of real numbers and for matrices. For real numbers, the numbers 0 and 1 play the unique role that x + 0 = 0 + x = x and x. 1 = 1. x = x for any real number x, 0 and 1 are the identity elements for the reals under the operations of addition and multiplication respectively. Similarly, the $n \times n$ zero matrix 0 and the $n \times n$ identity (multiplicative) matrix I are such that for any $n \times n$ matrix A, A + 0 = 0 + A = A and $A_I = I_A = I$. Hence, an elegant way of defining the identity function under the operation of composition would be to imitate the above well-known facts.

IDENTITY FUNCTION

Definition

Identity. *The identity function, under composition, is a function from A onto A, denoted by i (or, more specifically, i_A) such that foi = iof = f for all functions from A to A.*

At alternate description is that the identity function on A is the function i (a) = a for all $a \in A$. This can be proven from the above definition.

Inverse Function

We will introduce the inverse of a function with a special case: the inverse of a function on a set. After you've taken the time to understand this concept, you can read about the inverse of a function from one set into another.

The reader is encouraged to reread the definition of the inverse of a matrix in the following definition of the inverse function is a direct analogue of that definition.

Definition

Inverse Function. *Let $f : A \rightarrow A$. If there exists a function $g : A \rightarrow A$ such that gof = fog iA, then g is called the inverse of the function f and is denoted by f^{-1}, read "f inverse."*

An alternate description of the inverse of a function, will which can be proven from the definition, is as follows :

Let $f : A \rightarrow A$ be such that f (a) = b. Then, when it exist, $f^{-1}$is a function from A to A such that f^{-1} (b) = a. Note that f–1 "undoes" what f does.

Theorem 4: *Let $f : A \rightarrow A$. f^{-1} exists if and only if f is one to one and onto.*

Proof **:** ($\Rightarrow$) Assume that f^{-1} is a function. In this half of the proof, we wish to show that f is one to one and onto. To prove that f is one to one, let (a, b) and (c, b) be in f and show that a = c. If (a,b), (c, b) $\in$ f, then (b, a) and (b, c) are in f^{-1} Since $f^{-1}$is a function, a and c must be equal, so f is one to one.

Next, to prove that f is onto, observe that for f^{-1} to be a function, it must use all of its domain, namely A. Let be be any element of A. Then b has an image under f^{-1},f^{-1}(b). Another way of writing this is (b, f^{-1} (b) $\in$ f. By the definition of the inverse, this is equivalent of (f^{-1} (b), b) $\in$ f. Hence, b is in the range of f. Since b was chosen arbitrarily, this shows that the range of f must be all of A.

($\Rightarrow$) Assume f is one to one and onto to prove f^{-1} exists. We leave this half of the proof to the reader. #

Definition

Permutation. A bijection of a set A into itself is called a permutation of A. Next, we will consider the situation where $f : A \rightarrow B$ and B is not necessarily equal to A. How do we define inverse in this case?

Definition

Inverse of a Function (General Cases). *Let $f: A \rightarrow B$. If there exists a function $g: B \rightarrow A$ such the gof = i_A and fog = i_B, then g is called the inverse of f and is denoted by f^{-1}, read "f inverse."*

Note the slightly more complicated condition for the inverse in this case because the domains of fog and gof are different if A and B are different.

MAPPING OR FUNCTION

The concept of mapping of one set into another is of great importance in mathematics. It is not a new concept to any of us as we have been considering mapping from the beginning of our mathematical training. For example, plotting of the relation $y = x^2$ is nothing but to study the particular mapping which takes every real number into its square. The following discussion will make the concept of mapping clear.

Suppose A and B are any two non-empty sets. Let A = {a, b, c, d}, B = {x, y, z}. Suppose by some rule or other, we assign to each element of A unique element of B. Suppose a is associated to x, b is associated to y, c is associated to x and d is associated to z. The set of such assignments is called a *'function'* or *'mapping'* from A to B. If we denote this set by f than we write

$f : A \rightarrow B$

Which is read as *"f is a function of A to B"* or *"f is a mapping from A to B"*.

Loosely speaking, a mapping from one set into another may be defined as given below :

Definition : *Let A and B be two given sets. Suppose there exists a rule denoted by f, which associates to each member of A, a unique member of B. Then f is called a function or a mapping of A to B. The mapping f of A to B is denoted by f :*

$A \rightarrow B$ or by $A \xrightarrow{f} B$.

Further, if $a \in A$, then the element in B which is assigned to a is called the f image of a or the value of the function f for a and is denoted by f(a).

Now, we think of a definition which serves to make the concept of a mapping precise and thus formally, we define mapping as follows:

Definition : *If A and B are nom-empty sets then a mapping from A to B is a subset C of $A \times B$ such that for every $a \in A$ there is a unique $b \in B$ such that the ordered pair (a, b) is in C.*

For all practical purposes the following notion of mapping will be used hereafter and thus we arrive at another form of definition.

Definition : *A mapping $f : A \rightarrow B$, is a rule which associates any element $a \in A$ with some element $b \in B$, the rule being associate (or map) $a \in A$ with $b \in B$ if $(a, b) \in C$, C being the subset of $A \times B$.*

Note : The rule f should possess the characteristic that there may be some elements of the set B which are not associated to any element of the set A but each element of the set A must be associated to one and only one element of the set B. Two or more elements of the set A may be associated to the same element of the set B but association of one element of A to more than one element in B is not permissible.

Domain, Co-domain and Range of Functions : Let f be a mapping of A into B. Then A is called the *'domain'* of the function f and B the *'co-domain'* of the function f. It is evident from the definition that each element of B need not appear as the image of an element in A. We define the *'range'* of f to consist of all those elements in B which appear as f image of atleast one element in A. There can be more than one elements of A which have the same image in B. The image set f [A] is called the range of f.

Functions Defined as Sets of Ordered Pairs : Let A and B are any two non-empty sets, then a mapping f of A to B is a subset f of A × B satisfying the following conditions :

(i) for each $a \in A$, $(a, b) \in f$, for some $b \in B$;

(ii) if $(a, b) \in f$ and $(a, b') \in f$, then $b = b'$.

The first condition ensures that we have a rule that assigns to each element a ε A some element b ε B. Thus each element in A will have image The second condition guarantees that the image is unique. Accordingly, f is a function from A to B.

Note : If $f : A \to B$, it is important to distinguish between a function f and the value f(x) of f for any element x. While f is a subset of A × B, f(x) is an element of the set B.

GROWTH OF FUNCTIONS

The growth of a function is described using a special notation O-notation (read as *"big-oh notation"*. By this notation we can compare relative sizes of functions that is very useful in the analysis of computer algorithms.

The way we compare any complexity function with one of the standard functions is to use the functional "big O" notation which we define as follows :

Definition : *Let f(x) and g(x) be arbitrary functions defined on the set of real numbers R or a subset of R. Then f(x) is of order g(x), written as*

$f(x) = O(g(x))$

if there exists a real number R and a positive constant c such that, for all x > R, we have

$|f(x)| \leq c|g(x)|$.

We also write

$f(x) = h(x) + O(g(x))$

when

$f(x) - h(x) = O(g(x))$.

To show f(x) is O(g(x)), we need only find one pair of constants c and k such that f(x) < c g(x) if x > k. However, a pair c, k that satisfies the definition is never unique. Moreover, if one such pair exists, there may be infinitely many such pairs. If c, k is one such pair, any c', k' with C < c' and k < k' also satisfies the definition, since f(x) < c'g(x) whenever x > k' > k.

Big-Omega and Big-Theta Notations : If f(x) is Og(x), then we can say that except for constants and a finite number of exceptions, f(x) is bounded above by g(x), so g(x) grows at least as fast as f(x). For example if f(x) = x and g(x) = 2^x, than f(x) is O g(x), but g(x) grows considerably faster than f. Clearly, the statement f(x) is Og(x) says nothing about lower bound for f(x). For this we use *big-Omega notation.* When lower bound on the size of a function f(x) relative to a reference function g(x), we use big-theta notation.

Definition : *Let f(x) and g(x) be functions from the set of integers or the set of real numbers to the set of real numbers. We say that f(x) is Ω g(x), if there are positive constants c and k such that* $|f(x)| \geq c|g(x)|$ *whenever* $x > k$ *which is read as "f(x) is big-Omega of g(x)".*

Let f(x) and g(x) be functions from the set of integers or the set of real numbers to the set of real numbers. We say that f(x) is Θ g(x) if f(x) is O g(x) and f(x) is Ω g(x). When f(x) is Θ g(x), we say that "f(x) is big-theta of g(x)" and we say f(x) is of order g(x).

Rules for Determining the Θ-class of a Function :

1. Θ (1) functions are constant and have zero growth, the slowest growth possible.
2. Θ (log (n)) is lower that Θ (n^k) if k > 0. This means that any logarithmic function grows more slowly than any power function with positive exponent.
3. Θ (n^a) is lower than Θ (n^b) if and only if $0 < a < b$.
4. Θ (a^n) is lower than Θ (b^n) if and only if $0 < a < b$.
5. Θ (n^k) is lower than Θ (a^n) for any power n^k and any a > 1. Obviously, any exponential function with base greater than 1 grows more rapidly than any power function.
6. If r is not zero, than Θ (rf) = Θ (f) for any function f.
7. If h is a non-zero function and Θ (f) is lower than (or the same as) Θ (g), than Θ (f h) is lower than (or the same as Θ (g h).
8. If Θ (f) is lower than Θ (g), than Θ (f + g) = Θ (g).

RECURSIVELY DEFINED FUNCTIONS

A function is said to be *recursively defined* if the function's definition refers to itself. Recursion refers to several related concepts in computer science and mathematics.

The function definition must have the following two properties:

(i) There must be certain arguments, called *base values,* for which the function does not refer to itself.

(ii) Each time the function does refer to itself, the argument of the function must be closer to a base value.

A recursive function with these two properties are said to be *well-defined.*

Primitive Recursive Function : *Primitive recursive functions are the functions that can be generated by primitive recursion from a set of initial functions, employing methods similar to the ones used in the definition of addition and multiplication.*

The formation rules for the primitive recursive expressions are as follows:

1. 0 is expression
2. Every variable is an expression
3. If f is a function and $t_1, t_2, \ldots, t_d$ are expressions, then $f(t_1, t_2, \ldots, t_d)$ is an expression.

Initial Functions : The initial functions over set of natural numbers are:

1. **Zero Function :** $Z(x) = 0$ for all x.
2. **Successor Function :** $S(x) = x + 1$, for all X.
3. **Projection Function :** $\cup_i^n (x_1, x_2, \ldots, x_n) = x_i$ for all n tuples $(x_1, x_2, \ldots, x_n)$ for $1 \leq i \leq n$.

The initial function provide an infinite set of functions from which other function can be built up by using.

1. **Composition :** If f is an n-ary function and $g_1, g_2, \ldots, g_n$ are k-ary functions then $f(g_1, g_2, \ldots, g_n)$ is a k-ary function, where
   $f(g_1, g_2, \ldots, g_n)(x_1, x_2, \ldots, x_k)$
   $= f(g_1(x_1, x_2, \ldots x_k), \ldots, g_n(x_1, x_2, \ldots, x_k))$
2. **Primitive Recursion :** A function f of m + 1 variables is defined by recursion if there exists a function g of m variables, and a function h of m + 2 variables, and f is defined as follows:
   $f(x_1, x_2, \ldots, x_m, 0) = g(x_1, x_2, \ldots, x_m)$
   $f(x_1, x_2, \ldots, x_m, y + 1) = h(x_1, x_2, \ldots x_m, y)$
   $f(x_1, x_2, \ldots, x_m, y))$
   Here, y is assumed to be the inductive variable such that the value of f at y + 1 is expressed in terms of the value of f at y. The variables $x_1, x_2, \ldots, x_m$ are *parameters* and are assumed to remain fixed throughout the definition. Functions g and h are assumed to be known.

LINEAR

The word linear comes from the Latin word *linearis,* which means *pertaining to or resembling a line.* In mathematics, a linear map or function $f(x)$ is a function which satisfies the following two properties:

- Additivity (also called the superposition property): $f(x + y) = f(x) + f(y)$. This says that f is a group homomorphism with respect to addition.
- Homogeneity of degree 1: $f(\alpha x) = \alpha f(x)$ for all α.

It can be shown that additivity implies the homogeneity in all cases where α is rational; this is done by proving the case where α is a natural number by mathematical induction and then extending the result to arbitrary rational numbers. If f is assumed to be continuous as well then this can be extended to show that homogeneity for α any real number, using the fact the rationals form a dense subset of the reals.

In this definition, x is not necessarily a real number, but can in general be a member of any vector space. A less restrictive definition of linear function, not coinciding with the definition of linear map, is used in elementary mathematics.

The concept of linearity can be extended to linear operators. Important examples of linear operators include the derivative considered as a differential operator, and many constructed from it, such as del and the Laplacian. When a differential equation can be expressed in linear form, it is particularly easy to solve by breaking the equation up into smaller pieces, solving each of those pieces, and adding the solutions up.

Linear algebra is the branch of mathematics concerned with the study of vectors, vector spaces (also called linear spaces), linear transformations (also called linear maps), and systems of linear equations.

For a description of linear and nonlinear equations. Nonlinear equations and functions are of interest to physicists and mathematicians because they can be used to represent many natural phenomena, including chaos.

Integral Linearity

For a device that converts a quantity to another quantity there are three basic definitions for integral linearity in common use: independent linearity, zero-based linearity, and terminal, or end-point, linearity. In each case, linearity defines how well the device's actual performance across a specified operating range approximates a straight line. Linearity is usually measured in terms of a deviation, or non-linearity, from an ideal straight line and it is typically expressed in terms of percent of full scale, or in ppm (parts per million) of full scale. Typically, the straight line is obtained by performing a least-squares fit of the data. The three definitions vary in the manner in which the straight line is positioned relative to the actual device's performance. Also, all three of these definitions ignore any gain, or offset errors that may be present in the actual device's performance characteristics.

Many times a device's specifications will simply refer to linearity, with no other explanation as to which type of linearity is intended. In cases where a specification is expressed simply as linearity, it is assumed to imply independent linearity.

Independent linearity is probably the most commonly-used linearity definition and is often found in the specifications for DMMs and ADCs, as well as devices like potentiometers. Independent linearity is defined as the maximum deviation of actual performance relative to a straight line, located such that it minimizes the maximum deviation.

In that case there are no constraints placed upon the positioning of the straight line and it may be wherever necessary to minimize the deviations between it and the device's actual performance characteristic.

Zero-based linearity forces the lower range value of the straight line to be equal to the actual lower range value of the device's characteristic, but it does allow the line to be rotated to minimize the maximum deviation. In this case, since the positioning of the straight line is constrained by the requirement that the lower range values of the line and the device's characteristic be coincident, the non-linearity based on this definition will generally be larger than for independent linearity.

For terminal linearity, there is no flexibility allowed in the placement of the straight line in order to minimize the deviations. The straight line must be located such that each of its end-points coincides with the device's actual upper and lower range values. This means that the non-linearity measured by this definition will typically be larger than that measured by the independent, or the zero-based linearity definitions. This definition of linearity is often associated with ADCs, DACs and various sensors.

A fourth linearity definition, absolute linearity, is sometimes also encountered. Absolute linearity is a variation of terminal linearity, in that it allows no flexibility in the placement of the straight line, however in this case the gain and offset errors of the actual device are included in the linearity measurement, making this the most difficult measure of a device's performance.

For absolute linearity the end points of the straight line are defined by the ideal upper and lower range values for the device, rather than the actual values. The linearity error in this instance is the maximum deviation of the actual device's performance from ideal.

Linear Equation

A linear equation is an algebraic equation in which each term is either a constant or the product of a constant and (the first power of) a single variable.

Linear equations can have one or more variables. Linear equations occur with great regularity in applied mathematics. While they arise quite naturally when modeling many phenomena, they are particularly useful since many non-linear equations may be reduced to linear equations by assuming that quantities of interest vary to only a small extent from some "background" state.

QUADRATIC FUNCTION

A quadratic function, in mathematics, is a polynomial function of the form

$$f(x) = ax^2 + bx + c, \quad a \neq 0.$$

The graph of a quadratic function is a parabola whose axis of symmetry is parallel to the y-axis.

The expression $ax^2 + bx + c$ in the definition of a quadratic function is a polynomial of degree 2 or second order, or a 2nd degree polynomial, because the highest exponent of x is 2.

If the quadratic function is set equal to zero, then the result is a quadratic equation. The solutions to the equation are called the roots of the equation.

LOGARITHM

The logarithm of a number is the exponent by which another fixed value, the base, has to be raised to produce that number. For example, the logarithm of 1000 to base 10 is 3, because 1000 is 10 to the power 3: $1000 = 10^3 = 10 \times 10 \times 10$. More generally, if $x = b^y$, then y is the logarithm of x to base b, and is written $\log_b(x)$, so $\log_{10}(1000) = 3$.

Logarithms were introduced by John Napier in the early 17th century as a means to simplify calculations. They were rapidly adopted by scientists, engineers, and others to perform computations more easily and rapidly, using slide rules and logarithm tables. These devices rely on the fact—important in its own right—that the logarithm of a product is the sum of the logarithms of the factors:

$$\log_b (xy) = \log_b (x) + \log_b (y).$$

The present-day notion of logarithms comes from Leonard Euler, who connected them to the exponential function in the 18th century.

The logarithm to base $b = 10$ is called the common logarithm and has many applications in science and engineering. The natural logarithm has the constant e (≈ 2.718) as its base; its use is widespread in pure mathematics, especially calculus. The binary logarithm uses base $b = 2$ and is prominent in computer science.

Logarithmic scales reduce wide-ranging quantities to smaller scopes. For example, the decibel is a logarithmic unit quantifying sound pressure and voltage ratios. In chemistry, pH is a logarithmic measure for the acidity of an aqueous solution. Logarithms are commonplace in scientific formulas, and in measurements of the complexity of algorithms and of geometric objects called fractals. They describe musical intervals, appear in formulas counting prime numbers, inform some models in psychophysics, and can aid in forensic accounting.

In the same way as the logarithm reverses exponentiation, the complex logarithm is the inverse function of the exponential function applied to complex numbers. The discrete logarithm is another variant; it has applications in public-key cryptography.

Computational Complexity

Analysis of algorithms is a branch of computer science that studies the performance of algorithms (computer programs solving a certain problem). Logarithms are valuable for describing algorithms which divide a problem into smaller ones, and join the solutions of the subproblems.

For example, to find a number in a sorted list, the binary search algorithm checks the middle entry and proceeds with the half before or after the middle entry if the number is still not found. This algorithm requires, on average, $\log_2(N)$ comparisons, where N is the list's length. Similarly, the merge sort algorithm sorts an unsorted list by dividing the list into halves and sorting these first before merging the results. Merge sort algorithms typically require a time approximately proportional to $N \cdot \log(N)$. The base of the logarithm is not specified here, because the result only changes by a constant factor when another base is used. A constant factor, is usually disregarded in the analysis of algorithms under the standard uniform cost model. A function $f(x)$ is said to grow logarithmically if $f(x)$ is (exactly or approximately) proportional to the logarithm of x. (Biological descriptions of organism growth, however, use this term for an exponential function.) For example, any natural number N can be represented in binary form in no more than $\log_2(N) + 1$ bits. In other words, the amount of memory needed to store N grows logarithmically with N.

Fractals

Logarithms occur in definitions of the dimension of fractals. Fractals are geometric objects that are self-similar: small parts reproduce, at least roughly, the entire global structure. The Sierpinski triangle (pictured) can be covered by three copies of itself, each having sides half the original length. This causes the Hausdorff dimension of this structure to be $\log(3)/\log(2) \approx 1.58$. Another logarithm-based notion of dimension is obtained by counting the number of boxes needed to cover the fractal in question.

Inverses of other Exponential Functions

Exponentiation occurs in many areas of mathematics and its inverse function is often referred to as the logarithm. For example, the logarithm of a matrix is the (multi-valued) inverse function of the matrix exponential. Another example is the p-adic logarithm, the inverse function of the p-adic exponential. Both are defined via Taylor series analogous to the real case. In the context of differential geometry, the exponential map maps the tangent space at a point of a manifold to a neighborhood of that point. Its inverse is also called the logarithmic (or log) map.

Further logarithm-like inverse functions include the *double logarithm* $\ln(\ln(x))$, the *super-or hyper-4-logarithm* (a slight variation of which is called iterated logarithm in computer science), the Lambert W function, and the logit. They are the inverse functions of the double exponential function, tetration, of $f(w) = we^w$, and of the logistic function, respectively.

PERMUTATION

In mathematics, the notion of permutation is used with several slightly different meanings, all related to the act of permuting (rearranging) objects or values. Informally, a permutation of a set of objects is an arrangement of those objects into a particular order. For example, there are six permutations of the set {1,2,3}, namely (1,2,3), (1,3,2), (2,1,3), (2,3,1), (3,1,2), and (3,2,1). One might define an anagram of a word as a permutation of its letters. The study of permutations in this sense generally belongs to the field of combinatorics.

The number of permutations of n distinct objects is $n\times (n-1)\times(n-2)\times\ldots\times2\times1$, which number is called "n factorial" and written "$n!$".

Permutations occur, in more or less prominent ways, in almost every domain of mathematics. They often arise when different orderings on certain finite sets are considered, possibly only because one wants to ignore such orderings and needs to know how many configurations are thus identified. For similar reasons permutations arise in the study of sorting algorithms in computer science.

In algebra and particularly in group theory, a permutation of a set S is defined as a bijection from S to itself (i.e., a map $S \to S$ for which every element of S occurs exactly once as image value). This is related to the rearrangement of S in which each element s takes the place of the corresponding $f(s)$. The collection of such permutations form a symmetric group. The key to its structure is the possibility to compose permutations: performing two given rearrangements in succession defines a third rearrangement, the composition. Permutations may *act* on composite objects by rearranging their components, or by certain replacements (substitutions) of symbols.

In elementary combinatorics, the name "permutations and combinations" refers to two related problems, both counting possibilities to select k distinct elements from a set of n elements, where for k-permutations the order of selection is taken into account, but for k-combinations it is ignored. However k-permutations do not correspond to permutations as discussed in this article (unless $k = n$).

History

The rule to determine the number of permutations of n objects was known in Hindu culture at least as early as around 1150: the Lilavati by the Indian mathematician Bhaskara II contains a passage that translates to

The product of multiplication of the arithmetical series beginning and increasing by unity and continued to the number of places, will be the variations of number with specific figures.

A first case in which seemingly unrelated mathematical questions were studied with the help of permutations occurred around 1770, when Joseph Louis Lagrange, in the study of polynomial equations, observed that properties of the permutations of the roots of an equation are related to the possibilities to solve it. This line of work ultimately resulted, through the work of Évariste Galois, in Galois theory, which gives a complete description of what is possible and impossible with respect to solving polynomial equations (in one unknown) by radicals. In modern mathematics there are many similar situations in which understanding a problem requires studying certain permutations related to it.

Generalities

The notion of permutation is used in the following contexts.

In group theory

In group theory and related areas, one considers permutations of arbitrary sets, even infinite ones. A permutation of a set S is a bijection from S to itself. This allows for permutations to be composed, which allows the definition of groups of permutations. If S is a finite set of n elements, then there are $n!$ permutations of S.

In combinatorics

In combinatorics, a permutation is usually understood to be a sequence containing each element from a finite set once, and only once. The concept of *sequence* is distinct from that of a *set*, in that the elements of a sequence appear in some order: the sequence has a first element (unless it is empty), a second element (unless its length is less than 2), and so on. In contrast, the elements in a set have no order; {1, 2, 3} and {3, 2, 1} are different ways to denote the same set. In this sense a permutation of a finite set S of n elements is equivalent to a bijection from $\{1, 2, \ldots, n\}$ to S (in which any i is mapped to the *i*-th element of the sequence), or to a choice of a total ordering on *S* (for which $x < y$ if *x* comes before *y* in the sequence). In this sense there are also *n*! permutations of *S*.

Permutations in Group Theory

In group theory, the term *permutation* of a set means a bijective map, or bijection, from that set onto itself. The set of all permutations of any given set *S* forms a group, with composition of maps as product and the identity as neutral element. This is the symmetric group of *S*.

Up to isomorphism, this symmetric group only depends on the cardinality of the set, so the nature of elements of *S* is irrelevant for the structure of the group. Symmetric groups have been studied most in the case of a finite sets, in which case one can assume without loss of generality that $S=\{1,2,...,n\}$ for some natural number *n*, which defines the symmetric group of degree *n*, written S_n.

Any subgroup of a symmetric group is called a permutation group. In fact by Cayley's theorem any group is isomorphic to some permutation group, and every finite group to a subgroup of some finite symmetric group.

However, permutation groups have more structure than abstract groups, allowing for instance to define the cycle type of an element of a permutation group; different realizations of a group as a permutation group need not be equivalent for this additional structure. For instance S_3 is naturally a permutation group, in which any transposition has cycle type (2,1), but the proof of Cayley's theorem realizes S_3 as a subgroup of S_6 (namely the permutations of the 6 elements of S_3 itself), in which permutation group transpositions get cycle type (2,2,2). So in spite of Cayley's theorem, the study of permutation groups differs from the study of abstract groups.

Notation

There are three main notations for permutations of a finite set *S*. In *two-line notation*, one lists the elements of *S* in the first row, and for each one its image under the permutation below it in the second row. For instance a particular permutation of the set {1,2,3,4,5} can be written as:

$$\sigma = \begin{pmatrix} 1 & 2 & 3 & 4 & 5 \\ 2 & 5 & 4 & 3 & 1 \end{pmatrix};$$

this means that σ satisfies $\sigma(1)=2$, $\sigma(2)=5$, $\sigma(3)=4$, $\sigma(4)=3$, and $\sigma(5)=1$.

In *one-line notation*, one gives only the second row of this array, so the one-line notation for the permutation above is 25431. (It is typical to use commas to separate these entries only if some have two or more digits.)

Permutations in combinatorics

In combinatorics a permutation of a set S with n elements is a listing of the elements of S in some order (each element occurring exactly once). This can be defined formally as a bijection from the set { 1, 2,..., n } to S. Note that if S equals { 1, 2,..., n }, then this definition coincides with the definition in group theory. More generally one could use instead of { 1, 2,..., n } any set equipped with a total ordering of its elements.

One combinatorial property that is related to the group theoretic interpretation of permutations, and can be defined without using a total ordering of S, is the cycle structure of a permutation σ. It is the partition of n describing the lengths of the cycles of σ. Here there is a part "1" in the partition for every fixed point of σ. A permutation that has no fixed point is called a derangement. Other combinatorial properties however are directly related to the ordering of S, and to the way the permutation relates to it. Here are a number of such properties.

Ascents, descents and runs

An *ascent* of a permutation σ of n is any position $i < n$ where the following value is bigger than the current one. That is, if $\sigma = \sigma_1\sigma_2...\sigma_n$, then i is an ascent if $\sigma_i < \sigma_{i+1}$.

For example, the permutation 3452167 has ascents (at positions) 1,2,5,6.

Similarly, a *descent* is a position $i < n$ with $\sigma_i > \sigma_{i+1}$, so every i with $1 \leq i < n$ either is an ascent or is a descent of σ.

The number of permutations of n with k ascents is the Eulerian number $\left\langle {n \atop k} \right\rangle$; this is also the number of permutations of n with k descents.

An *ascending run* of a permutation is a nonempty increasing contiguous subsequence of the permutation that cannot be extended at either end; it corresponds to a maximal sequence of successive ascents (the latter may be empty: between two successive descents there is still an ascending run of length 1). By contrast an *increasing subsequence* of a permutation is not necessarily contiguous: it is an increasing sequence of elements obtained from the permutation by omitting the values at some positions. For example, the permutation 2453167 has the ascending runs 245, 3, and 167, while it has an increasing subsequence 2367.

If a permutation has k–1 descents, then it must be the union of k ascending runs. Hence, the number of permutations of n with k ascending runs is the same as the number $\left\langle {n \atop k-1} \right\rangle$ of permutations with k–1 descents.

Inversions

An *inversion* of a permutation σ is a pair (i,j) of positions where the entries of a permutation are in the opposite order: $i < j$ and $\sigma_i > \sigma_j$. So a descent is just an inversion at two adjacent positions. For example, the permutation $\sigma = 23154$ has three inversions: (1,3), (2,3), (4,5), for the pairs of entries (2,1), (3,1), (5,4).

Sometimes an inversion is defined as the pair of values (σ_i, σ_j) itself whose order is reversed; this makes no difference for the *number* of inversions, and this pair (reversed) is also an inversion in the above sense for the inverse permutation σ^{-1}. The number of inversions is an important measure for the degree to which the entries of a permutation are out of order; it is the same for σ and for σ^{-1}. To bring a permutation with k inversions into order (i.e., transform it into the identity permutation), by successively applying (right-multiplication by) adjacent transpositions, is always possible and requires a sequence of k such operations. Moreover any reasonable choice for the adjacent transpositions will work: it suffices to choose at each step a transposition of i and $i + 1$ where i is a descent of the permutation as modified so far (so that the transposition will remove this particular descent, although it might create other descents). This is so because applying such a transposition reduces the number of inversions by 1; also note that as long as this number is not zero, the permutation is not the identity, so it has at least one descent. Bubble sort and insertion sort can be interpreted as particular instances of this procedure to put a sequence into order. Incidentally this procedure proves that any permutation σ can be written as a product of adjacent transpositions; for this one may simply reverse any sequence of such transpositions that transforms σ into the identity. In fact, by enumerating all sequences of adjacent transpositions that would transform σ into the identity, one obtains (after reversal) a *complete* list of all expressions of minimal length writing σ as a product of adjacent transpositions.

Counting Sequences without Repetition

In this section, a k-permutation of a set S is an ordered sequence of k distinct elements of S. For example, given the set of letters {C, E, G, I, N, R}, the sequence ICE is a 3-permutation, RING and RICE are 4-permutations, NICER and REIGN are 5-permutations, and CRINGE is a 6-permutation; since the latter uses all letters, it is a permutation of the given set in the ordinary combinatorial sense. ENGINE on the other hand is not a permutation, because of the repetitions: it uses the elements E and N twice.

PERMUTATIONS IN COMPUTING

Algorithms to Generate Permutations

In computing it may be required to generate permutations of a given sequence of values. The methods best adapted to do this depend on whether one wants some randomly chosen permutations, or all permutations, and in the latter case if a specific ordering is required. Another question is whether possible equality among entries in the given sequence is to be taken into account; if so, one should only generate distinct multiset permutations of the sequence.

An obvious way to generate permutations of n is to generate values for the Lehmer code (possibly using the factorial number system representation of integers up to $n!$), and convert those into the corresponding permutations. However the latter step, while straightforward, is hard to implement efficiently, because it requires n operations each of selection from a sequence and deletion from it, at an arbitrary position; of the obvious representations of the sequence as an array or a linked list, both require (for different reasons) about $n^2/4$ operations to perform the conversion. With n likely to be rather small (especially if generation of all permutations is needed) that is not too much of a problem, but it turns out that both for random and for systematic generation there are simple alternatives that do considerably better. For this reason it does not seem useful, although certainly possible, to employ a special data structure that would allow performing the conversion from Lehmer code to permutation in $O(n \log n)$ time.

Random Generation of Permutations

For generating random permutations of a given sequence of n values, it makes no difference whether one means apply a randomly selected permutation of n to the sequence, or choose a random element from the set of distinct (multiset) permutations of the sequence. This is because, even though in case of repeated values there can be many distinct permutations of n that result in the same permuted sequence, the number of such permutations is the same for each possible result. Unlike for systematic generation, which becomes unfeasible for large n due to the growth of the number $n!$, there is no reason to assume that n will be small for random generation.

The basic idea to generate a random permutation is to generate at random one of the $n!$ sequences of integers $d_1, d_2, \ldots, d_n$ satisfying $0 \leq d_i < i$ (since d_1 is always zero it may be omitted) and to convert it to a permutation through a bijective correspondence. For the latter correspondence one could interpret the (reverse) sequence as a Lehmer code, and this gives a generation method first published in 1938 by Ronald A. Fisher and Frank Yates. While at the time computer implementation was not an issue, this method suffers from the difficulty sketched above to convert from Lehmer code to permutation efficiently. This can be remedied by using a different bijective correspondence: after using d_i to select an element among i remaining elements of the sequence (for decreasing values of i), rather than removing the element and compacting the sequence by shifting down further elements one place, one swaps the element with the final remaining element. Thus the elements remaining for selection form a consecutive range at each point in time, even though they may not occur in the same order as they did in the original sequence. The mapping from sequence of integers to permutations is somewhat complicated, but it can be seen to produce each permutation in exactly one way, by an immediate induction. When the selected element happens to be the final remaining element, the swap operation can be omitted. This does not occur sufficiently often to warrant testing for the condition, but the final element must be included among the candidates of the selection, to guarantee that all permutations can be generated.

Generation in Lexicographic Order

There are many ways to systematically generate all permutations of a given sequence. One classical algorithm, which is both simple and flexible, is based on finding the next permutation in lexicographic ordering, if it exists. It can handle repeated values, for which case it generates the distinct multiset permutations each once. Even for ordinary permutations it is significantly more efficient than generating values for the Lehmer code in lexicographic order (possibly using the factorial number system) and converting those to permutations. To use it, one starts by sorting the sequence in (weakly) increasing order (which gives its lexicographically minimal permutation), and then repeats advancing to the next permutation as long as one is found. The method goes back to Narayana Pandita in 14th century India, and has been frequently rediscovered ever since.

The following algorithm generates the next permutation lexicographically after a given permutation. It changes the given permutation in-place.

1. Find the largest index k such that $a[k] < a[k + 1]$. If no such index exists, the permutation is the last permutation.
2. Find the largest index l such that $a[k] < a[l]$. Since $k + 1$ is such an index, l is well defined and satisfies $k < l$.
3. Swap $a[k]$ with $a[l]$.
4. Reverse the sequence from $a[k + 1]$ up to and including the final element $a[n]$.

After step 1, one knows that all of the elements strictly after position k form a weakly decreasing sequence, so no permutation of these elements will make it advance in lexicographic order; to advance one must increase $a[k]$. Step 2 finds the smallest value $a[l]$ to replace $a[k]$ by, and swapping them in step 3 leaves the sequence after position k in weakly decreasing order. Reversing this sequence in step 4 then produces its lexicographically minimal permutation, and the lexicographic successor of the initial state for the whole sequence.

Generation with Minimal Changes

An alternative to the above algorithm, the Steinhaus–Johnson–Trotter algorithm, generates an ordering on all the permutations of a given sequence with the property that any two consecutive permutations in its output differ by swapping two adjacent values. This ordering on the permutations was known to 17th-century English bell ringers, among whom it was known as "plain changes". One advantage of this method is that the small amount of change from one permutation to the next allows the method to be implemented in constant time per permutation. The same can also easily generate the subset of even permutations, again in constant time per permutation, by skipping every other output permutation.

SOFTWARE IMPLEMENTATIONS

Calculator Functions

Many scientific calculators and computing software have a built-in function for calculating the number of k-permutations of n.

- Casio and TI calculators: nPr
- HP calculators: PERM
- Mathematica: FallingFactorial.

Spreadsheet Functions

Most spreadsheet software also provides a built-in function for calculating the number of k-permutations of n, called PERMUT in many popular spreadsheets. Apple's Numbers '08 software notably did not include such a function but this was rectified in Apple's Numbers '09 software package.

Applications

Permutations are used in the interleaver component of the error detection and correction algorithms, such as turbo codes, for example 3GPP Long Term Evolution mobile telecommunication standard uses these ideas. Such applications raise the question of fast generation of permutation satisfying certain desirable properties. One of the methods is based on the permutation polynomials.

Bibliography

Bajpai, R B : *Research Methodology : Data Presentation*, APH, 2007.

Balandier, G. : *Political Anthropology,* New York: Random House, 1970.

Bhanwar Lal Garg: *An Introduction to Research Methodology*, RBSA Pub, 2002.

Biolsi, Thomas : *Indians and Anthropologists: Vine Deloria, Jr., and the Critique of Anthropology,* Tuscon, University of Arizona Press, 1997.

Bock, K.: *Handbook of Psychological Anthropology,* Westport, Greenwood Press, 1994.

Boyle, J: *Critical Issues in Qualitative Research Methods*, England: University Press, 2006.

Burnette, D.: *Teaching Qualitative Research: A Compendium of Model Syllabi*, Alexandria: Council on Social Work Education, 2003.

Cox, D.R.: *Theoretical Statistics*. London: Chapman & Hall, 1974.

Crump, Thomas: *The Anthropology of Numbers*, England, Cambridge University Press, 1990.

Cyril, S.: *The Identification of Values in Anthropology*, American Journal of Sociology, 1959.

Dahlberg, Andrea: *In Contesting the Sacred: The Anthropology of Christian Pilgrimage*, London, Routledge, 1991.

Dasgupta, Manas: *Research Methodology in Economics : Problems and Issues*, Deep and Deep, 2007.

David, F.: *Quantitative Methods in Social Work: State of the Art,* New Delhi: Oxford University Press, 2001.

Eade, John: *Contesting the Sacred: Anthropology of Pilgrimage*, London, Routledge, 1991.

Francis, M.: *Dinka Response to Christianity: The Pursuit of Well-Being in a Developing Society,* Oxford, JASO, 1988.

Gaillard, Gerald, : *The Routledge Dictionary of Anthropologists*, London, Routledge, 2003.

Gans, Eric: *Originary Thinking: Elements of Generative Anthropology*, Stanford, Stanford University Press, 1993.

Garg, Ajit Lal : *An Introduction to Research Methodology*, RBSA Pub, 2002.

Gillies, Eva: *Vernacular Christianity: Essays in the Social Anthropology of Religion Presented to Godfrey Lienhardt*, Oxford, JASO, 1988.

Girish Saxena: *Basic Concept of Media Economics: Theory and Practice*, Vista International Pub, Delhi, 2010.

Grinnell, Jr., R.M.: *Social Work Research and Evaluation: Quantitative and Qualitative Approaches*, Itasca, IL.: F.E. Peacock Publishers.

Harrigan, K. R.: *Strategies for Declining Businesses*. Lexington, MA: Heath, 1980

Ian, Shaw: *Qualitative Research in Social Work,* New Delhi: Oxford University Press, 2001.

Isadore, Newman: *Qualitative-quantitative Research Methodology: Exploring,* Philippines: Oxford University Press, 2006.

John, M.: *Introduction to Library Research in Anthropology,* Boulder, Westview Press, 1998.

Judy, L.: *Research for Effective Social Work Practice,* Philippines: Oxford University Press, 2006.

Kalton, Graham: *Introduction to Survey Sampling.* Beverly Hills, CA: Sage, 1983.

Kanti Bagchi: *Research Methodology in Social Sciences: A Practical Guide,* Abhijeet Pub, 2007.

Kapila Mittal: *Research Methodology in Social Sciences,* Vista International, 2006.

Kemper, V.: *History of Anthropology: A Research Bibliography,* New York, Garland, 1977.

LeCompte, M.: *Ethnography and Qualitative Design in Educational Research,* San Diego: Academic Press, 2004.

MacKinley, A.C.: *The Econometrics of Financial Markets.* Princeton University Press, 1996.

Margaret, Alston: *Research for Social Workers: An Introduction to Methods,* New Delhi: Oxford University Press, 2001.

McGlynn, Frank, and Arthur Tuden : *Anthropological Approaches to Political Behavior,* Pittsburgh, PA: University of Pittsburgh, 1991.

Michael V. Angrosino: *Field Projects in Anthropology: a Student Handbook,* Prospect Heights, Waveland Press, 1992.

Monette, D.R.: *Applied Social Research: Tool for the Human Services,* New York: Holt, 2002.

Padgett, Deborah: *Qualitative Methods in Social Work Research: Challenges and Rewards,* New Delhi: Oxford University Press, 2001.

Pilcher, D.M.: *Data Analysis for the Helping Professions: A Practical Guide,* Newbury Park, CA: Sage, 2005.

Reid, W.J.: *Research in Social Work,* New York: Columbia University Press, 2006.

Robert, H.: *Dictionary of Concepts in Cultural Anthropology,* New York, Greenwood Press, 1991.

Russell, K.: *Fundamentals of Social Work Research,* New Delhi: Oxford University Press, 2001.

Spencer, Frank: *History of Physical Anthropology,* New York: Garland, 1997.

Stephen, D.: *Sacred Journeys: The Anthropology of Pilgrimage,* Westport, Greenwood Press, 1992.

Sutton, C.: *A Handbook of Research for the Helping Professions,* New York: Routledge, 2000.

Thomas R.: *Dravidian Kinship, Cambridge Studies in Social Anthropology,* New York, Cambridge University Press, 1981.

Vatuk, Sylvia: *American Studies in the Anthropology of India,* New Delhi, Manohar, 1978.

Weeks, M.: *Introduction to Library Research in Anthropology,* Boulder, Westview Press, 1998.

Winthrop, H.: *Dictionary of Concepts in Cultural Anthropology,* New York, Greenwood Press, 1991.

Index

❑❑❑